Q&A® 4 QuickStart

Que® Development Group

Text and graphics developed by
George Beinhorn
David W. Solomon
Hilary J. Adams
Donna Dowdle

Q&A® 4 QuickStart.

Copyright © 1991 by Que® Corporation.

Library of Congress Catalog No.: 90-63250

ISBN 0-88022-653-6

93 92 91   6 5 4 3 2 1

Interpretation of the printing code: the rightmost double-digit number is the year of the book's printing; the rightmost single-digit number, the number of the book's printing. For example, a printing code of 91-1 shows that the first printing of the book occurred in 1991.

Q&A® 4 QuickStart is based on Release 4 of Q&A.

Publisher: Lloyd J. Short

Associate Publisher: Karen A. Bluestein

Acquisitions Manager: Terrie Lynn Solomon

Product Development Manager: Mary Bednarek

Managing Editor: Paul Boger

Book Design: Scott Cook

Production Team: Jeff Baker, Brad Chinn, Sandy Grieshop

Product Director
Cheryl S. Robinson

Editors
Joanna Arnott
Cindy Morrow
Laura Wirthlin

Technical Editors
Vince Lackner
Andrew Young

*Composed in Garamond and Macmillan
by Que Corporation.*

Trademark Acknowledgments

Contents at a Glance

Table of Contents

Introduction

T his book is intended to be a self-teach manual
that you can use as time permits. With each chapter you
build on your knowledge of Q&A. On the right side of
each chapter opening, you see a list of topics covered.
This listing enables you to find quickly the information
you need.

Q&A is divided into five modules. The chapters are
organized is such a manner that you progress from
introductory information to more complex material.
Following the chapters is an appendix that provides
installation instructions.

How is This Book Organized?

The book is broken into the following chapters.

Chapter 1 addresses the basics of using Q&A. Use of the
keyboard, function keys, menu navigation, and help
screens are also discussed. Instructions are given on
starting the program and running the tutorial that comes
with the software.

Chapter 2 discusses database design. You learn how to
set up the form on-screen.

Chapter 3 discusses how to move around the database form, add data to the form, and how to customize the form.

Chapter 4 teaches you how to retrieve information from the database and how to make modifications to the data.

Chapter 5 introduces you to the programming functions of Q&A. You learn how to use functions and lookup statements.

Chapter 6 shows you how to print from the File module so that you can make use of the information contained in the database.

Chapter 7 concentrates on generating reports in the Report module from data within the File module.

Chapter 8 teaches you how to print the reports that you generate.

Chapter 9 introduces the Write module and explains its word processing capabilities.

Chapter 10 discusses how to retrieve and edit documents you have created with Write.

Chapter 11 describes the formatting and text enhancements you can use to refine your documents.

Chapter 12 explains the print commands in Write that control justification, line spacing, and document queues; the mail merge facilities that incorporate information stored in the File module; and how to generate mailing labels.

Chapter 13 explains some of the artificial intelligence strengths of Q&A. The chapter explains how you can use common, everyday phrases to make requests of a database.

Chapter 14 teaches you how to install printers, set default directories, issue DOS commands from within Q&A, and run other programs from the Q&A Main menu.

Chapter 15 discusses macros and their many uses within Q&A. The chapter studies writing and saving macros that you can use in any module of Q&A.

Chapter 16 presents using Q&A in a multiuser (network) environment. You learn basic network and data integrity principles. The chapter explains assigning and maintaining database passwords and provides suggestions for using and choosing passwords.

The appendix contains installation instructions.

Who Should Use This Book?

This book is recommended for those who are first getting to know Q&A and for those who want to examine specific areas of Q&A in detail. The book is designed to demonstrate different principles of design and implementation, but it is not meant to replace the documentation that came with the software. This book does not discuss all features of Q&A; it discusses only those features that give you a basic understanding of the program. You can then build on that basic understanding and advance into some of the more complex features of the software.

Because of its design, this book is intended also to serve as a refresher guide to specific tasks within Q&A. Most exercises can apply to almost any database, report, or word processing document. The samples that you develop in each chapter highlight the program's capabilities; you can replace or modify these samples easily so that they accomplish your particular task.

In addition, Que Corporation has a full line of reference books that can accompany this book. *Using Q&A*, 2nd Edition focuses in detail on each specific feature and is an excellent source for research. An easy and portable companion, *Q&A Quick Reference* presents step-by-step instructions in a task-oriented format.

Conventions Used in This Book

Certain conventions are used throughout the text and graphics of *Q&A 4 QuickStart* to help you better understand the book's subject.

Text you should type is displayed in **boldface blue type**. When you press a key combination, such as Alt-F6, the keys are shown as they appear on the keyboard (Alt-F6). In this book, a key combination is joined by a hyphen. You press and hold down the Alt key and then press the F6 key.

Screen messages appear in a special typeface.

Getting Started with Q&A

Q&A is a database and word processing software package that combines the practicality and ease of a highly functional database with the power and flexibility of a full service word processor. With its fully integrated word processing and file management capabilities, Q&A offers outstanding performance with highly advanced features. Unlike some database and word processing packages, Q&A is easy to learn and enables you to be highly productive in a short amount of time. The software consists of separate modules. Because of Q&A's modular construction, you can learn what you need to know immediately, and then proceed with other areas of the system as time permits.

This chapter introduces you to the five modules of Q&A and gives you a brief description of the available features. You also learn how to navigate through the menus of the software and how to use some primary function key assignments. The chapter reviews navigation keys on your keyboard, as well as some keys that provide special functions, such as Insert, Delete, Home, and so on.

Understanding the advantages of Q&A

Navigating the menu structure

Learning Q&A's modules

Using the keyboard

Using the mouse

Starting Q&A

Getting help

1

You do not need prior knowledge of the software before beginning this chapter. Some exposure to basic principles of DOS is helpful, but not necessary.

You need to install Q&A software on your computer before you continue. For installation instructions, refer to the Appendix or your Instruction Manual.

Key Terms Used in This Chapter	
Module	The way in which Q&A organizes its various applications. Q&A contains five modules: File, Report, Write, Utilities, and Assistant.
Random Access Memory	The computer's primary working memory in which program instructions and data are stored so that they are accessible directly to the central processing unit (CPU).

What is Q&A?

Q&A is a database and word processing software package for personal computers. The program is constructed using modules, with each module focusing on a different type of application. You can learn to use the modules as you need them. The modules are not interdependent, but they can work together when you want to exchange information between applications. When printing a document from the word processing module, for example, you can include information that you stored in the database module. You can exchange data between all parts of Q&A easily.

Not only can you share data between modules of Q&A, you also can use Q&A's highly functional Import menu to import information from other databases or documents into Q&A documents. Imported data is not restricted to personal computer software packages; Q&A also shares information with minicomputers. You can import data into Q&A, update the data, use it for reports and documents, and then send it back to the host computer through export facilities.

You can use Q&A on both personal computers that are independent of any other computers or on a network system that uses a file server. This versatility enables your computer system to grow with your needs.

1

Because your needs grow and evolve, software must be able to keep up with your expanding requirements. Q&A is flexible and enables you to develop basic applications initially; as your expertise increases, you can use the more advanced features of the software. Database designs and report formats are evolutionary and you can modify them over time. You can make changes to the information in your database quickly and easily. You can add and move fields, change labels, or complete whatever modification is required to make the database more workable—even if you make these changes years after you created the database.

Q&A consists of five modules: File, Report, Write, Utilities, and Assistant. The modules are linked together in such a way that they can exchange data freely. You can create a database that contains addresses and then use those addresses in mailings without having to retype the information or convert the data from one file format to another.

The File Module

The File module is the core of Q&A. File is a full-featured database management program, which you can use to design and maintain databases. In fact, File can stand alone as an application.

With File, you can create a database, add records, manipulate those records, or redesign the database at any time. You can view the data in Form view, which shows one record at a time, or in Table view, which shows records arranged in columns by field. Both views make it easy for you to browse through the database.

Organization is a snap with Q&A. You can organize data alphabetically, numerically, or by keywords. You also can search for records that meet certain criteria and display only those records rather than all the records in the database.

The Report Module

The Report module is an extension of the database module that enables you to retrieve data and display it in ways that are easily understood. Q&A has preprogrammed report formats, which you can customize to create reports that suit your needs. After you create a report, you can use the Write module to dress up the report. With this module, you can create any report ranging from a simple list of information to a complex crosstab with summary fields.

1

The Write Module

Q&A's Write module is a full-featured word processor that can be used to create any type of document. With Write, you can create headers and footers, work with multiple column documents, and run a spelling check. The mail merge features of Write enable you to print mailing labels, envelopes, and form letters with ease. Write even contains predefined formats for most types of mailing labels.

The Intelligent Assistant

Q&A's Intelligent Assistant enables you to retrieve information from databases using simple English statements and questions. The Assistant is a natural-language program with a vocabulary of around 600 words. To use this module effectively, you must conform to its fairly strict syntax. But because you can issue commands in English, you don't have to learn Q&A's regular query language.

Using Q&A's artificial intelligence, you can use common, everyday phrases to issue requests and generate reports. The software can "learn" terminology that is unique to your industry or working environment; this knowledge enables you to use expressions and phrases with which you are familiar.

The Utilities Module

Q&A's Utilities module is several different programs that enable you to perform file management and housekeeping tasks. You can use Utilities to customize Q&A to suit your needs; to modify font files for your printer; and to list, rename, copy, and delete files.

Q&A is a menu-driven system. You select your choices from a menu instead of a command line. As you work your way through Q&A's menus, previous menus are visible and layered one on top of another, with the most recent menu being on top. Because of this stacking method, you can see the menus that you accessed to arrive at your current location in the system.

What Do You Need To Use Q&A?

1

To run Q&A 4.0, you must have the following equipment:

- An IBM-compatible personal computer with at least one floppy disk drive and a hard disk drive.
- At least 3.5 megabytes of free storage space on your hard disk.
- At least 512K of RAM (random access memory). (If you plan to run Q&A on a network, note that each computer should have 484K of free memory.)
- A color or monochrome monitor.
- DOS version 2.1 or later. (You must have DOS 3.1 or later for network use.)

The following equipment, though not necessary, is recommended:

- A printer (dot-matrix, laser, or inkjet).
- A Microsoft-compatible mouse or trackball.
- Expanded memory.

Navigating within Q&A

Q&A uses menus to guide you through the system. Each menu contains a series of options. Using a layered menu system makes learning Q&A easier and aids in menu navigation.

```
                    Q&A MAIN MENU

               F - File
               R - Report
               W - Write
               A - Assistant
               U - Utilities
               X - Exit Q&A




Q&A Version 4.0   125N  Copyright (C) 1985-1991, Symantec   All rights reserved.
Reminder: Select Utilities to customize Q&A for your printer.
X-Exit to DOS            F1-Description of choices          ←┘ Continue
```

The system begins with the Q&A Main menu.

1

To the left of each option is a letter that represents the selection. You can use the following methods to navigate through menus:

- Press the cursor-movement keys to highlight the selection you want and press ⏎Enter.

- Press the letter to the left of the selection and press ⏎Enter.

- Press the number sequence of the selection. To access the Write menu from the Main menu, for example, you press 3.

- Press the space bar to move the highlight bar to the selection you want and press ⏎Enter.

- Use the mouse to point to the selection you want and click once to select the choice. Click twice to activate your choice.

Use the method that is most comfortable to you. As you become more familiar with Q&A and learn the menu sequence, you can advance to faster navigation techniques.

You can set Q&A to make menu navigation easier. You can change the program execution from manual, which requires you to press Enter to confirm menu selections, to automatic. When you use automatic execution, you just press the letter to the left of the selection. You do not have to press ⏎Enter to confirm the selection.

Many of the instructions in this book tell you to "select" an option. Use the following guidelines to select an option:

- If you have execution set for manual, press the cursor-movement keys to highlight the selection and press ⏎Enter.

- If you have execution set for automatic, press the letter that precedes the option. You do not have to press ⏎Enter.

Using the Keyboard

You can use many different styles of keyboards with Q&A. Some keyboards are more elaborate than others, but they all function identically.

Most people use either a Personal Computer AT keyboard or an Enhanced keyboard. Keyboards contain the following areas:

- The function keys, labeled F1 to F12 at the top of the IBM Enhanced keyboard (or F1 through F10 at the left of the Personal Computer AT keyboard).

- The alphanumeric, or "typing," keys, located in the center of the keyboard.

1

- The numeric and cursor-movement keys, found at the right side of the keyboard.

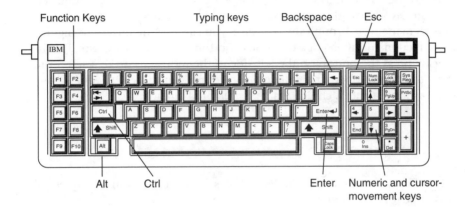

Personal Computer AT keyboard

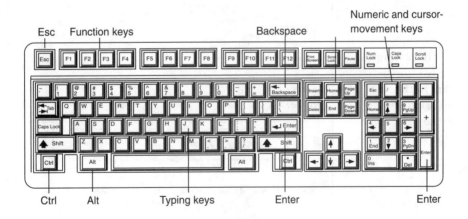

Enhanced keyboard

Function Keys

Many of the commands in Q&A are initiated by pressing function keys. Q&A uses only the first ten function keys. These keys are used to trigger special tasks within Q&A. You use function keys alone or in combination with the Ctrl, Alt, or ⇧Shift keys. To use a key combination such as ⇧Shift-F1, hold down the ⇧Shift key and press F1. This key combination initiates your request. Q&A displays function keys and key combinations on the bottom line of the screen.

1

Using Q&A with a Mouse

You can use a mouse to navigate through documents and make menu selections in Q&A. Instead of using navigational keys such as the cursor-movement keys to maneuver through the software, you can use the mouse to highlight the selection and then click the mouse button. When clicking with a mouse, quickly press the button on the left side of the mouse to make a selection. Press the button once to highlight a choice; press it twice (called *double-clicking*) to activate a choice that is highlighted already.

Navigating the Directory Structure

Q&A offers several menus with lists of files for your function or request. These lists appear throughout Q&A.

When viewing a file list, the first item on the list is \.. (Except in the root directory).

```
                      LIST OF FILES IN C:\QA\WRITE\*.*

   \..                    QUEUE
   ABBREAK.V04             REPORT.INX
   ANNOUNCE                SUBCALCS
   BADDEBIT                TEST
   BADDEBIT.110
   LETTER
   MACROS
   OPERATOR
   PROPOSAL
   PXASSIST.405
   Q-REPORT.403


         File name: C:\QA\WRITE\


   Esc-Exit    F1-Help    F3-Delete    F5-Copy    F7-Search    F8-Rename    F10-Continue
```

Select the \ to go back one directory. Generally, directories are structured in a hierarchy. To move up one step in the hierarchy, select \.. and press ⏎Enter.

```
                    LIST OF FILES IN C:\QA\*.DTF

\..
\FILE
\WRITE
EMPLOYEE.DTF
PROPERTY.DTF
WRIGHT.DTF




        File name: C:\QA\


 Esc-Exit  F1-Help  F3-Delete  F5-Copy  F7-Search  F8-Rename  F10-Continue
```

All directories contained in a list appear first, with individual files following in alphabetical order.

To go to a directory that is one level below your current directory, highlight the directory name (\WRITE or \FILE) and press ⏎Enter.

You then can assign a description to any Q&A file. This option appears when you highlight the file on a file listing.

```
                    LIST OF FILES IN C:\QA\WRITE\*.*

\..              QUEUE
ABBREAK.V04      REPORT.INX
ANNOUNCE         SUBCALCS
BADDEBIT         TEST
BADDEBIT.110
LETTER
MACROS
OPERATOR
PROPOSAL
PXASSIST.405
Q-REPORT.403


        File name: C:\QA\WRITE\LETTER


LETTER        Size: 1,357     Date edited: 11/18/90    Time edited: 17:50
No description available.  Press F6 to add one.
Esc-Exit  F1-Help  F3-Delete  F5-Copy  F7-Search  F8-Rename  F10-Continue
```

See the message line for instructions regarding this option.

1

Descriptions can be up to 72 characters long and can be appended to any database or word processing file.

Using Q&A Help Screens

Q&A has an extensive and very detailed set of help screens that are available throughout the system. The following figure shows a sample of a help screen for the File module. Many times, more help screens are available than just the first one that you see on-screen. If more help screens are available, you are instructed to press F1 for more information. The additional help screen appears. If the current help screen contains more information than can fit on one screen, you are asked to press PgDn to view additional screens. Some help screens are many pages long and cover tasks in great detail.

Notice how the screen gives a brief description of the available functions, followed by a cross-reference to the Instruction Manual.

```
                        BUILT-IN MATH FUNCTIONS              Pg. F-154

Note: In the following, n can be a number, a field identifier, or an expres-
sion. x can be a text value, field id, or expression. list is a list of field
identifiers separated by commas, double dots (to express a range), or both.

@ABS(n)         Returns the absolute value of n.
@ASC(x)         Returns the ASCII decimal value of the first character of x.
@AVG(list)      Produces the average of the values of all items in the list.
@EXP(n,m)       Raises n to the mth power.
@INT(n)         Returns the integer portion of n.
@MAX(list)      Returns the maximum of all items in the list.
@MIN(list)      Returns the minimum of all items in the list.
@MOD(x,y)       Returns x modulo y.  See Pg. ?? of manual for more information.
@NUM(x)         Returns the number represented by x.
@ROUND(n,m)     Rounds off n to m decimal digits.
@SGN(x)         Returns the sign of x.
@SQRT(n)        Returns the square root of n
@STD(list)      Calculates the standard deviation of the items in the list.
@SUM(list)      Returns the sum of the values of all the items in the list.
@VAR(list)      Returns the variance of all non-blank items in the list.
@WIDTH(n)       Returns the width of field n.

Esc-Exit              → PgDn-More ←      → PgUp-Previous ←
```

This help format is consistent throughout the software. The cross-reference gives you a starting point from which to research your task further.

Develop the habit of using the help screens as often as possible. After you become more familiar with the software and documentation, you may not use the screens as much. New users, however, will find the help screens an invaluable source of information. The cross-references can save you time and much frustration when you are trying to execute a task. Help screens are used repeatedly throughout this book to help you get into the practice of using them as your first line of reference.

Starting Q&A

The following start-up procedures assume that you are accessing Q&A at the DOS prompt. If you are using Q&A on a network or are using a menu system from which to load software, you may need to follow a different start-up procedure.

Before loading the software onto your computer, make a backup of the software disks. Refer to the Q&A Instruction Manual for backup instructions.

The following instructions are for computers with Q&A installed and ready to run on a hard or fixed disk. Because most hard disks are named drive C, the following steps follow that assumption. Q&A software should already be installed in the QA subdirectory, as recommended in the installation instructions. If you are using a different subdirectory name, substitute that subdirectory name for QA in the following procedures.

To start Q&A, follow these instructions:

1. Turn on your computer.

   The C: prompt appears. The Q&A software is stored in a subdirectory on drive C.

2. At the C: prompt, type **CD QA** to access the QA subdirectory in which the Q&A software is stored.

3. Press ⏎Enter .

   You are taken into the subdirectory that contains the software files.

4. Type **QA** and press ⏎Enter to start the program.

   The software loads and you are taken to the Q&A Main menu.

Using the Q&A Tutorial

Q&A comes with a tutorial program that is meant to acquaint you briefly with the software. The tutorial examines all Q&A modules quickly, and it gives you an idea of how you can accomplish tasks in Q&A. Try to complete the tutorial before beginning this book, although completing the tutorial is not necessary for understanding the QuickStart. The tutorial explains issues that are discussed in greater detail in the book. To complete the tutorial, you must have the tutorial files copied on your hard disk.

1

To complete the tutorial, follow these steps:

1. Change to the directory in which Q&A is stored.
2. Follow the steps in the Instruction Manual using the practice database WRIGHT.DTF.

2

Starting the File Module

This chapter helps you design and set up a database. Before you begin, make sure that Q&A is installed and ready to use (see the Appendix for detailed installation instructions). Although you should complete the tutorial that comes with the software, it is not a requirement to proceed with this chapter. The tutorial, however, only takes about an hour to work through and will help you learn quickly.

This chapter assumes that you have minimal knowledge of Q&A. Exercises are designed to establish a good basis from which to grow and expand your knowledge of databases. Not all features available in the File module are examined. You examine only the key features needed to begin the learning process.

Make sure that you understand Q&A's function keys, cursor movement, and menu navigation before you begin this chapter. Your understanding of this information is necessary to execute the exercises contained in this chapter. If you are familiar with computers and keyboards, you may want to briefly review this information. If computers are new to you, please read Chapter 1 completely before beginning.

Understanding File

Designing a database

Adding fields

Defining the format spec

Understanding global options

Redesigning a database

2

Key Terms Used in This Chapter

Data	Actual information pertaining to a field. Data in an address database can contain the name of a street (Elm Street), the name of the city (Indianapolis), and the name of the state (IN). Fields consist of data.
Database	An electronic filing cabinet of information pertaining to a general topic. Databases consist of records, fields, and data. Information is grouped into classifications, such as address books, expense reports, and budgets. These classifications represent a unique group of information. Databases make retrieval and sorting of data easy.
Field	A group of labels that describe a form. Suppose, for example, that you have an address database. The fields in this database may contain first and last name, street address, city, state, and phone number. Fields make up forms.
Records	A group of fields that belong to one topic. For example, records contain information about a specific thing, person, or company. In a filing cabinet database of addresses, for example, a record is the name of each person whose address the database includes. Records make up a database.

Understanding File

You use databases on a daily basis. Examples of databases include the Yellow Pages of your telephone directory, cookbooks, or possibly a parts list for your car. All these general groups of information represent a database. Sometimes you don't think of them as databases, but nonetheless, they are a grouping of information pertaining to a general topic. When you need specific details, you go to the general group to retrieve the needed information. Q&A gives you a similar opportunity to develop databases of information. This information is stored in the File module of Q&A.

With the File module, you create electronic databases. These databases are electronic filing cabinets that supply information in numerous ways. When thinking of a database as a filing cabinet, compare the filing cabinet with your computer. A filing cabinet can contain different types of information on a variety of topics. The information can include financial statements from a spreadsheet program, names and addresses from a database program, and correspondence from a word processing program. Each part of the cabinet serves a beneficial purpose, although the types of information stored can be very different. Software programs used to store this information can be compared to the drawers in a filing cabinet.

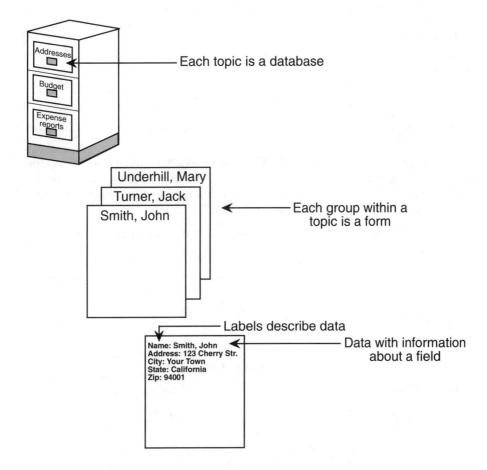

If you look at the drawer containing names and addresses, the file folders contained in the drawers represent forms in a database. Each piece of information within the file folder is a field in the database. Databases consist of many individual fields that contain data.

19

2

The fields and data within them are identified using labels (a description of the data) followed by a blank area in which you type the information.

```
                              BUDGET
        ─────────────────────────────────────────────────────
        Check Number:▮▮▮▮▮▮          Date of Expense:
        Payee:
        Amount:
        Description:
        Type:
        Check Cleared?:
        Date Entered:
        Time Entered:




        ─────────────────────────────────────────────────────
        BUDGET.DTF     New Form 1    of 1      Total Forms: 5    Page 1  of 1

        Esc-Exit   F1-How to add   F3-Delete form   F7-Search   F8-Calc   F10-Continue
```

Facts are entered in the database and organized in a way that makes it easy for you to find and sort the information. All fields within a database can be used in a retrieval or sorting routine so that you can search for information in any field in a database.

To enter the File module of Q&A, start from the Q&A Main menu and select File.

The File menu is displayed.

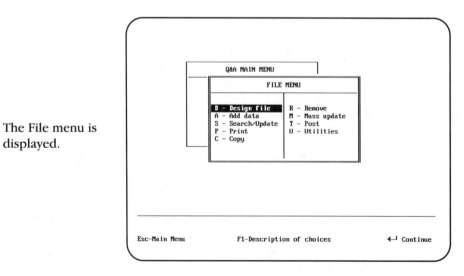

```
                    Q&A MAIN MENU
                    ┌──────────────────────────────────┐
                    │           FILE MENU              │
                    │                                  │
                    │  D - Design file    R - Remove   │
                    │  A - Add data       M - Mass update│
                    │  S - Search/Update  T - Post     │
                    │  P - Print          U - Utilities│
                    │  C - Copy                        │
                    │                                  │
                    └──────────────────────────────────┘

        ─────────────────────────────────────────────────────
        Esc-Main Menu          F1-Description of choices      ←┘ Continue
```

The File menu provides you with the following options:

- Use the Design file option to design a database, redesign an existing database, or customize a database to use some of Q&A's special features.
- Use the Add data option to add information or data to an existing database.
- Use the Search/Update option to search for previously entered forms and to update those forms.
- Use the Print option to print information contained in a database.
- Use the Copy option to copy database designs or selected forms from one database to another within the Q&A software package.
- Use the Remove option to delete all forms or selected forms from a database.
- Use the Mass update option to change all the information or data in fields at one time instead of updating data one form at a time.
- Use the Post option to take data from one database and automatically send it to another field in another database.
- Use the Utilities options to back up or copy a database onto a disk, provide a link to an SQL database, import and export data, and recover damaged databases.

Designing a Database

Designing a database is an easy process. Think of all the pieces of information you want to capture and then group that information together. For example, suppose that you want to design a database to track receipts. First gather the receipts and see whether you can group the receipts in general headings. Each general heading becomes a field, and all the headings combined become your database.

Now consider which pieces of information you want included in the database. These pieces of information will become the database fields. Then consider the kinds of questions you may ask about the information. This process helps you formulate the reporting requirements and aids in field development. Try to gather any documents or reports you want the database to generate. Remember, however, that you do not have to finalize the database design at this time. With Q&A, you easily can change and customize your basic design.

When you design a Q&A database, you must remember the following information:

- Field names within a database should always be different.

  As your skill level evolves and you begin using programming statements and mail merge facilities, not repeating field names becomes even more important. Unless you use special programming procedures, Q&A looks for requested fields by name. If it finds two identical field names, Q&A takes the information out of the first field it encounters. This field may not be the one you want.

- Enter field names one after another, each on its own line.
  Do not be concerned with sequence or cosmetic appearance. After the field names are on-screen, you can go back and indicate the length of the field. This procedure makes it easier for you to capture more of your relevant fields the first time and minimizes the time spent redesigning the form.

- Always try to estimate the length needed to input data in a field.
  Use the greater-than symbol (>) to indicate where a field ends. If you do not use the greater-than sign, Q&A assumes that you need the entire line (80 spaces) for data entry. If you do not define field length, problems can result when you print reports or move fields. You accidentally can move or add fields on top of existing data.

The following example illustrates a database that is used for tracking household expenses. This database contains all monthly household bills along with daily expenses, such as groceries, shopping, and entertainment. The fields contain information about the date of expenditure, payee, amount spent, check number, description, and type of expense.

To create a database, follow these steps:

1. From the Main menu, select File.
2. Select Design a new file.

2

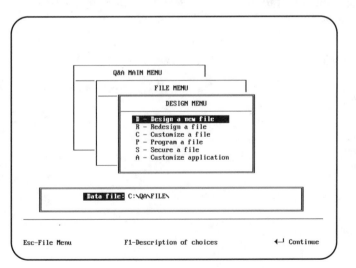

```
              Q&A MAIN MENU
                   FILE MENU
                      DESIGN MENU
                 D - Design a new file
                 R - Redesign a file
                 C - Customize a file
                 P - Program a file
                 S - Secure a file
                 A - Customize application




   Esc-File Menu      F1-Description of choices      ←┘ Continue
```

The Design menu
is displayed.

The Design menu consists of the following choices:

- Use the **D**esign a new file option to design a new file or database.
- Use the **R**edesign a file option to redesign an existing file or database. With this option, you can add new fields, move existing fields, or delete fields.

```
              Q&A MAIN MENU
                   FILE MENU
                      DESIGN MENU
                 D - Design a new file
                 R - Redesign a file
                 C - Customize a file
                 P - Program a file
                 S - Secure a file
                 A - Customize application

     Data file: C:\QA\FILE\


   Esc-File Menu      F1-Description of choices      ←┘ Continue
```

You are
prompted to
enter a name for
the database you
want to design.

2

- Use the Customize a file option to customize or enhance an existing database. You can develop tables, help screens, and use the programming features of Q&A.

- Use Program a file to develop programming statements, control cursor movement, control update ability for fields, and develop field names.

- Use Secure a file to restrict access to a file or to certain fields within the file.

- Use Customize application to create custom menus and control customized Q&A applications. You also use this option to lock a database or protect a macro file.

    Database names can be up to eight characters long and can contain alphabetic and numeric characters. Select a name that reminds you of the content of the database.

3. Type a name for the database and press ⏎Enter.

    Because this sample database contains information pertaining to a monthly budget, type **BUDGET**.

You will see three screens as you go through the design process. The first screen contains the field names and lengths of the fields, the second screen tells Q&A what kind of data you will enter in the fields, and the third screen tells Q&A how to display the data (numbers with decimals, for example). Do not worry about skipping any of these screens. Q&A automatically takes you through the correct process.

The screen you see now resembles a blank sheet of paper. The four lines of information at the bottom of this screen help you design your database.

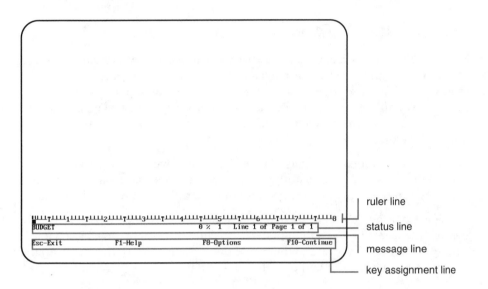

The last line on the screen, the key assignment line, shows frequently used function key assignments. You can view additional function key assignments by pressing F1.

The blank line above the key assignment line is the message line. This line is blank now because the software does not have a message or instruction to give you at the moment. When you complete a process, this line tells you what is happening and may ask for additional information needed to complete the process.

The third line from the bottom of the screen is the status line. This line tells you the name of the database, whether any special keys are invoked (Caps Lock, Ins), the amount of memory used for the database design, and the location of the cursor on the form.

The ruler line is directly above the status line. Cursor location is displayed on this line as well as any tabs that you set.

Notice that the top part of the screen is blank. This area will hold your fields. You are looking at Page 1 of 1 of your new database. Even though you see only one page, your databases can be up to 10 pages long. To access additional pages, press the PgDn key. Press the PgUp key to return to the first page.

Creating the File Form

As you design a database, remember that you can use the additional pages behind Page 1. In some circumstances, you may want to use Page 1 for one group of data and use Page 2 for another group of data. Suppose, for example, that you work in an office where your computer is easily viewed by passers by. You may want to have the confidential data, such as salary or bonus information, hidden on Page 2.

Think of the computer screen as a piece of paper or worksheet. Enter each field label on a separate line, until you have most fields listed that are needed. You then can redesign and change the sequence or appearance of the form.

On Line 1 type a title for each database you design. This title helps you quickly identify the database. Even though the status line displays the database name, your eyes naturally gravitate to the top of the form first. Move the cursor to the first position on the form and type the database title.

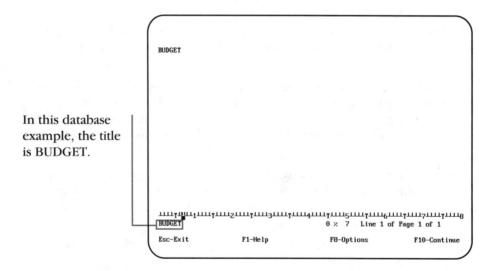

In this database example, the title is BUDGET.

Do not be concerned about the positioning of the title at this time. You will center it on the form later. Press ↵Enter twice to move the cursor down two lines on the form.

2

Now you need to add the fields that will contain your data. Fields are comprised of these parts:

- A label, which describes the data.
- A colon (:), which indicates where the label ends and the data begins.
- A greater-than symbol (>), which identifies where the data and the field ends.

Adding Fields

You add fields to a database using the first screen in the design process. Just type the names of the fields. Whether you are designing a new database or redesigning an existing database, the first screen you see in the design process contains the fields.

To add fields to a database, complete the following steps:

1. Type the field label.
2. End the field label by typing a colon (:).
3. Designate the size of the blank by moving the cursor the required number of spaces, and then type a greater-than symbol (>) to indicate the end of the blank.

   You can create blanks of up to one page in length, but you cannot extend the field from one page to another.

4. Press ⏎Enter to advance the cursor to the next line.

   For example, to add a field to the sample database, type **Date of Expense:**, move the cursor 10 spaces, type **>**, and press ⏎Enter. Continue with this procedure to add the sample field labels. The numbers in parentheses represent the amount of space you should leave for each blank.

   Payee: (40)

   Amount: (10)

   Check Number: (6)

   Description: (40)

   Type: (25)

2

This screen
illustrates what
the sample
database looks
like.

```
BUDGET

Date of Expense:              >
Payee:                                >
Amount:              >
Check Number:          >
Description:                          >
Type:                        >




LLLLᵀLLLL₁LLLLᵀLLL₂LLLLᵀLLL₃▮▮▮ᵀLLLL₄LLLLᵀLLL₅LLLLᵀLLL₆LLLᵀLLL₇LLLLᵀLLL₈
BUDGET                              0 % 32 Line 8 of Page 1 of 1

Esc-Exit          F1-Help          F8-Options          F10-Continue
```

5. Press F10 after you enter all fields for the database.

As Q&A saves the field names, the `Saving Design` message appears on the
message line. You are now at the second screen in the design process.

Adding Multiple Line Fields

If you need to specify more than one line of space for a particular field, you
can set up a multiple line field. The process for adding multiple line fields is
identical to adding a single line field. Note that if you want the left edges of
the blank to line up, you must insert the less-than symbol (<) instead of a
colon at the beginning of the field. If you start the field with a colon, successive lines begin at the left edge of the screen.

Defining the Format Spec

After you save the field names, you see the Format Spec screen. Use this
screen to describe the data you plan to type in each field in the database.

```
  BUDGET
  Date of Expense: T
  Payee: T
  Amount: T
  Check Number: T
  Description: T
  Type: T




      In each field, type a letter to say what TYPE of information
      goes in that field.  The information types are:

       T = Text           N = Number          D = Dates
       Y = Yes/no         M = Money           H = Hours (time)
       K = Keywords (as in properties, categories)

      You can also enter format OPTIONS.  Press F1 for more information.


  BUDGET.DTF              Format Spec                Page 1  of 1

  Esc-Exit    F1-How to format   F3-Clear Spec   F6-Expand field    F10-Continue
```

A help screen automatically appears to show you the available format options.

By indicating fields as being Date, Hour, Number, or Money type, you can perform calculations and determine age, time, numeric, and financial considerations. Unless you designate otherwise, Q&A assumes that all fields will contain text and places the letter "T" in each field. Not all fields will be text fields, however. Some fields will contain numbers, dollar amounts, keywords, and dates. Changing format specifications is easy. Just type the correct format directly over the top of the current format.

Text Type

Text fields require no special formatting features. These fields can contain alphabetic and numeric information. Q&A automatically assigns all fields as this type by default. Although you often may think of text fields as containing only numeric information, they often contain other data. For example, the phone number (555)555-1212 contains a hyphen and parentheses.

Date Type

You can specify dates in a variety of formats. For example, December 31, 1991 can be entered as 2/31/91 or Dec. 31, 1991. Each type of date format requires a different number of spaces on the form. In order to accommodate all date formats, insert 10 spaces as you design the date field.

All date fields are formatted the same and can have date calculations performed on them. Entries are validated to ensure each month reflects the correct number of days. If you try to add the date September 31, 1991 in a date field, for example, Q&A tells you that it is not a valid entry (September has only 30 days).

Hour Type

With this format type, you can enter time in the 12- or 24-hour format. Although Q&A displays time in the 12-hour format (such as 5:00 p.m.), it can interpret the 24-hour format (17:00).

Money Type

Money type fields contain currency amounts. When entering data into a Money type field, it is not necessary to type the currency symbol—the symbol is added for you. If you enter a whole number with no decimal places, you do not need to type the decimal followed by zeros. If you do not indicate decimals, the number is whole, and Q&A automatically places the decimal and zeros for you.

Number Type

Number type fields only contain numeric entries. If you try to make an entry other than numeric, the entry is not accepted. Numbers entered in this type of field do not receive a decimal unless you enter it at the time of entry.

Keyword Type

A keyword data type enables you to retrieve criteria that may not be apparent from any other field in the database. You type each keyword and separate entries with a semicolon. It is possible that expenses can be more than one type. For example, an expense can be a utility expense and a phone bill. Groceries may be food expenses and a special expense for entertainment. To allow for multiple types of expenses, use the Keyword format for this field.

2

Yes/No Type

A Yes/No field is used to store an answer to a question that can be answered either in the positive or the negative. Positive conditions are indicated by yes, Y, true, T, or 1; negative values can be no, N, false, F, or 0.

You may find this type of field helpful when you want to indicate those customers who receive preferred pricing, for example. Using this field type, you quickly can retrieve the preferred customer listings so that you can send out sale flyers.

Setting Sample Field Types

If you are following the BUDGET database example, follow these steps to specify field types:

1. Change the "Date of Expense" field format to indicate that all entries in this field will be calendar dates. Place the cursor in the "Date of Expense:" field, and type a **D** directly over the top of the T.

2. Change the "Amount" field format to indicate that this field will contain a money entry by placing the cursor directly over the "T" and typing **M**.

3. Change the "Check Number" field to indicate that this field will contain a numeric entry. Place the cursor directly over the "T" and type **N**.

4. Change the "Type" field format to indicate that this field may contain more than one type of expense. Place the cursor directly over the "T" and type **K**.

5. After you define the type of information you want to locate in each field, press F10.

Setting Global Format Options

When you create field types, the Global Format Options screen is displayed as the last screen in the design process. You use this screen to indicate how you want the information you requested to appear.

2

Regardless of how you make database entries, setting global formats ensures that the entries are formatted per your specifications and consistent in their appearance.

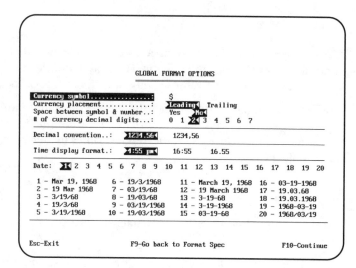

```
                        GLOBAL FORMAT OPTIONS
                        ─────────────────────

   Currency symbol.................:   $
   Currency placement..............:   Leading   Trailing
   Space between symbol & number...:   Yes    No
   # of currency decimal digits....:   0   1   2   3   4   5   6   7

   Decimal convention..:  1234.56    1234,56

   Time display format.:  4:55 pm    16:55    16.55

   Date:  1  2  3  4  5  6  7  8  9  10  11  12  13  14  15  16  17  18  19  20
    1 - Mar 19, 1968     6 - 19/3/1968     11 - March 19, 1968   16 - 03-19-1968
    2 - 19 Mar 1968      7 - 03/19/68      12 - 19 March 1968    17 - 19.03.68
    3 - 3/19/68          8 - 19/03/68      13 - 3-19-68          18 - 19.03.1968
    4 - 19/3/68          9 - 03/19/1968    14 - 3-19-1968        19 - 1968-03-19
    5 - 3/19/1968       10 - 19/03/1968    15 - 03-19-68         20 - 1968/03/19


   Esc-Exit              F9-Go back to Format Spec           F10-Continue
```

Suppose, for example, that you enter April 15, 1990 in a database. You can type this entry in several of the following formats: 4/15/90, Apr. 15, 1990, April 15, 1990, or 4-15-90. Data always is formatted to the format currently specified on the Global Options screen, however.

You can change global formats easily at a later time. When you change formats, all entries in the database automatically reflect the change. Additional editing by you is not necessary.

To move around this screen, use the cursor-movement keys or mouse pointer. Highlight the selection you want to change by pressing the up- and down-arrows. Press the right- and left-arrow keys to move to the right of the title. You also can use the space bar to move to the right of the titles. If you are using a mouse, move the pointer to the option you want to select and click the left mouse button. After you make your selections, press F10 .

The Global Format Options screen is divided into four types of formats. The following sections discuss each format.

Currency

The first section of the Global Format Options screen applies to money fields. Use this group to indicate the currency symbol you want to use. You also can indicate whether you want that symbol placed before or after the number,

2

whether you want a space between the symbol and the entry, and how many decimal places you want displayed in the figure. If you are located within the United States or Canada, Q&A's standard currency symbol is a dollar sign ($).

If you want to use a foreign currency standard, check your DOS manual for a chart of ASCII characters and numeric equivalents. To change this symbol to other currency symbols, press and hold down the Alt key and type the ASCII decimal equivalent of the symbol using the numeric key pad on your keyboard. Among the currency symbols that Q&A can display are the Italian lira, British pound, Japanese yen, and the Dutch guilder.

You also may determine the positioning of the currency symbol, the space between the symbol and the number, and the number of decimals displayed.

Decimal Convention

The second area of the Global Format Options screen enables you to set up decimal conventions. Two options are displayed. The first option follows the decimal standard. Use the second option if you prefer to separate whole numbers from partial numbers by a comma. Press ←, →, ↑, or ↓ to select the desired conventions.

Time Display Format

Use this option to select how you want a "time" field displayed. The first choice is standard time, the second choice is military time (24 hours), and the third choice follows European standards.

Date

This area of the screen enables you to choose from 20 different date formats. An example of the date March 19, 1968 is shown using all the selection options. All dates entered in fields in the database are reformatted to conform to your selection. If you decide to change the format you originally selected, press the arrow keys to select the number that appears next to the format you want to use. You also can change the format of a date field when it is being used in another module of Q&A by indicating one of the selections shown. In the BUDGET database, the Date format is style 7.

After you set all global format options, save the design by pressing F10 . The design is saved with all field names, format types, and global format options. You then return to the File menu.

Redesigning A Database

After you save a database, you can redesign it at any time—even after you enter the data. Databases usually evolve over a period of time and gradually grow to meet your needs. You will find it rare that you design a database once, and then never need to make a change. Most people don't know what they need from a database until they have used it for a while. The redesign process is easy and involves the same Q&A screens you used in the design process. You can move existing fields or add new fields to a database.

To redesign an existing database, follow these steps:

1. From the File menu, select **D**esign file.

The Design menu screen is displayed.

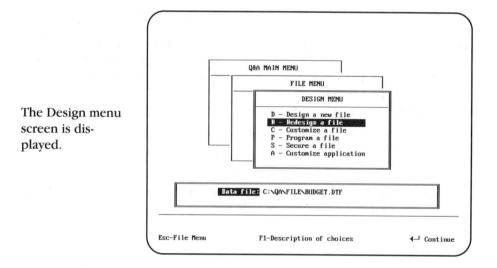

You originally used the first option on this menu to set up your database. You now will use the second option to redesign the database.

2. From the Design menu, select **R**edesign a file.

Q&A prompts you to enter the name of the database file. If the name in the prompt is correct, press ⏎Enter to confirm the choice. If the displayed name is not correct, press the space bar to delete the name. You can press ⏎Enter to see a listing of available files.

If you were just working in the BUDGET.DTF database file, the system should remember this name and the prompt should be correct. (If the prompt is not correct, press the backspace key to delete everything in the prompt and type **BUDGET**.)

3. Press ↵Enter to begin the redesign process.

```
BUDGET

Date of Expense:AA          >
Payee:AB                              >
Amount:AC          >
Check Number:AD    >
Description:AE                        >
Type:AF                >




Ͱ‖‖‖‖ᴛ‖‖‖‖₁‖‖‖ᴛ‖‖‖‖₂‖‖‖ᴛ‖‖‖‖₃‖‖‖ᴛ‖‖‖‖₄‖‖‖ᴛ‖‖‖₅‖‖‖ᴛ‖‖‖‖₆‖‖‖ᴛ‖‖‖‖₇‖‖‖ᴛ‖‖‖‖₈
BUDGET                              0 %  1   Line 1 of Page 1 of 1

Esc-Exit          F1-Help          F8-Options          F10-Continue
```

The screen you
see closely
resembles the one
you created in the
design process.

To the right of each field label and colon, however, there is a two-letter
designation (AA, AB, AC). These multiple letter additions are called field tags.
Q&A uses the field tags to internally connect the data to the correct field on
the form. Field tags always appear in alphabetical sequence. When you move
or delete fields from a form, remember that the field tag is part of the field. Be
sure to include the field tag (along with the label, colon and greater-than
symbol) no matter how you redesign the form.

If you accidentally delete a field tag, just retype the tag in the proper alphabetical sequence. If you want to add a new field, don't worry about the field
tag. Because you are adding a brand new field, the system automatically
assigns a field tag and adjusts everything in the system appropriately. If you
delete a field tag and cannot remember it, press Esc to stop the design
process and start from Step 1.

Adding New Fields

After using a database, you may decide that you need to add some fields to
make the database more useful. For example, in the BUDGET.DTF database,
you may find it helpful to have a field indicating whether a check has cleared
the bank so that you can balance your checkbook. In addition, you may want
to know on what date the entry was added to your database and at what time

2

of the day the entry took place. Suppose that the bank charges you 15 cents for each check processed, and you want to track this amount to verify monthly service charges. You also may want to add a debit field so that you can combine the amount of expense with the service charge.

Adding new fields to a database is simple. Just type the new fields where you want them to appear on the form. To add a new field, follow these steps:

1. Move the cursor directly below the field where you want the line inserted.

2. Type the field label or labels you want to add, including a colon.

3. Move the cursor to designate the field space and type a greater-than sign to indicate the end of the field.

4. Press ⏎Enter.

In this example, the fields Check Cleared, Service Charge, Total Debit, Date Entered, and Time Entered were added to the database form.

```
 BUDGET

 Date of Expense:AA          >
 Payee:AB                              >
 Amount:AC        >
 Check Number:AD    >
 Description:AE                    >
 Type:AF                >
 Check Cleared?:    >
 Service Charge:      >
 Total Debit:          >
 Date Entered:            >
 Time Entered:        >



 ⌊⌊⌊⌊ᴛ⌊⌊⌊⌊₁⌊⌊⌊⌊ᴛ⌊⌊⌊⌊₂⌊⌊ᴛ⌊⌊⌊⌊₃⌊⌊⌊⌊ᴛ⌊⌊⌊⌊₄⌊⌊⌊⌊ᴛ⌊⌊⌊⌊₅⌊⌊⌊⌊ᴛ⌊⌊⌊⌊₆⌊⌊⌊⌊ᴛ⌊⌊⌊⌊₇⌊⌊⌊⌊ᴛ⌊⌊⌊⌊₈
 BUDGET                                    0 %  23  Line 13 of Page 1 of 1

 Esc-Exit          F1-Help          F8-Options          F10-Continue
```

Moving Fields

You can rearrange the order of the fields on your form at any time. After using a database for a while, you may realize that a field would serve a better purpose in another location on the form. For example, suppose that after examining the BUDGET database file, you think it would be more practical to have the Check Number field appear first on the form beside the Date of Expense field.

To move existing fields in a database, follow these steps:

1. Place the cursor on the first character of the field label you want to move.

2. Make sure that you are in Insert mode by pressing `Ins` until `Ins` appears on the status line.

3. Press `F8` to display the Options menu.

4. Select **B**lock Operations.

5. Select Move.

6. Use the cursor-movement keys to select the text you want to move, and then press `F10`.

7. Move the cursor to the new location and press `F10` again.

   The field appears in the new location.

```
┌─────────────────────────────────────────────────────────┐
│                                                          │
│   BUDGET                                                 │
│                                                          │
│   Check Number:AD    >Date of Expense:AA        >        │
│   Payee:AB                               >               │
│   Amount:AC           >                                  │
│   Check Number:AD   >                                    │
│   Description:AE                              >          │
│   Type:AF                    >                           │
│   Check Cleared?:   >                                    │
│   Service Charge:    >                                   │
│   Total Debit:         >                                 │
│   Date Entered:       >                                  │
│   Time Entered:      >                                   │
│                                                          │
│                                                          │
│                                                          │
│   ⊥⊥⊥⊤⊥⊥⊥⊥1⊥⊥⊥⊥⊤⊥⊥⊥2⊥⊥⊥⊤⊥⊥⊥⊥3⊥⊥⊥⊤⊥⊥⊥⊥4⊥⊥⊥⊤⊥⊥⊥⊥5⊥⊥⊥⊤⊥⊥⊥6⊥⊥⊥⊤⊥⊥⊥⊥7⊥⊥⊥⊤⊥⊥⊥8   │
│   BUDGET                      Ins  0 %  21  Line 3 of Page 1 of 1   │
│                                                          │
│   Esc-Exit          F1-Help        F8-Options      F10-Continue    │
│                                                          │
└─────────────────────────────────────────────────────────┘
```

In this example, the cursor was placed on the "D" in the Date of Expense field and the Check Number field was inserted.

37

2

You add more
space between
the fields by
pressing the
space bar. Note
that you must be
in Insert mode.

```
BUDGET

Check Number:AD    >                    Date of Expense:AA      >
Payee:AB                                               >
Amount:AC       >
Check Number:AD    >
Description:AE                                    >
Type:AF                          >
Check Cleared?:       >
Service Charge:      >
Total Debit:          >
Date Entered:          >
Time Entered:        >




⌐⌐⌐⌐T⌐⌐⌐⌐1⌐⌐⌐⌐T⌐⌐⌐⌐2⌐⌐⌐⌐T⌐⌐⌐⌐3⌐⌐⌐⌐T⌐⌐⌐⌐4⌐⌐⌐⌐T⌐⌐⌐⌐5⌐⌐⌐⌐T⌐⌐⌐⌐6⌐⌐⌐⌐T⌐⌐⌐⌐7⌐⌐⌐⌐T⌐⌐⌐⌐8
BUDGET                                   Ins  0 %  41  Line 3 of Page 1 of 1

Esc-Exit            F1-Help              F8-Options          F10-Continue
```

Deleting Fields

To delete a field, follow these steps:

1. Place the cursor on the first space in the field you want to delete.

2. Press ⬆Shift - F4 to delete the line.

   The field is no longer on the screen and the balance of the form
   moves up one line.

```
BUDGET

Check Number:AD    >                    Date of Expense:AA      >
Payee:AB                                               >
Amount:AC       >
Description:AE                                    >
Type:AF                          >
Check Cleared?:       >
Service Charge:      >
Total Debit:          >
Date Entered:          >
Time Entered:        >




⌐⌐⌐⌐T⌐⌐⌐⌐1⌐⌐⌐⌐T⌐⌐⌐⌐2⌐⌐⌐⌐T⌐⌐⌐⌐3⌐⌐⌐⌐T⌐⌐⌐⌐4⌐⌐⌐⌐T⌐⌐⌐⌐5⌐⌐⌐⌐T⌐⌐⌐⌐6⌐⌐⌐⌐T⌐⌐⌐⌐7⌐⌐⌐⌐T⌐⌐⌐⌐8
BUDGET                                   Ins  0 %  1   Line 6 of Page 1 of 1

Esc-Exit            F1-Help              F8-Options          F10-Continue
```

Now the fields are
in the correct
sequence.

Restoring Deletions

To restore a field that you deleted, follow these steps:

1. Place the cursor on the first character of the line in which the deleted field was positioned.
2. Press F8 to display the Options menu.
3. Select Other Options.
4. Select Restore.

Note that only the most recent deletion is restored.

Improving Database Design

You can improve the form appearance in several ways. For example, centering the title and drawing a dividing line between the title and the fields that contain data greatly improves both the look and functionality of the form.

The Options menu offers several choices. Some choices cannot be activated at this time because their use is confined to the Write module. The following four options can be activated at this time:

- Lay out page enables you to set tabs and to draw lines.
- Align Text enables you to move text and field labels to the left or center of the page.
- Block Operations enables you to copy, move, and delete field labels and other text. You also can use Block Operations to copy or move text blocks to a disk file, print blocks, and convert blocks to all uppercase text.
- Other Options activates a spell check and thesaurus. You also can see database statistics, use search and replace, restore, and perform calculations.

The following sections discuss how to use the preceding options.

Centering a Title

To center a title on the database form, follow these steps:

1. Position the cursor on the line you want to center.
2. Press F8.

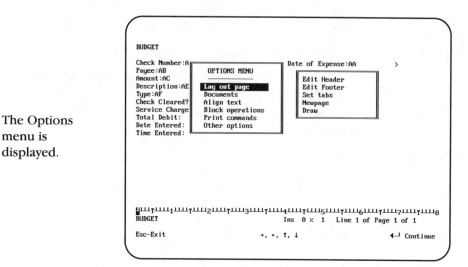

The Options
menu is
displayed.

3. Select **A**lign Text.

   The cursor jumps to the second window to the right, which enables you to select left or center alignment of text.

4. Select **C**enter.

   The title is centered on the form.

When you center text, you can position the cursor anywhere on the line. Cursor position is not important as long as it is located on the line you want centered. To remove the centering format, repeat Steps 1 through 3, but select Left instead of the Center option. Then press ⏎Enter to realign the text with the left margin.

Drawing Lines

With Q&A's Draw feature, you can enhance the appearance of a database form. Areas of the form can be emphasized by drawing lines or boxes around frequently-read fields. Use this technique to instantly focus attention to a particular part of a form.

First, position the cursor where you want to begin drawing the line. The line should start at the far left of the screen and run all the way across the form.

To draw a line on a form, follow these steps:

1. Use the cursor-movement keys to place the cursor where you want to begin drawing.

   For example, move the cursor to the first space on the blank line between the title (BUDGET) and the first field (Check Number) in the sample database you created.

2. Press F8.

   The Options menu is displayed.

3. Select Lay out Page.

   The cursor jumps to the window to the right of the Options menu.

4. Select Draw.

```
                           BUDGET

 Check Number:AD    >            Date of Expense:AA      >
 Payee:AB                              >
 Amount:AC      >
 Description:AE                             >
 Type:AF               >
 Check Cleared?:    >
 Service Charge:     >
 Total Debit:        >
 Date Entered:          >
 Time Entered:       >
```

You are now in Draw mode. The message line provides drawing instructions. The key assignment shows you the available options.

```
|ᴸᴸᴸᴸ┬ᴸᴸᴸᴸ₁ᴸᴸᴸᴸ┬ᴸᴸᴸ₂ᴸᴸᴸ┬ᴸᴸᴸ₃ᴸᴸᴸ┬ᴸᴸᴸ₄ᴸᴸᴸ┬ᴸᴸᴸ₅ᴸᴸᴸ┬ᴸᴸᴸ₆ᴸᴸᴸ┬ᴸᴸᴸ₇ᴸᴸᴸ┬ᴸᴸᴸ₈
▮BUDGET                               0 ⅍ 1   Line 2 of Page 1 of 1
Use the cursor keypad to draw.  Press F8 to erase.  Press F10 when done.
Esc—Exit      →←↓↑   Shift →←↑↓    F6—Pen up    F8—Erase    F10—Resume editing
```

5. To draw a single line, press down and hold →.

2

A line is drawn
across the length
of the form.

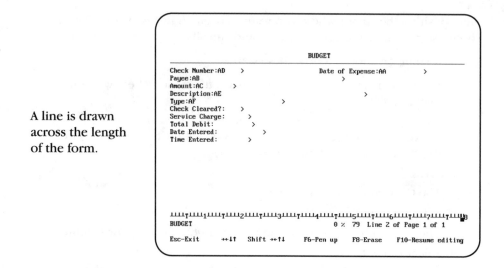

6. Press F10 to save the new line and return to the redesign process.

   You now can resume editing the design of the form.

The following table illustrates the function key assignments for Draw mode:

Table 2.1
Function Key Assignments

Key	Function
Esc (Exit)	Cancels Draw mode and returns you to Edit mode.
←, ↑, →, ↓	Draws a single solid line in the direction of the arrow.
⇧Shift-arrow keys	Draws a double line in the direction of the arrow.
F6 (Pen up)	Lifts the pen up from the form so that you can move the pen to another location.
F8 (Erase)	Erases lines already drawn on the form.
F10 (Resume editing)	Saves drawings and returns you to Edit mode.

2

Remember that you can make changes at any time. Fields can be moved, deleted, and added. Lines or boxes can be drawn around areas of the form. You can insert extra space between lines by pressing ⏎Enter. You even can make changes after you enter data. As long as you move the field tags along with the label, colon, and greater-than sign, the data is not lost.

Changing Field Formats

After you make the necessary changes to your database file and press F10, you are taken to the Format Spec screen. Notice that the new fields you added are formatted as T (Text). You must make sure that the format types are correct. For example, in the sample database you added a Check Cleared? field. This field should be formatted as a Yes/No field. Make the necessary change. All other field formats remain as you defined them when you first designed the form.

```
                              BUDGET

    Check Number: N              Date of Expense: D
    Payee: T
    Amount: M
    Description: T
    Type: K
    Check Cleared?: Y
    Service Charge: M
    Total Debit: M
    Date Entered: D
    Time Entered: H




    BUDGET.DTF              Format Spec           Page 1 of 1

    Esc-Exit    F1-Help    F3-Clear Spec    F6-Expand field    F10-Continue
```

In this example, you see the correct format specs.

Press F10 to save the changes and continue the redesign process.

You again see the Global Format Options screen. Review all settings to make sure that they are correct for any information that you added. If you specified any information as number, money, time, or date, you must make the necessary adjustments in the settings.

All settings on this screen should be correct for the sample you created except for the Time Display setting. This setting should be set at the Hour option, which is the first option on the screen. Press F10 to save the database.

Adding New Data in File

In the last chapter, you designed a form that represents the fields of data you want Q&A to use to track budget information. Of course, you can design other databases that track other types of information, but records have a primary element in common. Each record is a visual representation of the manner in which Q&A stores and manipulates data within each database.

Although you now have the necessary form to represent the budget information you want to track, no budget information yet exists in the budget database. Now you will enter sets of data into the form. A set of data is information entered into each field of the form. Each set of data is called a *record*. You add information to the budget database through the budget form one record at a time.

Moving around the database

Using data entry shortcuts

Customizing forms

Creating customized help screens

3

Key Terms Used in This Chapter

Status line	A line at the bottom of the screen that displays current status information such as the name of the database.
Message line	A line below the status line that displays pertinent messages about an operation or an action.
Key assignment line	A line below the message line that displays many of the useful function key assignments that operate a screen's features.
Ditto functions	A set of field, form, date, and time operations that copy information from a previous record to the current one.
Restricted value	An entry into a field whose value must meet certain criteria, such as being after a preset date or within a range of numbers.
Initial value	A value automatically assigned to a field of a new record when the field's value is often the same as in other records.
Speed-up search field	A field whose value is kept in an internal index by Q&A. Q&A uses the index to locate specific information quickly.
Custom help	User provided text that displays through the F1 help facilities and enables specific field information to be displayed.

Adding records, in the simplest form, consists of satisfying the information requirement of each field of the form. You add records by accessing the form, entering information into each field of the form, and finally, saving your entries. Q&A files the completed records and provides the means to retrieve the information you entered. You can view the information on-screen, modify the information through editing, and print the information in a report.

The record ensures a certain level of data checking during your input. Data checking tends to prevent inappropriate data entry into your database. You wouldn't want to find a name in a date field when you are printing records by date order, for example. Recall that the form design process enables you to specify length and type of each field's data. By selecting the field's length and type, you indicate your general information intention for the field. You satisfy a date type field by entering a date, a number type field by entering a number, and a text type field by entering characters. Field types are fundamental to adding appropriate data to a form. Your information isn't of much use if you store a name in a number field or a time in a date field.

You also specify the global formats for field types, such as dates and times, to ensure that only one mode of data entry satisfies field information entry. If you select a 12 hour time format, represented as *hh:mm am*, Q&A does not accept 24 hour format entry. Global formats go a bit beyond field types in ensuring appropriate data input.

You will discover that Q&A offers features to enhance adding appropriate data. You can change field format values, restrict values to conform to various specifications, establish initial values for fields, and include other data adding integrity checks.

In this chapter, you learn to move around on the form as you add data. You learn some shortcuts for data entry. Finally, you learn why and how to customize your forms to ensure appropriate data input.

Accessing and Navigating the Add Mode

You use the Add mode to add new records to a database. After adding a few records, you may decide to customize the database form that you are using. For now, assume that you want to add records to the budget database without adding any custom-design features. You learn about custom design and other features later in the chapter.

Adding information in Q&A File is as easy as typing the data into the appropriate field of the appropriate form. The information in this chapter applies to any Q&A V4 database. You created a database to keep track of household expenses in Chapter 2, and you continue to learn File functions by using this sample database in this and other chapters.

To access the Add mode and add information to a database, follow these steps:

    1. From the File menu, select Add Data.

3

Notice that you are prompted to enter the name of the database to which you want to add information. If no file name appears, type BUDGET.

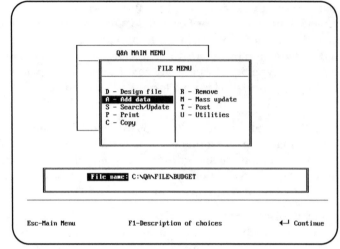

```
                  Q&A MAIN MENU
                        FILE MENU

        D - Design file      R - Remove
        A - Add data         M - Mass update
        S - Search/Update    T - Post
        P - Print            U - Utilities
        C - Copy


        File name: C:\QA\FILE\BUDGET


Esc-Main Menu        F1-Description of choices        ← Continue
```

If you have just worked with a database, Q&A volunteers the file name for you. As you saw in Chapter 2, you can blank an incorrect name by pressing the space bar key and then pressing ⏎Enter.

Q&A shows you a list of available files and waits for you to type the correct file name.

```
                LIST OF FILES IN C:\QA\FILE\*.DTF

        \..
        BUDGET.DTF




        File name: C:\QA\FILE\BUDGET


Esc-Exit   F1-Help   F3-Delete   F5-Copy   F7-Search   F8-Rename   F10-Continue
```

2. Type the name of the database you want to use or confirm that the file name displayed in the prompt is correct and press ⏎Enter to continue. Remember, you don't have to include the .DTF extension because Q&A adds it automatically.

You are going to add information to the BUDGET.DTF file. This file name may already appear in the prompt.

```
                                  BUDGET
        _____

        Check Number:█████████         Date of Expense:
        Payee:
        Amount:
        Description:
        Type:
        Check Cleared?:
        Service Charge:
        Total Debit:
        Date Entered:
        Time Entered:




        _____

        BUDGET.DTF      New Record 1    of 1     Total Records: 0      Page 1  of 1

        Esc-Exit   F1-Help     F3-Delete form    F7-Search    F8-Calc    F10-Continue
```

Now you can see what the Budget database form actually looks like.

Understanding the Screen

You are in the Add mode. Look at the bottom of the screen. The line below the horizontal line is the status line. The status line informs you about the current database status. You use the current database name as a verification check to ensure that you're adding records to the database you intend to use. The status line shows you the number of the current record. As you add records, the current number will increment for each record you add. The number does not increment if you don't save a record after you have filled in the form. You learn how to save a record in the next section.

The status line also shows you how many records the database contains and what page of the form is displayed. The current page information is useful when you work with a multi-paged form.

The blank line you see below the status line serves as a message line. The message line is blank because you have not yet entered any data. Information is displayed on this line as you add new forms. If, for example, you press ⏎Enter while in the last field of the form, the message line displays:

```
        This is the last accessible field on your form.
```

The bottom line, the key assignment line, shows frequently used function keys assignments that apply to the Add mode. You use the function keys as operation indicators. The F3 key, for example, performs an operation that deletes from the database the contents of the current record, and the F1 key accesses help text for you to read. Function key assignments may change in the different Q&A modules. Therefore, always check this line so that you know the proper function of each key.

The following list illustrates the function keys and their uses in the Add mode of File:

Key	Function
Esc (Exit)	Takes you out of Add mode and returns you to the File menu.
F1 (Help)	Displays a help screen that shows function key assignments used during the add process.
F3 (Delete form)	Deletes the data from the form of the displayed database.
F7 (Search)	Takes you from Add Data to Search/Update, bypassing the File menu.
F8 (Calc)	Executes programming statements for the current database.
F10 (Continue)	Adds the new form to the database.

As you begin to add records in Q&A, you may have to refer to the key assignments often. Most Q&A users learn the key assignments in short order, however. Before long, you'll be comfortable with the various key assignments too.

Getting Help

Q&A has an extensive help screen facility built throughout the system. Although you are currently working with the Add mode screen, help facilities are available from almost any screen. In most cases, the text presented by the help facilities pertains to the general operation you are performing. This context-sensitive nature makes Help a very useful learning aid or reminder system. Until you are more familiar with Q&A, you may find it useful to review the Help screens before you perform each task. The Help screens often refer you to a page in the Q&A documentation that addresses the function you want to perform, giving you a starting place to further research the procedure.

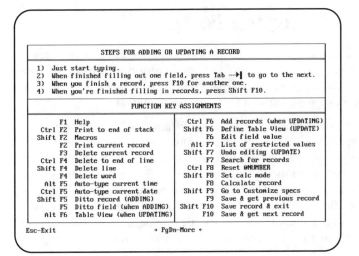

3

Press F1 to see the Help screen.

Steps for adding or updating a form are displayed. Notice that many more function keys are displayed here than were shown on the key assignment line. Keep in mind that the key assignment line shows only the most frequently used keys.

Review the function key assignments shown. Often more information is available than can appear on one screen. When additional pages of information are available, you see PgDn-More flashing at the bottom of the screen.

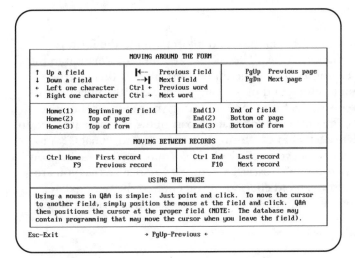

Press the PgDn key to see additional information. To access the preceding Help screen, press PgUp. To cancel the Help screen and return to the File form, press Esc.

3

Navigating Around the Form

The form shows field names or labels. Each label provides an adjacent data entry area. You may want to skip an entry field and enter data into a later field. Or perhaps you want to return to a field that you entered data into earlier. Q&A enables you to navigate around a form any way you want.

Several keys help you move around and enter information in your form. As you add information, you use the Tab↹ key to move from one field to another in sequence. Pressing ↵Enter in a field also moves to the next field, unless the current field is the last field of the form. Press ⇧Shift Tab↹ to move back, one field at a time. Use the arrow keys for up and down movement. The ↓ key moves you to the first field on the line below the cursor. The ↑ key moves you to the first field on the line directly above the cursor. Choose the method of navigating fields that is the most comfortable for you to use as you complete a form.

Within each field, the ← and → keys move the cursor correspondingly. The �←Backspace key deletes the character or number to the left of the cursor while the Del key deletes the character at the cursor's position. The Ins key toggles the typing mode between Insert and Overtype.

Navigating the forms and their fields is easy. In the next section, you put the navigating keys into practice.

Entering Data

To make your database useful, you must add information to the form you created. Adding information to Q&A File is easy. To enter information in the database, move the cursor to the first field (if it's not already there), type the information you want to enter, and press Tab↹ to move to the next field. As you enter field contents in the form, Q&A is storing your entry as tentative data. In other words, the entries aren't made a part of the database just yet. In fact, you can complete each field of a form and press Esc to signal Q&A to discard your entry. Of course, you can blank the form using the F3 key you learned about earlier. You might discard an entry if you realize that you are entering information from an old check or if you entered the wrong date, amount, and description. Sometimes, it's easier to start again with a "blank sheet of paper."

```
                              BUDGET

        Check Number: 435              Date of Expense:
        Payee:
        Amount:       ┌─────────────────────────────────────┐
        Description:  │           ! Warning !               │
        Type:         │                                     │
        Check Cleared?: │  This record will be deleted PERMANENTLY. │
        Service Charge: │                                   │
        Total Debit:  │  Are you sure you want to delete it? │
        Date Entered: │                                     │
        Time Entered: │      Y - Yes      █ N - No █        │
                      └─────────────────────────────────────┘



        ─────────────────────────────────────────────────────────

        BUDGET.DTF    New Record 1    of 1    Total Records: 0    Page 1 of 1

        Esc-Cancel                                    ↵ Continue
```

Q&A doesn't want you to delete data accidentally though and issues a verification prompt. You answer by selecting Yes or No.

Most often, though, you will want your information included in the database. You signal Q&A that the data is no longer tentative and that you want to save the information. After you enter information in all the fields, press F10 and Q&A saves your entries in the database you are working with.

To continue with the household budget example, next you add fictitious entries to the database. Because these entries are for your practice, you can delete these entries later and replace them with authentic data. Assume that you want to enter a check for groceries purchased last week. Enter the following data in the BUDGET.DTF database:

Check Number: **1095**

Date of Expense: **02/14/91**

Payee: **Ollie's Market Basket**

Amount: **$56.73**

Description: **weekly grocery shopping**

Type: **food**

Check Cleared?: **N** (No)

Service Charge: **.15**

Total Debit: **$56.88**

Date Entered: **03/01/91**

Time Entered: **10:23 am**

53

Note that the time is reformatted per the Global Format Options screen. When you make time entries, you can enter only the hour and minutes. Q&A does not acknowledge seconds as valid entries.

Now that this form is completed, press F10 to add the form to the database and to see another blank form. Look at the status line. Notice that some of the information has changed.

3

You now see New Record 2 of 2 and Total Records: 1. Two new function keys are listed on the key assignment line.

```
                              BUDGET
_____

Check Number:████████              Date of Expense:
Payee:
Amount:
Description:
Type:
Check Cleared?:
Service Charge:
Total Debit:
Date Entered:
Time Entered:




BUDGET.DTF     New Record 2    of 2    Total Records: 1    Page 1 of 1
Esc-Exit  F1-Help   F5-Ditto   F7-Search   F8-Calc   F9-Go back   F10-Continue
```

One of these keys, F5, produces a "ditto" function and the other key, F9, enables you to go back to the form you just added.

Using the Ditto Function

As you enter information into the File form, you may notice that much of what you are entering repeats the information from the previous form entry. You may, for example, find that you enter the current date over and over again. The File Add mode provides you with a data-entry shortcut that carries over the last form's contents to the current form. You can copy (ditto) data by using the F5 key. Use this feature to copy the contents of a field from the prior form to the current form. When used with other keys, F5 provides a range of ditto options. The following list illustrates the ways in which you can use the ditto feature:

F5 combinations	Use
F5	Copies the contents of one field.
⇧Shift-F5	Copies all fields from the previous form.
Ctrl-F5	Types the current date in the field.
Alt-F5	Types the current time in the field.

3

As you enter data, try these key combinations to develop a feel for their usefulness. Most users find that, after some time, the effort of becoming familiar with shortcut keys repays itself in dividends of faster, more accurate data entry.

Copying One Field at a Time

Suppose that you want to add a second form to the BUDGET.DTF database. This form contains information about your gas and electric bills. As you fill in the form, you notice that several of the fields contain the same information. Instead of retyping this information in the second form, just press F5. Q&A copies the needed information from the same field of the first record to the second (current) record.

```
                              BUDGET

Check Number: 1095              Date of Expense: 02/14/91
Payee: Ollie's Market Basket
Amount: $56.73
Description: weekly grocery shopping
Type: food
Check Cleared?: N
Service Charge: $0.15
Total Debit: $56.88
Date Entered: 03/01/91
Time Entered:10:23 am




BUDGET.DTF     New Record 1    of 1    Total Records: 1    Page 1  of 1

Esc-Exit   F1-Help      F3-Delete form    F7-Search    F8-Calc   F10-Continue
```

In this example, you see Form 1 of the BUDGET.DTF database.

In this example, you see the copied Date of Expense information.

```
                                    BUDGET
            _____

            Check Number: 1096          Date of Expense: 02/14/91
            Payee:
            Amount:
            Description:
            Type:
            Check Cleared?:
            Service Charge:
            Total Debit:
            Date Entered:
            Time Entered:




            BUDGET.DTF      New Record 2    of 2    Total Records: 1      Page 1 of 1

            Esc-Exit  F1-Help   F5-Ditto   F7-Search   F8-Calc   F9-Go back   F10-Continue
```

After you finish with the new form, press F10. You now see New Form 3 of 3 and Total Forms 2 for the database.

Copying an Entire Form

You can copy an entire form when you use the F5 key in combination with the ⇧Shift key. Suppose that you paid your gas and electric bills this month. All that would differ on the Q&A file form would be the check numbers, the amount, and the total debit. Use the Ditto Form feature to fill out the next form.

To use the Ditto Form feature, follow these steps:

1. Place the cursor in the first field of the new blank form.

   In the sample BUDGET.DTF database, place the cursor in the first field of Form 3 of 3.

2. Press ⇧Shift-F5.

   The entire contents of the prior form are copied onto the new form.

3. Enter any information that may differ in the new form.

   In this case, type the new check number, amount, and new total debit amount.

4. Press F10 to save the new form.

Using Ditto To Enter Time and Date

In addition to copying forms, you also can insert the current date and time. This date is retrieved from the date that displays when you first turn on your computer. You can ask Q&A to read this date and insert it into a field. Press `Ctrl`-`F5` to enter the current date. You also can add the current time by pressing `Alt`-`F5`.

Customizing a Database

You can see that as you enter information into a database, the process can be repetitious and tedious. Q&A provides options to make data entry and processing easier. You can automate simple tasks and, with the help of Q&A, recall them as needed. The Customize feature of Q&A is part of the Design menu.

To access the Customize features, follow these steps:

1. From the File menu, select Design File.
2. Select Customize a file.

   A prompt appears at the bottom of the screen asking which database you want to customize.
3. Type the name of the file you want to customize if the name does not appear correctly. Then press `↵Enter`.

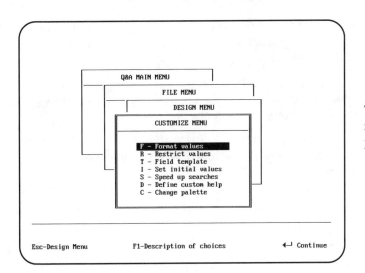

The Customize menu is displayed.

This part of the system is where you can use the power of Q&A to create useful databases. Use Customize to maximize the efficiency of your design. Each of the features performs a particular function. A brief description of these functions follows:

- Use Format values to change the format type of the data you want to enter in a database. You used this screen in the Design/Redesign process, but you also can access the screen here.

- Use Restrict values to set restrictions on what kind of data you can enter into a field. You also use this option to specify whether a field is a "required" field (it must contain data).

- Use Field template to create a template for your data, such as phone numbers like (317)555-1212.

- Use Set initial values to have frequently entered information automatically typed in a field as you add new forms.

- Use Speed up searches to maximize the performance of a database and to check for duplicate entries.

- Use Define custom help to build your own Help screens for a database.

- Use Change palette to adjust the monitor display of a database. Fields or labels can be highlighted in several different ways to vary color and contrast.

Changing the Format Values Screen

Format values are used to tell Q&A what type of information you will enter into each field. You can select types of information such as dates, numbers, money, and text with this option.

You first review the selections you made in the Design/Redesign procedure. To review the previously selected formats of a database, place the cursor on the Format values option of the Customize menu and press ⏎Enter.

You see the Format Spec screen. Notice that the frequently used function keys are shown on the key assignment line. The function key assignments for Format Spec are as follows:

Key	Function
Esc (Exit)	Returns you to the Customize menu.
F1 (Help)	Displays a Help screen with examples of different formatting options.
F3 (Clear Spec)	Deletes all format types previously selected.
F6 (Expand field)	Expands the size of the fields to contain additional format options.
F10 (Continue)	Saves changes and returns you to the Customize menu.

Also displayed is a Help screen explaining the available options. Frequently, more than one screen of help text is accessible. If more information is available, you are told to press F1 for more information or press PgDn to see additional screens.

```
       HOW TO FORMAT: THE FORMAT SPEC        pg. F-22, 109

   In each field, enter an information TYPE followed optionally by format
   OPTIONS:

   ┌──────┬─────────┬────────────────────────────────────────────────┐
   │ TYPE │ MEANING │              FORMAT OPTIONS                     │
   ├──────┼─────────┼────────────────────────────────────────────────┤
   │  T   │ Text    │ JR = Justify Right      U = Uppercase           │
   │  K   │ Keyword │ JC = Justify Center     L = Lowercase           │
   │  Y   │ Yes/No  │ JL = Justify Left       I = Initial caps        │
   │      │         │                                                 │
   │  N   │ Number  │ JR, JL, JC                                      │
   │  M   │ Money   │ 0-7 = # of decimal digits (for N only)          │
   │      │         │ C   = insert commas                             │
   │      │         │                                                 │
   │  D   │ Date    │ JR, JL, JC                                      │
   │  H   │ Time    │                                                 │
   └──────┴─────────┴────────────────────────────────────────────────┘

   Examples:  N,2,JR,C  =  This field contains numbers, and they should have
                           two decimal digits, be right justified, with commas.
              T,U        =  This field contains text, in uppercase.

 Esc-Exit
```

In addition to a one-letter format type, you can control justification, case, number of decimal digits, and comma placement.

Secondary format type symbols are added to the primary format type, separating each symbol with a comma. Suppose that you want all entries in the Check Cleared? field to be uppercase regardless of how the information is entered. You press Esc to clear help from the screen. You see the Format Spec with primary format options. Move the cursor to the Check Cleared? field and type **Y,U**. Then press F10.

Next, you see the Global Format Options screen. This screen is displayed for any modifications you want to make. To continue saving changes and to return to the Customize menu, press $\boxed{F10}$.

Using Restrict Values

3

By using the Restrict values option, you can restrict or set limitations on data entered into a database. You can ask that entries fall within a range, meet date requirements, or be of a definite nature.

To access the Restrict Spec, follow these steps:

1. From the Customize menu, select Restrict values.

```
                              BUDGET
     _____

     Check Number:▮▮▮▮▮▮        Date of Expense:
     Payee:
     Amount:
     Description:
     Type:
     Check Cleared?:
     Service Charge:
     Total Debit:
     Date Entered:
     Time Entered:




     _____
     BUDGET.DTF              Restrict Spec          Page 1 of 1

     Esc-Exit         F1-Help        F6-Field editor      F10-Continue
```

Notice that the Restrict Spec has many of the same function key assignments as the Format Spec.

2. Press $\boxed{F1}$.

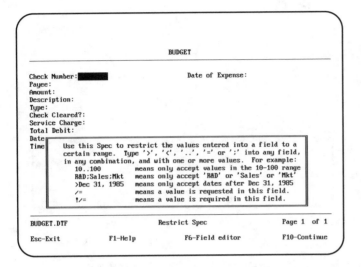

```
                         BUDGET

Check Number: ▓▓▓▓▓▓▓          Date of Expense:
Payee:
Amount:
Description:
Type:
Check Cleared?:
Service Charge:
Total Debit:
Date
Time    Use this Spec to restrict the values entered into a field to a
        certain range.  Type '>', '<', '..', '=' or ';' into any field,
        in any combination, and with one or more values.  For example:
           10..100        means only accept values in the 10-100 range
           R&D;Sales;Mkt  means only accept 'R&D' or 'Sales' or 'Mkt'
           >Dec 31, 1985  means only accept dates after Dec 31, 1985
           /=             means a value is requested in this field.
           !/=            means a value is required in this field.


BUDGET.DTF              Restrict Spec           Page 1  of  1

Esc-Exit        F1-Help        F6-Field editor      F10-Continue
```

The Restrict Spec Help screen appears. You can set a variety of restrictions for a database. Only one screen of information is available for the Restrict Spec, but the samples shown are very explicit.

3. Move the cursor to the field that you want to restrict and type the restricted values.

4. Press F10 to save the changes.

Suppose that you want to use this spec to set two restrictions on data entered in the BUDGET.DTF database. You want all dates entered in the Dates of Expense field to be after June 1, 1990. You can update this date as each calendar year changes. Requesting a date as a restriction reduces data input errors. You also want to specify that the Type field must contain data, which means that this field must contain data on every form added to this database.

To complete these two requirements, begin with the cursor in the Date of Expense field. You must expand this field because it is not large enough to hold the restriction criteria you will type. To expand this field, press F6.

3

The cursor moves
from the top of
the Restrict Spec
to the bottom and
appears in an
editing box
directly above the
status line.

```
                              BUDGET

Check Number:                      Date of Expense:▮▮▮▮▮▮▮▮▮
Payee:
Amount:
Description:
Type:
Check Cleared?:
Service Charge:
Total Debit:

┌─────────────────────────────────────────────────────────┐
│                                                          │
│                                                          │
│                                                          │
│                                                          │
└─────────────────────────────────────────────────────────┘

Date of Expe                       0 %  1   Line 1 of 1
BUDGET.DTF                    Restrict Spec            Page 1 of 1

Esc-Exit      F2-Print      F7-Search      F8-Options     F10-Exit editor
```

When you use F6 to expand a field, the size of the field increases to 480
characters. Type **>May 31, 1990** in the editing box.

If you make an
entry with a date
before June 1,
1990, an error
message tells you
that the entry
does not meet the
restrictions as
defined on the
Spec.

```
                              BUDGET

Check Number: 1098                 Date of Expense:▌04/04/90 ▐
Payee:
Amount:     ┌──────────────────────────────────────────────────┐
Descript    │  Value not in specified range.  Please verify before continuing. │
Type:       └──────────────────────────────────────────────────┘
Check Cleared?:
Service Charge:
Total Debit:
Date Entered:
Time Entered:

BUDGET.DTF      New Record 1     of 1     Total Records: 3     Page 1 of 1

Esc-Exit   F1-Help      F3-Delete form    F7-Search     F8-Calc   F10-Continue
```

Press F10 to exit the editing box with the new restriction in effect.

```
                              BUDGET
                                _____

  Check Number:              Date of Expense: >May 31, 1+
  Payee:
  Amount:
  Description:
  Type:
  Check Cleared?:
  Service Charge:
  Total Debit:
  Date Entered:
  Time Entered:




  Expand field:>May 31, 1990
  BUDGET.DTF              Restrict Spec            Page 1 of 1

  Esc-Exit        F1-Help        F6-Field editor      F10-Continue
```

An arrow pointing to the right appears in the expanded field, indicating that more information can be displayed.

You also want to make the restriction that a field must contain information. This restriction is called a *required field*. You use /= as your restriction criteria. The forward slash (/) indicates *not*. When combined with the equal sign (=), you are telling Q&A that the field cannot be equal to blank. To complete this restriction, move the cursor to the Type field and type /=.

```
                              BUDGET
                                _____

  Check Number:              Date of Expense: >May 31, 1+
  Payee:
  Amount:
  Description:
  Type: /=
  Check Cleared?:
  Service Charge:
  Total Debit:
  Date Entered:
  Time Entered:




  BUDGET.DTF              Restrict Spec            Page 1 of 1

  Esc-Exit        F1-Help        F6-Field editor      F10-Continue
```

The Restrict Spec should now look like this screen.

Using Set Initial Values

The Set Initial Values option automatically enters frequently used information into a field when you are adding new forms. You may keep a phone book database, for example. If you are adding new names, addresses, and phone numbers to a database and most of the people live in Florida, you can use this option to fill the State field with *Florida* on every new form added to the database. For those people who do not live in Florida, simply type the correct state name directly over the word *Florida*. You can edit Initial Values to conform to exceptions; they are only suggestions. In addition to filling fields with text information, you also can complete fields with the current date or hour. This information is taken from the computer system internal clock that is activated when you first turn on the computer.

To access the Initial Values Spec, select Set Initial Values from the Customize menu. Set Initial Values looks similar to the Restrict Spec, but it performs a different function. If you are in a hurry or have your work interrupted while customizing a database, you could be using the wrong menu item without realizing it. To make sure that you are looking at the correct Spec, check the status line. The Spec name is always shown in the center of this line.

The Key Assignment line offers the same selections as seen on the Restrict Spec.

You may want to review the help screens when you are first learning the customize features. To access the help screen, press F1.

```
                              BUDGET
    _____

    Check Number:█████        Date of Expense:
    Payee:
    Amount:
    Description:
    Type:
    Check Cleared?:
    Service Charge:
    Total Debit:
    Dat┌──────────────────────────────────────────────────────┐
    Tim│                                                        │
       │ Use this spec to pre-fill new records with the most common values │
       │ for each field. When you select "Add data" from the File Menu,    │
       │ you will get a new record with these values already typed. Also:  │
       │                                                        │
       │      @date    will produce the current date           │
       │      @time    will produce the current time           │
       │      @number  will produce a unique number            │
       └──────────────────────────────────────────────────────┘
    _____

    BUDGET.DTF          Initial Values Spec        Page 1 of 1

    Esc-Exit       F1-Help        F3-Clear Spec      F10-Continue
```

Not only can you fill new forms with frequently entered data, you also can ask that the current date, current time, and a sequential number be inserted into fields. The BUDGET.DTF database has Date and Time-Entered fields that you can fill by using this Spec.

To insert the correct date, time, and sequential order into all fields, follow these steps:

1. Type @date in the Date Entered field.

2. Move the cursor to the Time Entered field.

3. Type @time in the Time Entered field:

   The last option on this screen uses the @number criteria. Use this option to number a field sequentially. An example of an application that uses the @number criteria is a purchase order database. Each purchase order number should be unique (no duplicates), and the numbers should be consecutive. When using @number, the system keeps track of the last number assigned and uses the next available number when a new purchase order is added to the database. Because BUDGET.DTF does not require consecutive numbering, this feature is not used in the database.

4. Press F10 to save the Initial Values criteria and return to the Customize menu.

Speeding Up Searches

The Speed-up searches option on the Customize menu enables you to customize a Speed-up Spec. Speed-up Spec searches enable you to do search and sort routines on a database. If searching and sorting are foreign concepts to you, don't worry. You'll see them explained before you need to use them. For now, you learn the principles of using a Speed-up Spec to locate a record or records using the contents of a specified field.

In principle, creating a Speed-up Spec is similar to creating a library book index. In fact, Q&A does index Speed-up Spec fields. If you needed a certain book, by title for instance, you could go to the library book shelves and sequentially scan each title until you found the title you had in mind. Likewise, Q&A can scan database records, by check number for instance, to locate a check that you had in mind. While computer searches are faster than human searches, a sequential search in either case isn't very efficient.

3

In a library, the librarian may create a card file containing book titles arranged alphabetically and by the shelf locations. When library patrons need to search for a book by its title, they use the indexed cards to locate the shelf location. Once the shelf is located, the process to retrieve the book is rather speedy. Q&A enables you to use internal indexing provisions to index your choice of fields in much the same way. Instead of searching a large database with data in random order, Q&A is capable of searching the index of "speedy" fields to find the location of the desired record.

You can select many fields to index, although the number should be kept as small as possible (perhaps five to eight fields). When you index fields in this manner, adding new forms to the database takes slightly longer because each new form has to store the speed up search index as it is saved. Generally, the time difference is not noticeable when the size of a database is small (less than a few hundred records), but the difference becomes more noticeable as the size of the database grows. Even so, the time you invest in the beginning of a project means a quicker, more responsive database.

As an example of the use of the Speed-up Spec, you will follow steps to indicate that the Check Number field should be indexed. To access the Speed-up Spec, from the Customize menu, select Speed up searches and note the appearance of the text Speed-up Spec on the status line.

The Speed-up Spec appears. The key assignment line is the same as in Set Initial Values.

```
                              BUDGET
         ─────────────────────────────────────────────────
         Check Number:███████      Date of Expense:
         Payee:
         Amount:
         Description:
         Type:
         Check Cleared?:
         Service Charge:
         Total Debit:
         Date Entered:
         Time Entered:




         BUDGET.DTF              Speed-up Spec         Page 1 of 1
         Esc-Exit        F1-Help        F3-Clear Spec    F10-Continue
```

```
                              BUDGET

  Check Number: ███████           Date of Expense:
  Payee:
  Amount:
  Description:
  Type:
  Check Cleared?:
  Service Charge:
  Total Debit:
  Dat┌─────────────────────────────────────────────────────┐
  Tim│ Type "S" in each field for which you frequently give search │
     │ restrictions. For example, if you search frequently for     │
     │ specific cities, type an "S" in your "City" field. Optionally, │
     │ type "SU" to require that new values in that field are unique, or │
     │ "SE" to require that new values already exist (are NOT unique). │
     │                                                     │
     │ SUGGESTION: Each speedy field will slow down the adding and │
     │ updating of records. Use them sparingly.            │
     └─────────────────────────────────────────────────────┘

  BUDGET.DTF            Speed-up Spec              Page 1 of 1

  Esc-Exit         F1-Help        F3-Clear Spec      F10-Continue
```

To review the help screen associated with this function, press F1.

To indicate that a field is repeatedly requested for searches, follow these steps:

1. Type S in the Check Number field, which indicates that this field is often used for searching.

   Several of the other fields, such as Payee, Type, and Check Cleared?, may be used frequently for searching. You may want to index these fields too.

2. Move your cursor to the Payee field and press S if you want to index that field.

3. Move your cursor to the Check Cleared? field and press S if you want to index that field.

4. Press F10 to save your selections and return to the Customize menu.

   Your data file is rearranged to reflect the new settings. The process should take only a few seconds.

Eliminating Duplicate Entries

The Unique Values option checks whether any forms have duplicate information in designated fields. If so, it warns you that a duplicate exists in the database and asks you to confirm your data. Select these fields by typing U (indicating Unique) after the S in the field area. You can, for example, use this option to make sure that duplicate purchase orders or Social Security numbers are not entered accidentally.

In the budget database, you don't want to enter any check number more than once. You already indexed the check number field and now you indicate that the contents of the field should be unique for each record. Again, access the Speed up Searches item from the Customize menu, and follow these steps:

1. Type ⑤⑪ in the Check Number field to indicates that this field is to be indexed for searching and that it must always be unique (no duplicates).

2. Press ⑩ to save your selections and return to the Customize menu.

   Your data file is rearranged to reflect the new settings.

Now, the check number field is indexed, and Q&A will display a warning when you attempt to reenter a check number.

Ensuring Prior Entries

The Existing Values option tells you whether a duplicate exists in the database. This option indicates that a duplicate value does not exist and asks if you want to continue. Use this option to make sure that information going into a database is consistent. An example of this application would be a job classification or job title. If a job title is abbreviated accidentally—VP instead of Vice President—you receive a warning. Select these fields by typing **E** (indicating Existing) after the S in the field area.

The Type field of the budget database, for example, will provide more uniform information when the number of different types included is small and each type conveys the same meaning when entered into a record. Access the Speedup Spec for this example.

To select the Type field and indicate that it should already exist, follow these steps:

1. Move the cursor to the Type field and type ⑤⑤.

```
                              BUDGET

   Check Number: SU              Date of Expense:
   Payee: S
   Amount:
   Description:
   Type: ███SE██████████
   Check Cleared?: S
   Service Charge:
   Total Debit:
   Date Entered:
   Time Entered:




   BUDGET.DTF             Speed-up Spec          Page 1 of 1

   Esc-Exit        F1-Help        F3-Clear Spec     F10-Continue
```

This procedure indicates that a user must enter a value that already exists in the database.

2. Press F10 to save your selections and return to the Customize menu.

   Your data file is rearranged to reflect the new settings. Indexing should take only a few seconds.

Developing Custom Help Screens

Sometimes, offering help information that pertains to your database is preferable to accessing Q&A's built-in help text. You can provide custom help for yourself and other users of your database. In addition to displaying a custom Help screen when the user presses the F1 key, you can display custom help when a user enters a field, when a user enters data that fails to conform with field requirements, and in many other circumstances.

Define Custom Help is used to add your own Help screens to a database. When you press F1, your customized Help screen appears first, and the Q&A Help screen appears the second time you press F1.

A Help screen that shows the different types of expenses, for example, would be helpful when you use the example BUDGET.DTF database. The Help screen would ensure that data going into this field is consistent, and it could list several types of expenses, such as utility, rent, food, and entertainment.

To create the Help screen, follow these steps:

1. From the Customize menu, select Define Custom Help.

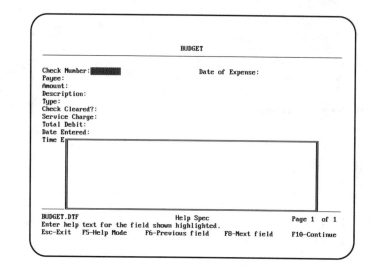

The Help Spec
appears.

The box that appears at the bottom of the screen contains the help text for the highlighted field. The box can hold 480 characters (60 characters across, 8 lines down). To move to help text boxes for other fields, press [F6] (Previous field) and [F8] (Next field). Suppose, for example, that you want to add a Help screen for the Type field. To move to the Type field help text box, press [F8] (Next Field).

2. Press [F8] until the field for which you want to add a help screen is highlighted. For this example, highlight the Type field.

In this example,
you see the Type
field highlighted.

```
                              BUDGET

      Check Number:                    Date of Expense:
      Payee:
      Amount:
      Description:
      Type:
      Check Cleared?:
      Service Charge:
      Total Debit:
      Date Entered:
      Time E ┌─────────────────────────────────────────────┐
             │                                             │
             │                                             │
             │                                             │
             │                                             │
             │                                             │
             │                                             │
             │                                             │
             └─────────────────────────────────────────────┘
      BUDGET.DTF                     Help Spec            Page 1 of 1
      Enter help text for the field shown highlighted.
      Esc-Exit   F5-Help Mode    F6-Previous field    F8-Next field    F10-Continue
```

3. With your cursor in the first space, enter a title for this Help screen, followed by the kinds of expenses. For this example, type **Expense Types** for the title.

4. Add the types of expenses, each on its own line:

   utility

   food

   rent

   entertainment

   Now you need to create the second Help screen, which is for the Check Cleared? field. This Help screen tells the user to enter a Y for Yes or an N for No.

5. Press F8 to move your cursor to the Check Cleared? field.

6. Enter the following information on the Help screen:

   If this is a check and it has not cleared your bank account, enter N for No.

   If this is a check and it has cleared your bank account, enter Y for Yes.

   If this is not an expense that you issued a check for, enter N for No.

Your Help screen should look like this.

```
                               BUDGET
         _____

         Check Number:                   Date of Expense:
         Payee:
         Amount:
         Description:
         Type:
         Check Cleared?:▓▓▓
         Service Charge:
         Total Debit:
         Date Entered:
         Time E┌──────────────────────────────────────────────────┐
               │ If this is a check and it has not cleared your bank│
               │ account, enter N for NO.                           │
               │                                                    │
               │ If this is a check and it has cleared your bank account,│
               │ enter Y for YES.                                   │
               │                                                    │
               │ If this is not an expense you issued a check for enter N│
               │ for NO.                                            │
               └──────────────────────────────────────────────────┘
         BUDGET.DTF                  Help Spec            Page 1  of 1
         Enter help text for the field shown highlighted.
         Esc-Exit   F5-Help Mode   F6-Previous field   F8-Next field   F10-Continue
```

7. Press F10 to save your custom help screens. You are returned to the Customize menu.

Reviewing Customized Modifications

To see how these modifications make data entry easier, you must return to the File menu, and then add a new form to your database. To add a new form, press Esc twice to return to the File menu. Select the Add Data option, and then select the database for which you want to add data. For this example, select the BUDGET.DTF database that you created earlier.

You are now in the Add mode. To add a new form and see whether your customized selections work correctly, follow these steps:

1. In the Check Number field, enter a check number that you entered earlier. Press the Tab⇄ key. For this example, enter 1097.

An error message appears that tells you that this is not a unique check number. (You added this number to the database earlier.)

```
                              BUDGET

Check Number: 1097                      Date of Expense:
P
A │  This field should be unique.  Please verify before continuing. │
D
Type:
Check Cleared?:
Service Charge:
Total Debit:
Date Entered: 03/17/91
Time Entered:11:46 am




BUDGET.DTF    New Record 1    of 1     Total Records: 3     Page 1  of 1

Esc-Exit   F1-Help        F3-Delete form     F7-Search     F8-Calc    F10-Continue
```

2. Correct the Check Number to read 1099 and move your cursor to the next field.

3. Enter the date May 27, 1990 and press ↵Enter.

   You receive an error message that tells you this is not within a specified range (this field was instructed not to accept any entries earlier than June 1, 1990).

4. Correct the date to the current date and move the cursor to the next field.

5. Fill the Payee, Amount, and Description fields as if this information were a food vendor check; move to the Type field.

6. Press F1 to view the help screen that you created for this field.

```
                              BUDGET
_____

Check Number: 1099                Date of Expense: 08/22/90
Payee: Joe's Hot Dog Stand
Amount: $14.60
Description: lunch for my friend and I
Type: ████████████████████████
Check Cleared?:
Service Charge:
Total Debit:
Date Entered: 03/17/91
Time E ┌──────────────────────────────────────────────┐
       │  Expense Types                               │
       │  utilities                                   │
       │  food                                        │
       │  rent                                        │
       │  entertainment                               │
       │                                              │
       │                                              │
       └──────────────────────────────────────────────┘

BUDGET.DTF      New Record 1      of 1    Total Records: 3      Page 1  of 1

Esc-Exit   F1-Help      F3-Delete form    F7-Search    F8-Calc   F10-Continue
```

In this example, you see the Type field highlighted.

Your custom Help screen appears; the screen displays the different type classifications that can be entered into this field.

7. Press Esc to clear the help screen.

8. Move to the next field.

9. Press F1 to view the Help screen that you created for this field.

You see a help screen that was created for the Check Cleared? field.

10. Press Z or N in the Check Cleared? field. For this example, press N.

11. Enter any service charges for the check in the Service Charge field. For this example, enter .15.

12. Enter the total debit for the check in the Total Debit field. For this example, enter 14.75.

The remaining two fields will be completed from information requested in Set Initial Values. Both date and time entered are completed.

13. Press F10 to save the new form.

14. Press Esc to exit to the File menu.

Looking for Information in a Database

Adding records to your databases ensures that your information is "on file" in your PC. Adding records electronically is similar to collecting paperwork manually. You may know that every thing you need to know is contained somewhere "in the file cabinet," but looking for and changing an item of information requires some sort of search technique. When searching for information in a file cabinet, you rely on the index tags of file folders. With an electronic database manager, like Q&A File, you use the search tools built into the software.

Once you add records to a Q&A database, you likely need to retrieve those records for information and updating. Q&A provides for you the Search/Update mode to perform this retrieval function. Unlike the single tab on a file folder, Q&A makes every field of a database available for use in a search. You can search on several fields at the same time, thus setting up a series of selection criteria that must be met. Although your computer and Q&A must do a considerable amount of work to retrieve your selected records, you will find the time required for the search to be very quick. The Q&A File Search/Update mode provides rapid and convenient access to your records based on your information requirements.

In this chapter, you learn the fundamentals of Q&A's search and update features. You see how to establish search criteria and restrictions. You learn to sort your records.

4

Key Terms Used in This Chapter

Retrieve	To access records from the database for viewing or updating.
Retrieve Spec	An entry screen where users specify values for fields to determine which of the records of a database are retrieved for modification or viewing.
Search Criteria	The field values or expressions entered by a user which make up the Retrieve Spec.
Criterion Expression	A value containing an operator (such as \, ;, or &) along with a literal value that determines the records retrieved in a search.
Wild card	The ? and the .. characters used in field criteria values that match single or multiple literal characters in the corresponding field of records being retrieved.
Table View	A format of data presentation where multiple records are displayed as horizontal columns of fields with one record per screen line.
Sort	An operation taken on random sequence records that provides a specified sequence of records as an output. Sorts can be ascending (0-9 or A-Z) or descending (9-0 or Z-A).
Sounds-Like Retrieval	A method of record retrieval where the search criterion's pronunciation, not exact spelling, is used to match the pronunciation of the corresponding field of the records.

Entering the Search/Update Mode

You access Search/Update from the File menu. You will complete a series of exercises using different search methods. These exercises are based on the BUDGET.DTF database. If you did not design that database using the preceding exercises, however, you can experiment with the topics covered by using the EMPLOYEE.DTF database. EMPLOYEE.DTF is a database that comes with the Q&A software and is used in the Q&A Tutorial.

From the Search/Update mode, you will specify search criteria using a Search Spec definition screen. The first search exercise introduces the Search Spec screen and selects all the records in the database.

To enter the Search/Update mode, follow these steps:

1. From the File menu, select Search/Update for the database that you want. For this example, select the BUDGET.DTF database. You see an empty Retrieve Spec screen.

```
                          BUDGET
 ┌──────────────────────────────────────────────────────────┐
 │                                                            │
 │  Check Number:              Date of Expense:               │
 │  Payee:                                                    │
 │  Amount:                                                   │
 │  Description:                                              │
 │  Type:                                                     │
 │  Check Cleared?:                                           │
 │  Service Charge:                                           │
 │  Total Debit:                                              │
 │  Date Entered:                                             │
 │  Time Entered:                                             │
 │                                                            │
 │                                                            │
 │                                                            │
 │                                                            │
 │  BUDGET.DTF           Retrieve Spec         Page 1 of 1    │
 │                                                            │
 │  Esc-Exit  F1-Help  F6-Expand  F8-Sort  Alt+F8-List  ↑F8-Save  F10-Continue │
 └──────────────────────────────────────────────────────────┘
```

Notice the key assignment line, which contains some new assignments not seen in Design or Add mode.

2. Press F1 to view the help screen. The help screen familiarizes you with basic retrieval functions.

```
                                    BUDGET

Check Number:                          Date of Expense:
Payee:
Amount:
Description:
Type:
Check Cleared?:
Service Charge:
Total Debit:
Dat
Tim    Use the Retrieve Spec to say what records you want to Retrieve.

       To retrieve ALL the records, leave the spec blank and press F10.

       To retrieve SELECTED records, enter restrictions into the fields.
       Press F1 for a summary of restrictions with examples.


BUDGET.DTF                     Retrieve Spec                  Page 1 of 1

Esc-Exit   F1-Help   F6-Expand   F8-Sort   Alt+F8-List   ↑F8-Save   F10-Continue
```

As you see in the help text, the method used to retrieve all records for subsequent display is to leave all of the Retrieve Spec fields blank. Q&A interprets a blank search specification to mean "retrieve all records." You learn how to retrieve records based on your criteria later in the chapter. For now, you learn some of the mechanics of Search/Update using a blank search specification.

Retrieving All or Any Forms in a Database

When the Retrieve Spec is empty (no search criteria in any of the fields), you can retrieve all records in your database by pressing the F10 key.

Because you did not enter any restrictions on the Retrieve Spec, Q&A retrieves and displays the first record of all records in the database. Follow these steps:

1. Press F10.

   A record is displayed on your screen in the same format that you saw in the Add mode.

```
                              BUDGET
        _____

        Check Number: 1695              Date of Expense: 11/02/90
        Payee: Fred's Fresh Food Market
        Amount: $56.73
        Description: weekly grocery shopping
        Type: food
        Check Cleared?: N
        Service Charge: $0.15
        Total Debit: $56.88
        Date Entered: 11/05/90
        Time Entered: 3:40 pm




        _____

        BUDGET.DTF    Retrieved form 1    of --    Total Forms: 5    Page 1  of 1

        Esc-Exit    F1-Help    Alt+F6-Table    F7-Search    F8-Calc    F10-Continue
```

Your status line shows the name of the database, the number of the record displayed and its sequence, shown here as dashes because you did not sort the records.

(You learn about sequence later in this chapter.) The status line also shows the total number of records in the database, and the page of the record that you are viewing. Again, the budget database form consists of a single page. You also have new key assignments displayed on the key assignment line. Remember to check the key assignment line when your screen changes.

Because Total Forms is equal to 5, records additional to the displayed record have been retrieved.

2. Press `F10` to view the next record. `F10` moves you forward through the retrieved records, one record per `F10` press.

   Form 2 is now displayed. You can view records one at a time by pressing `F10`.

3. Press `F9` enough times to go back until the first record is displayed.

Using this method is fine if you do not care that some records do not meet your needs or that the records do not appear in a convenient order. Active databases can grow quickly, however, and you don't want to wade through dozens or hundreds of records to see or change a few records.

Using Search Criteria for Selectivity

You can use other methods to retrieve records. Next you learn search methods
that enable you to be selective. Instead of retrieving all records, you can
restrict retrieved records to those you want to work with. To return to the
Retrieve Spec and begin another retrieve specification for a search, follow
these steps:

1. Press ⌷F7⌷ to access the Retrieve Spec screen again.

   Additional retrieval options appear on a help screen.

2. Press ⌷F1⌷ to view these additional retrieval options.

   A small Help screen appears containing the following message:

   Press F1 for a summary of restrictions with examples.

3. Press ⌷F1⌷ to view other ways of retrieving records.

   The second Help screen has many more symbols to use for record
   retrieval, as shown in the following figure.

```
                    HOW TO SEARCH: THE RETRIEVE SPEC          Pg. F-??

     Type symbols into individual fields to indicate what information you want.

     SYMBOL   MEANING                          EXAMPLES

     x        equal to x                       Boston    CA      4/12/85
     /x       not equal to x                   /CA       /Sales  /$100
     >x       greater than x                   >12:00 pm
     <x       less than x                      <10,000   <1/1/85
     >=x      greater than or equal to x       >=Jones   >=12:00 am
     <=x      less than or equal to x          <=1000    <=12/31/85
     >x..<y   greater than x and less than y   >10..<100
     x;y;z    x OR y OR z                      red;white;blue   9.99;10.00
     =        empty (i.e., equal to nothing)
     /=       not empty
     MIN n    retrieve n lowest values         MIN 5
     MAX n    retrieve n highest values        MAX 100
     x..      begins with x (if text field)    pre..
     ..x      ends with x (if text field)      ..ing
     ..x..    contains x (if text field)       ..esp..

     Esc-Exit                    ← PgDn-Using expressions →
```

At first, the information displayed on the Help screen may seem complex or
cryptic. You learn how to interpret the various symbols as you work through
the chapter. As a simple explanation, the Help screen shows how to form
examples of the data that you want to retrieve. You enter an example as a
specification in a field in the Retrieve Spec screen.

The SYMBOL column of the Help screen table shows the lowercase letters x, y, and z. The column also shows operators such as /, <, >, .., and ;. When you enter a retrieve specification, you enter a combination of an operator and a literal value. A literal value is a character or combination of characters that you expect to find in the database. In the table, the literal value is represented by x (or y or z). You do not use x, y, or z in the retrieve specification. The x, y, and z are displayed in the table to show you how the operators are positioned in the specification in relationship to your literal value. Used together, the operator > (greater than) and the literal number 100, for example, mean "greater than 100." What you actually enter into a field of the Retrieve Spec screen is >100. The >100 entry is called an expression because it expresses to Q&A the criteria all records must satisfy to be retrieved.

You enter the expression into a field of the retrieve specification. If you enter >100 into the Amount of Expense field, you tell Q&A to retrieve all records with expense in excess of $100.00. In column 1 of the Help table, the same expression is symbolically represented by >x where x could be any value.

As you can see from the table, there are many operators other than the > operator. The < (less than) operator, for instance, can be used to form the expression <100, which means "less than 100." As a specification in the Amount of Expense field, the expression <100 tells Q&A to retrieve all records with the amount of expense of under $100.00.

If you're still unsure about how to form expressions for retrieve specifications, you will get a better idea of how to form them in subsequent examples.

Equal To Retrievals

One expression that you will use often is the Equal To expression. As the term implies, an Equal To specification restricts the records retrieved to those which match the literal specification you place in the desired field of the Retrieve Spec screen. There is no operator associated with the Equal To expression. You might think that the operator would be the = character, but because Q&A needs only the sample literal to match in records, no operator is necessary. The = operator is implied.

You might, for example, want to retrieve all the records in a mailing database that have the City field equal to Boston. If you refer to the Help table, you see the first meaning as "equal to x." To form the specification, replace the meaning of the symbol x with the value *Boston* and press F10 to execute the retrieval.

You use a new Retrieve Spec to institute a new search. Suppose that you want to look up the payee for check number 1096. To return to the Retrieve Spec and institute a new search, follow these steps:

1. Press F7.

   The Retrieve Spec appears (check the status line to verify your exact location).

2. Press the Tab⁵ key to highlight the field for which you want to enter a specification. For this example, highlight the Check Number field.

3. Enter the expression in the field. For this example, enter 1096 in the Check Number field.

4. Press F10 to retrieve the record.

   If you entered the budget data previously, only one record will contain the check number 1096. If you press F10 again, Q&A tells you, on the message line, that no more records meet your criterion.

5. Press F10 again to view additional records.

In this example, you see that no more records exist for check number 1096.

```
                              BUDGET
      _____

      Check Number: 1096              Date of Expense: 11/02/90
      Payee: North Shore Gas & Electric
      Amount: $25.25
      Description: monthly gas and electricity
      Type: utility
      Check Cleared?: N
      Service Charge: $0.15
      Total Debit: $25.40
      Date Entered: 11/05/90
      Time Entered: 3:40 pm




      _____
      BUDGET.DTF     Retrieved form 1     of 1     Total Forms: 5    Page 1 of 1
      No more records. Press Esc to exit or F9 for previous form.
      Esc-Exit      F1-Help          Alt+F6-Table      F7-Search      F8-Calc
```

6. Press F7 to return to the Retrieve Spec screen.

Retrievals Using Wild Cards

Wild-card retrievals are a flexible means of retrieving records. Samples of wild-card retrievals are shown on the Retrieve Spec Help screen table as the last three examples. When in the Retrieve Spec screen, you press F1 twice to view the table in the Help screen.

In computer parlance, a wild card is a character whose meaning is reserved as a substitute for another character or characters. In a card game, a wild card is a card, like the Joker, that substitutes for any other card. Wild cards are useful in search criteria expressions because you can specify an expression that is close to what you want, yet Q&A retrieves matching records.

Wild-card expressions use two periods (..) as part of the retrieval criterion. If you are looking for all checks written to your utility company, for example, you need to type only the first two or three letters of the company name in the Payee field, followed by two periods as the wild card. The system looks for all records in which the Payee name starts with whatever "actual" characters you entered in the field and the wild card matches any ending characters of the field in the record.

Press Esc to cancel the help screen. Press F3 to clear the Retrieve Spec.

To execute a wild-card retrieval, follow these steps:

1. On the Retrieve Spec screen, use the Tab⇔ key to move to the Payee field.

2. Type the first three letters of your utility company name followed by two periods, **Gas..**, for example.

3. Press F10 to begin the retrieval.

   The first record is retrieved. The example budget database has two records that meet the criterion.

4. Press F10 to view another record.

Viewing Multiple Forms Using Table View

After using the database for a while, you may have many records. Even with restrictive search criteria, a search may retrieve many records. In a year, for example, you may have over a dozen records for your utility company. Seeing a synopsis of the group of records in a table is often more convenient than viewing each record as a form by pressing F10. You can build a table of records from your database and view the table rather than viewing each record separately.

To view a tabular presentation of your data, follow these steps:

1. Press Alt - F6.

In this example, you see the table of records for Gas & Electric.

Check Number	Date of Expense	Payee	Amount	Description
1096	11/02/90	North Shore Ga→	$25.25	monthly gas a→
1097	11/02/90	North Shore Ga→	$23.78	monthly gas a→

BUDGET.DTF   Retrieved record 2   of 2   Total records: 5

Esc-Exit F1-Help   { ↓ ↑ Home End PgUp PgDn }-Navigate   F10-Show form

All records that meet your previous retrieve specification are displayed. In a table view, you see as many of the currently retrieved records as will fit on the screen. Use the arrow keys and PgUp and PgDn keys to navigate through the table.

2. Press F10 to see the highlighted record as a form.

   If you want to make changes in the record, you can do so now.

3. Press Alt - F6 to return to the table.

The table displays five columns of information at once on your 80-column display. By default, these five columns are the first five fields in your database. You can move to additional columns which lie beyond the right boundary of the screen by moving right with the arrow key.

You may, however, want to limit the displayed fields or change the relative display order. If so, you can change the data that is displayed on the table. If you are reviewing your BUDGET.DTF database to see which utility checks have not yet cleared your bank, that information is not shown on the table's first five fields.

To change your table, follow these steps:

1. Press ⇧Shift - F6 .

   You are taken to the Table View Spec.

```
                              BUDGET
   ─────────────────────────────────────────────────────────
   Check Number: 10          Date of Expense: 20
   Payee: 30
   Amount: 40
   Description: 50
   Type: 60
   Check Cleared?: 70
   Service Charge: 80
   Total Debit: 90
   Date Entered: 100
   Time Entered: 110




   ─────────────────────────────────────────────────────────
   BUDGET.DTF           Table View Spec          Page 1 of 1

   Esc-Exit    F1-Help   Alt+F8-List specs  Shift+F8-Save specs  F10-Table View
```

In this example, you see the Table View Spec for the BUDGET.DTF database.

Each of the fields contains a number. This number represents a relative column offset. In other words, the lowest numbered field appears as the column at the left of the screen, and remaining numbered fields appear successively to the right. By default, these numbers are in increments of 10 relative to the prior field, but you can change the increment to 1. By providing gaps between the numbers, Q&A makes it easier for you to resequence some of the columns later, without having to renumber all of the fields at that time.

2. Move your cursor to the field that you want as column 10 and replace the field's current number with 10. In this case, the Check Number field is already number 10.

3. Move your cursor to the field that you want to make the next column and replace the existing number with 20. For this example, the Date of Expense is already the second column.

4. Continue tabbing to other desired fields and replacing existing numbers with numbers reflecting the new display order. For this example, the Check Cleared field number 70 is replaced with number 50. The Check Cleared field will appear as the fifth column in the table view.

5. Renumber additional fields or delete the numbers in any field that you do not care to see in the table view. In this example, the remaining fields have their numbers deleted, leaving Check Number, Date of Expense, Payee, Amount, and Check Cleared? as the incremental fields.

6. Press F10 to return to the Table View.

In this example, you now see the Check Cleared? field in the fifth column.

```
+---------------------------------------------------------------------------+
|                                                                           |
|  Check Number  Check Cleared?  Date of Expense    Payee        Amount     |
|  --------------------------------------------------------------------     |
|         1696 N                  11/02/90       North Shore Ga+   $25.25    |
|         1097 N                  11/02/90       North Shore Ga+   $23.78    |
|                                                                           |
|                                                                           |
|                                                                           |
|                                                                           |
|                                                                           |
|                                                                           |
|  ------------------------------------------------------------------       |
|  BUDGET.DTF     Retrieved record 1    of 2       Total records: 5        |
|  Esc-Exit  F1-Help    { ↓ ↑ Home End PgUp PgDn }-Navigate   F10-Show form |
+---------------------------------------------------------------------------+
```

You can change this table view as often as you want.

7. Press F10 to view the highlighted record as a form.

8. Press F7 to return to the Retrieve Spec and begin another search.

9. Press F3 to clear all retrieve criteria from the Retrieve Spec.

Using Greater Than/Less Than for a Retrieval

Specifying records whose field equals the field spec is only one form of restricting records. You also can make another kind of retrieval by using the greater-than sign (>) and the less-than sign (<). Help examples for the > and < operators are displayed as examples 3 and 4 of the Retrieve Spec Help table you have been seeing in examples.

Using the > operator, you can specify records that exceed the value you express in the field specification. Using the < operator, you can specify records that are less than your specification. You can combine >, <, and = operators for a variety of selection criteria. The Help table shows the symbolic expressions and examples.

You could, for example, retrieve all records for expenses greater than $15 and less than $80. An expression using both the < and > operators sets the range for the retrieval.

To complete this type of retrieval, follow these steps:

1. On the Retrieve Spec, use the Tab⇹ key to move to the field in which you want to set a range. For this example, move the cursor to the Amount field.

2. Type the criteria expression into the highlighted field. For this example, enter the following in the Amount field: >15..<80

   This command retrieves all records with expenses from $15.01 to $79.99.

3. Press F10 to start the retrieval.

   The first record to meet the specifications appears on the screen. If more than one record meets the criteria, press F10 to view the records one by one. Press Alt-F6 if you want to view a table of the selected records.

Notice that the .. characters appear between the >15 and <80 components of the specification. When the .. characters appear between parts of the specification they can be read as the word *through*. In this example, the >15..<80 expression means "greater than 15 through less than 80." Of course you can use the > or < operators individually in an expression such as >15 or <25.

Sorting Your Retrieved Forms

When you retrieve records, their normal order of appearance is the order of their entry. Records in their order of entry are said to be in *natural order*. For some database viewing and editing, natural order is fine. Other times, having records ordered by some field, say Check Number, is important to your work organization. Q&A gives you the ability to put records in order. The operation that orders records to your specification is called a *sort*.

For convenience, as you can retrieve records from a database, you also can sort these records. You can sort records alphabetically or numerically. Alphabetical sorts can be from A to Z (ascending) or from Z to A (descending). Numeric sorts can be from low to high (ascending 1 to 10) or high to low (descending 10 to 1). You store the sorting information on a Sort Spec that you access from the Retrieve Spec.

You are not limited to ordering your records based on a single field. You can perform multiple sorts simultaneously. If you have a database for addresses, for example, you may want to sort it alphabetically by the City field, and then alphabetically by the Last Name field. The resulting sort order gives you an alphabetical view of city names and an alphabetized order of last names for cities with more than one record. The first sort criteria is called a *primary sort*, and the second sort criteria is called a *secondary sort*. You can, for example, sort your BUDGET.DTF database primarily by Type, and then secondarily by cost, with the most costly expense first.

Before you start the sort activity, review the existing retrieve specification to ensure that it reflects your search criteria. Press F7 to return to the Retrieve Spec. Because you will sort all records in your database, the Retrieve Spec should be blank, which indicates that All records will be selected. To clear the Retrieve Spec of existing criteria, press F3.

Using the key assignment line at the bottom of your screen, notice that pressing F8 displays a Sort Spec.

```
                              BUDGET

Check Number:                   Date of Expense:
Payee:
Amount:
Description:
Type:
Check Cleared?:
Service Charge:
Total Debit:
Date Entered:
Time Entered:




BUDGET.DTF               Retrieve Spec            Page 1  of 1

Esc-Exit   F1-Help   F6-Expand   F8-Sort   Alt+F8-List   ↑F8-Save   F10-Continue
```

To sort your retrieved records, follow these steps:

1. Press F8 to display the Sort Spec.

2. Press F1 to review the help screen before proceeding with this exercise.

```
                              BUDGET

Check Number:                   Date of Expense:
Payee:
Amount:
Description:
Type:
Check Cleared?:
Service Charge:
Total Debit:
Date
Time
     Type a SORT LEVEL (a number from 1 - 9999) followed by a SORT
     ORDER abbreviation in the fields you want to sort on.

     Abbreviations:   AS or A = Ascending Sort (low to high, A to Z)
                      DS or D = Descending Sort (high to low, Z to A)

     Examples:     CITY: 2 DS          STATE: 1 AS


BUDGET.DTF                  Sort Spec              Page 1  of 1

Esc-Exit  F1-Help  F6-Expand  Alt+F8-List  ↑F8-Save   F9-Retrieve  F10-Continue
```

In this example, you see the Sort Spec help screen for the BUDGET.DTF database.

89

The screen asks you to type a sort level followed by a sort order. When you select search criteria, specify whether the field is the primary or secondary sort by entering either a **1** or **2** in the field. You then specify whether you want to sort the field by ascending or descending order by typing either **as** or **ds** after the number **1** or **2**.

To complete a sort, follow these steps:

1. From the Sort Spec screen, use the `Tab⇄` key to move to the field of your primary sort and enter a **1** followed by either **as**, to sort by ascending order, or **ds**, to sort by descending order. The **1** indicates to Q&A's sort mechanism that this field is the primary sort field. The **as** or **ds** indicates to Q&A your ordering preference for the field.

   For this example, move the cursor to the Payee field and enter **1as** to have Q&A sort first by payee name in ascending (A to Z) order.

2. Move to the field you want as the secondary sort field and enter **2** followed by either **as** or **ds**.

   For this example, move the cursor to the Amount field and enter **2ds** to have Q&A sort next by Amount paid in descending (most to least costly) order.

```
                              BUDGET                              ▪

        Check Number:                Date of Expense:
        Payee: 1as
        Amount: 2ds
        Description:
        Type:
        Check Cleared?:
        Service Charge:
        Total Debit:
        Date Entered:
        Time Entered:




        BUDGET.DTF                   Sort Spec              Page 1  of 1

        Esc-Exit  F1-Help  F6-Expand  Alt+F8-List  ↑F8-Save  F9-Retrieve  F10-Continue
```

3. Press `F10` to begin the sorted retrieval. Behind the scenes, Q&A is performing two operations in tandem: sorting and retrieving. If the database contains many records, you may have to wait momentarily for the operations to be completed.

The first record is retrieved. To view the retrieved records in a table, press the ⌊Alt⌋-⌊F6⌋ Table key.

```
┌──────────────┬───────────────┬────────────────┬──────────────┬──────────┐
│ Check Number │ Check Cleared?│ Date of Expense│    Payee     │  Amount  │
├──────────────┼───────────────┼────────────────┼──────────────┼──────────┤
│         1099 │N              │ 11/05/90       │Chicago Phone →│   $25.66 │
│         1098 │N              │ 10/29/90       │First National→│  $600.00 │
│         1095 │N              │ 11/02/90       │Fred's Fresh F→│   $56.73 │
│         1096 │N              │ 11/02/90       │North Shore Ga→│   $25.25 │
│         1097 │N              │ 11/02/90       │North Shore Ga→│   $23.78 │
│              │               │                │              │          │
├──────────────┴───────────────┴────────────────┴──────────────┴──────────┤
│ BUDGET.DTF      Retrieved record 1    of 5         Total records: 5      │
│                                                                          │
│ Esc-Exit  F1-Help      { ↓ ↑ Home End PgUp PgDn }-Navigate   F10-Show form│
└──────────────────────────────────────────────────────────────────────────┘
```

In this example, you see the table of sorted forms for the BUDGET.DTF database. You can see all records selected and their sequence of display.

Remember when completing different Specs (such as Retrieve or Sort) that Q&A is not case-sensitive when it reads your requests. You can use all capital letters, all lowercase letters, or a combination of both. In addition, when you complete the Sort Spec, you can abbreviate ascending requests by typing an **a** and descending requests by typing a **d**. To Q&A, the **1a** sort specifier means exactly the same thing as the **1as** sort specifier. You might want to include the **s** character anyway to help you identify the specification as a sort.

4. Use the arrow keys to highlight any record that you want to view or edit as a form. Press ⌊F10⌋ to revert from the table view to the form view. Pressing ⌊Alt⌋-⌊F6⌋ returns you to the table view.

Entering Multiple Criteria

As you have seen, you can retrieve records using an exact match specification. With an equal specification you can ask for records whose type is *food* or *utility*. Each of these requests is a separate retrieval requiring you to modify the retrieval specification before accessing the next type you're interested in. In other words, you first retrieve *food* type records, change the retrieve specification, and retrieve *utility* records.

Suppose, however, that you want to see records that contain either food or utility. Q&A provides an *or* operator that you use in retrieve specifications. The *or* operator is the ; character. The *or* operator retrieves records whose specified field meet one or more criteria. Using the or operator, you can retrieve records, for example, that have a Type field content of either food or utilities, performing the retrieval as one process instead of two.

To perform a keyword search, follow these steps:

1. Press F7 to return to the Retrieve Spec. You will retrieve all records containing either food or utilities in the Type field.

2. Tab to the field used for the search. In this case, move to the Type field.

3. Enter the search criteria separated by the ; character. For this search, type the following retrieval criteria:

   food;utilities

4. Press F10 to start the retrieval process.

5. To see more than one matching record at once, press Alt - F6 to view records in a table view.

```
                            BUDGET

Check Number: N                    Date of Expense: D
Payee: T
Amount: M
Description: T
Type: X
Check Cleared?: YU
Service Charge: M
Total Debit: M
Date Entered: D
Time Entered: H




BUDGET.DTF              Format Spec              Page 1 of 1

Esc-Exit    F1-Help    F3-Clear Spec    F6-Expand field    F10-Continue
```

6. To see fields to the right of the active screen, press Ctrl -→ , and to return the view to the left fields, press Ctrl -← .

```
┌─────────────────────────────────────────────────────────────┐
│         HOW TO SEARCH: THE RETRIEVE SPEC          Pg. F-??    │
│                                                              │
│ Type symbols into individual fields to indicate what information you want. │
│ ┌────────┬──────────────────────────────┬─────────────────────┐ │
│ │ SYMBOL │ MEANING                      │ EXAMPLES            │ │
│ ├────────┼──────────────────────────────┼─────────────────────┤ │
│ │ x      │ equal to x                   │ Boston   CA   4/12/85 │ │
│ │ /x     │ not equal to x               │ /CA     /Sales  /$100 │ │
│ │ >x     │ greater than x               │ >12:00 pm           │ │
│ │ <x     │ less than x                  │ <10,000   <1/1/85   │ │
│ │ >=x    │ greater than or equal to x   │ >=Jones   >=12:00 am │ │
│ │ <=x    │ less than or equal to x      │ <=1000    <=12/31/85 │ │
│ │ >x..<y │ greater than x and less than y│ >10..<100          │ │
│ │ x;y;z  │ x OR y OR z                  │ red;white;blue  9.99;10.00 │ │
│ │ =      │ empty (i.e., equal to nothing)│                    │ │
│ │ /=     │ not empty                    │                     │ │
│ │ MIN n  │ retrieve n lowest values     │ MIN 5               │ │
│ │ MAX n  │ retrieve n highest values    │ MAX 100             │ │
│ │ x..    │ begins with x (if text field)│ pre..               │ │
│ │ ..x    │ ends with x (if text field)  │ ..ing               │ │
│ │ ..x..  │ contains x (if text field)   │ ..esp..             │ │
│ └────────┴──────────────────────────────┴─────────────────────┘ │
│                                                              │
│ Esc-Exit            → PgDn-Using expressions ←               │
└─────────────────────────────────────────────────────────────┘
```

Here you see the right column displayed.

4

Notice that all records contain either food or utilities in the Type field. An or retrieval criteria is not restricted to two alternatives, it can contain as many items as you need to select.

Entering Multiple Criteria Using Keyword Fields

In this section, you discover why the Keyword field type is so useful for retrievals. If you have forgotten about assigning the Keyword field type to the budget database's Type field, you might want to review the customization section of Chapter 2 now.

You included a Type field in the budget database to record the record's type of expense. This Type field is called a *general category* field. Including a general category field makes sense for most databases. Using the category field for selective retrievals is a good way to get an overview of records that have some common characteristic.

When people organize their information into general categories, they begin to realize that some information fits logically into more than one category. A used car dealer, for example, may have a car that fits both the "one owner" and "convertible" categories. When searching for the car based on customer criteria, either category may be the important feature to the customer. The dealer needs a method of sorting cars that enables multiple categories to be used in the same search.

4

You also may need to sort your records using multiple categories. In the budget database, for example, you might want to sort your records containing a certain type of expenditure by whether the expenditure was expected or unexpected. With Q&A file, you have access to this enhanced categorization capability. The Keyword field is Q&A's provision for enabling multiple categories in a single field.

You enter multiple keywords in a Keyword field using the ; (or) operator to separate the entries. Following the example of the Type field in the budget database, you can add the keyword *unexpected* to the record for check number 1097. You retrieve the record by searching for 1097 in the Check Number field and then tabbing to the Type field. After the last character in the word utilities, you type ;**unexpected**.

```
                              BUDGET

 Check Number:                     Date of Expense:
 Payee:
 Amount:
 Description:
 Type: áphone:utility
 Check Cleared?:
 Service Charge:
 Total Debit:
 Date Entered:
 Time Entered:




 BUDGET.DTF                  Retrieve Spec           Page 1  of 1

 Esc-Exit   F1-Help   F6-Expand   F8-Sort  Alt+F8-List  ↑F8-Save  F10-Continue
```

When you press F10 or go to the Retrieve Spec by pressing F7, the new type is included in the record. The Type field contains both utilities and unexpected.

You can retrieve and edit the record for check number 1099 so that the Type field contains food or unexpected.

```
                              BUDGET

        Check Number: 1099          Date of Expense: 11/05/90
        Payee: Chicago Phone Company
        Amount: $25.66
        Description: November telephone bill
        Type: utility;phone
        Check Cleared?: N
        Service Charge: $0.15
        Total Debit: $25.81
        Date Entered: 11/06/90
        Time Entered:11:28 am




        BUDGET.DTF    Retrieved form 1    of --    Total Forms: 5    Page 1 of 1

        Esc-Exit    F1-Help    Alt+F6-Table    F7-Search    F8-Calc    F10-Continue
```

Now, when you search for records with utilities in the Type field, the record for check 1097 appears. When you search for records with a food expense, check 1099 appears. If you search for records of unexpected expenses, the records for both checks appear.

To retrieve both of these records, follow these steps:

1. Press F7 to access the Retrieve Spec and press F3, if necessary, to clear any previous specification.

2. Move to the Type field and enter the keyword you want to match.

```
                              BUDGET

        Check Number:              Date of Expense:
        Payee:
        Amount:
        Description:
        Type: unexpected
        Check Cleared?:
        Service Charge:
        Total Debit:
        Date Entered:
        Time Entered:




        BUDGET.DTF              Retrieve Spec        Page 1 of 1

        Esc-Exit   F1-Help   F6-Expand   F8-Sort   Alt+F8-List   ↑F8-Save   F10-Continue
```

In this case, enter the word **unexpected**.

3. Press F10 to continue with the retrieval. The matching records are retrieved.

4. Press Alt-F6 to see the records in table view.

4

As you can see, both records appear in the table.

```
┌─────────────┬────────────────┬──────────────┬─────────┬──────────────┐
│Check Number │ Date of Expense│    Payee     │ Amount  │ Description  │
├─────────────┼────────────────┼──────────────┼─────────┼──────────────┤
│1097         │ 02/14/91       │Gas & Electric│$78.15   │Last of Feb B→│
│1099         │ 08/22/90       │Joe's Hot Dog→│$14.60   │lunch for my →│
│             │                │              │         │              │
│             │                │              │         │              │
│             │                │              │         │              │
│             │                │              │         │              │
│             │                │              │         │              │
│             │                │              │         │              │
│             │                │              │         │              │
└─────────────┴────────────────┴──────────────┴─────────┴──────────────┘

 BUDGET.DTF      Retrieved record 1     of 2       Total records: 5

 Esc-Exit  F1-Help   ( ↓ ↑ → ← Home End PgUp PgDn )-Navigate      F10-Show form
```

5. When you are finished viewing the table, press F7 to return to the Retrieve Spec for additional searches.

Even though you have the ability to search for a single keyword in records that contain multiple keywords, you may want to ensure that your search finds records with more than one keyword. You can think of such searches as extended keyword searches. A car dealer, for example, might want to search the stock for a car that fits both the categories one owner and convertible.

In the budget database, you may want to search for Food records that are also Unexpected expenses. To perform these searches, you preface the criteria with the & symbol. Q&A retrieves only the records that meet your full specification.

To see the & character in action, follow these steps:

1. From the Retrieve Spec, clear any previous criteria by pressing F3.

2. Move to the desired Keyword field. In this example, move to the Type field.

3. Type an & followed by the first keyword. Type a ; followed by the second keyword. In this example you type:

&food;unexpected

```
                              BUDGET                              ■

  Check Number:                     Date of Expense:
  Payee:
  Amount:
  Description:
  Type: &food;unexpected
  Check Cleared?:
  Service Charge:
  Total Debit:
  Date Entered:
  Time Entered:




                                                                 4


  BUDGET.DTF                  Retrieve Spec              Page 1 of 1

  Esc-Exit   F1-Help   F6-Expand   F8-Sort   Alt+F8-List  ↑F8-Save   F10-Continue
```

4. Press F10 to initiate the retrieval and view the first record. To view more records press F10 again. In this example, the one record containing both food and unexpected in the Type field is displayed.

```
                              BUDGET                              ■

  Check Number: 1099                Date of Expense: 08/22/90
  Payee: Joe's Hot Dog Stand
  Amount: $14.60
  Description: lunch for my friend and I
  Type: food;unexpected
  Check Cleared?: N
  Service Charge:
  Total Debit:
  Date Entered:
  Time Entered:




  BUDGET.DTF     Retrieved form 1    of 1    Total Forms: 5   Page 1 of 1
  No more records. Press Esc to exit or F9 for previous form.
  Esc-Exit       F1-Help        Alt+F6-Table      F7-Search      F8-Calc
```

Retrieving Forms That Don't Match Criteria

You can select records that are exceptions to the rule. You might, for example, want to see all expenses except those that are Rent types. When retrieving records that are exceptions to the rule, use the forward slash (/) to indicate the word *not*. You encounter this not type of selection criteria all the time in daily life. When you ask friends to share in ordering a pizza, for example, they say "Get any topping but anchovies." Said another way, their criteria for the pizza is *not anchovies* or */anchovies*. Anchovies is the exception criteria. If you have some trouble recalling the not or other operator symbols, just access the retrieve specification Help example table as you have done before.

To request all expenses that are not Gas & Electric, you would enter */Gas & Electric* in the Type field.

To complete this retrieval, follow these steps:

1. Press [F7] to return to a Retrieve Spec.

2. Press [F3] to clear the Retrieve Spec of old criteria.

3. Move your cursor to the Type field.

4. Enter / and the value you want to exclude from the search criteria. For this example, type */Electric*.

```
          HOW TO SEARCH: THE RETRIEVE SPEC          Pg. F-??

  Type symbols into individual fields to indicate what information you want.

  ┌─────────┬───────────────────────────────┬───────────────────────────────┐
  │ SYMBOL  │ MEANING                       │ EXAMPLES                      │
  ├─────────┼───────────────────────────────┼───────────────────────────────┤
  │ x       │ equal to x                    │ Boston     CA      4/12/85    │
  │ /x      │ not equal to x                │ /CA      /Sales   /$100       │
  │ >x      │ greater than x                │ >12:00 pm                     │
  │ <x      │ less than x                   │ <10,000    <1/1/85            │
  │ >=x     │ greater than or equal to x    │ >=Jones   >=12:00 am          │
  │ <=x     │ less than or equal to x       │ <=1000    <=12/31/85          │
  │ >x..<y  │ greater than x and less than y│ >10..<100                     │
  │ x;y;z   │ x OR y OR z                   │ red;white;blue   9.99;10.00   │
  │ =       │ empty (i.e., equal to nothing)│                               │
  │ /=      │ not empty                     │                               │
  │ MIN n   │ retrieve n lowest values      │ MIN 5                         │
  │ MAX n   │ retrieve n highest values     │ MAX 100                       │
  │ x..     │ begins with x (if text field) │ pre..                         │
  │ ..x     │ ends with x (if text field)   │ ..ing                         │
  │ ..x..   │ contains x (if text field)    │ ..esp..                       │
  └─────────┴───────────────────────────────┴───────────────────────────────┘

  Esc-Exit              → PgDn-Using expressions ←
```

5. Press [F10] to continue and retrieve a record.

6. Press [F10] to continue viewing additional records. No records with your *not* criteria are presented.

Retrievals Based On Dates

You can use Date fields to retrieve records that use all the preceding methods except for Keyword type retrievals. Date ranges can be specified using equal to, wild-card, or greater/less than symbols.

To retrieve records with dates on or after July 1, 1990, for example, you would enter **>June 30, 1990** in the date field as the retrieve criterion. To retrieve records with dates on or after July 1, 1990 but before August 15, 1990, you would use **>June 30, 1990..<August 15, 1990**. You can type date criteria by using any Q&A recognized format for the date. The following figures show different ways to search for records whose Date of Expense falls between January 1, 1991 and May 1,1991.

In these examples, you see a search for all records with the same date range, yet each method of forming the date portion of the expression is unique. You should select a method of entering dates within expressions that is most comfortable for you.

Using the Question Mark as a Wild Card

You will recall that the .. wild card can stand for any single or group of characters. Using .., you can retrieve records containing both DAVID and DAVE, for example. You supply some core literal value, such as DAV, that Q&A must match. The .. wild card will match anything else in the field's value. Records containing DAVID, DAVE, DAVIE, and DAVY will be retrieved. In some cases, you will want more control over the wild-card matching process. For more exact control of wild-card matches, you need a wild card that matches anything in its character position.

You use a ? (question mark) to perform a wild-card retrieval when you want to replace a single character in the retrieval specifications. You might, for example, want to see all expenses for food. You can see all these expenses by using a ? as a wild-card symbol in place of one of the characters in food.

To find all expenses for food, complete the following steps:

1. Press F7 to return to the Retrieve Spec.
2. Press F3 to clear the Retrieve Spec of restrictions.
3. Move the cursor to the field for which you want to set up search criteria. For this example, move the cursor to the Type field.

4. Type the criteria with the ? representing a character. For this example, type fo?d.

5. Press F10 to continue the retrieval process. The first record to meet your request appears.

Caution: When using ? wild cards to retrieve date fields, you must enter the criteria preceded by a closed square bracket ( ]). A search for all records in the month of July, 1990 would be entered as]1990/07/??.

You cannot perform a ? wild-card retrieval on a field with a Format Type of number or money. Use the two-dot (..) wild-card symbols for these types of fields.

Executing Sounds Like Retrievals

As databases grow and become more complex, you might have more trouble remembering how properly to spell entries. Because of this spelling problem, Q&A has a unique retrieval feature to find records based on phonetic representation. Using a Sounds Like retrieval, you have a very good chance of retrieving a desired record even if you misspell the criterion text. You activate this retrieval by using the tilde (~) symbol in front of the criterion text.

If you want to search for a record of someone living in Cupertino, California and you are not sure how to spell *Cupertino*, you could find the record using any of the following spellings in the proper retrieve specification field:

~copertino

~kopertino

~koperteno

~cooprteno

You also can use Sounds Like retrievals to find misspellings in the database. An equals search for the last name SOLOMON will not include the errant record entry for SOLOMAN. The Sounds Like search will show records for both SOLOMON and SOLOMAN because the spellings sound nearly the same. You can correct the misspelling when you discover the problem.

To illustrate the Sounds Like capability, try the following example. Assume you want to find all phone expenses, but you are not sure how it was entered into your database. To use a sounds-like retrieval to final all matching records, follow these steps:

1. Press F7 to return to a Retrieve Spec.

2. Press F3 to clear the Retrieve Spec of all old restrictions.

3. Move your cursor to the Type field.

4. Enter the sounds-like criteria. For this example, enter ~**fon**. Remember that Q&A will search based on the sound of *fon*, not on the spelling.

5. Press F10 to continue the process and retrieve the first record. The record is displayed.

   Sounds like retrievals are especially handy when searching databases for first and last names of which you are unsure of the spelling.

6. Press F10 for additional matches or press Esc to return to the File menu.

4

Programming a Form in File

5

One of the most useful features of Q&A File is its provision for programming the data entry form for a database. To a Q&A newcomer, the idea of "programming" may be intimidating. Don't think, however, that Q&A form programming is difficult to learn. In fact, programming a form isn't like the programming that software specialists do. Programming a form involves entering command-like statements in a "programming specification." Q&A assists you in programming a form by offering familiar **F1** Help keys and by checking your statement entries for acceptable format. Even if you decide that programming a form is beyond your needs, you should browse through this chapter; you may find that you can apply the described programming features to entering your data into Q&A File. If you have learned the material in previous chapters without problems, you should work through this chapter in more detail.

Q&A has many features that you can use to improve performance and ease of data entry. You can automate and control data entry by using programming statements in a specification. These statements are associated with entry fields in your form.

Statements can be very basic or extremely complex, depending on the task you want to complete. The statements covered in this chapter are rather basic, but

Understanding programming capabilities

Using programming features

Writing calculation statements

Writing conditional statements

Using Lookup statements

Using @Functions

even basic programming enables you to invoke additional powers of Q&A and make your database work up to its maximum potential. This chapter doesn't attempt to teach you every method of programming—or even every instruction that a statement might contain. Rather, this chapter concentrates on introducing you to the programming specification and related screens as you complete exercises illustrating a few of the features of form programming.

5

Key Terms Used in This Chapter

Statement	A command or series of commands entered into a programming specification screen that are used for cursor control and data manipulation.
Calculation statement	A statement that uses values (such as field values) to calculate results and then places those results in a field.
Conditional statement	A statement that executes instructions if data meets specified conditions.
GoTo statement	A statement that moves the data entry to another field without operator intervention.
Lookup statement	A statement that uses values contained in a user-defined lookup table to substitute a value for the data entered by the user.
Function	An expression that substitutes a calculated value or action for a value entered by the user.

Previewing Programming Capabilities

In the chapter exercises, you will examine a variety of programming statements and applications. The exercises include statements that control cursor movement between fields, automatic display of Help screens or messages, retrieving data from tables for automatic entry, and financial calculations. Also included are conditional statements that require certain conditions to be met before execution. In these exercises, the chapter uses the budget database you have used in previous chapters.

You will learn how to write the following types of programming statements for your databases:

Calculation statement	This statement adds the contents of the Amount field to the contents of the Service Charge field and places the result in the Total Debit field.
If/Then statement	This statement checks whether the Check Number field contains an entry. If the field does contain a check number, the statement inserts a 15 percent charge in the Service Charge field.
GoTo statement	This statement moves the cursor through the Service Charge and Total Debit fields and executes the programming statements in those fields.
Lookup statement	This statement pulls information from a table and inserts it in the Type field.
@Functions	These functions are used to display a Help screen and to display a message on the message line.

As you can see from this list, you will use programming to automate and control the behavior of data entry. Although the exercises associate programming statements with specific fields, you can use the information presented in the exercises to program other fields in the budget database or in a database of your own design.

Accessing Programming Features

You access programming features from the **P**rogramming menu. To get to this part of the system, follow these steps:

1. From the **F**ile menu, select **D**esign file.
2. From the **D**esign menu, select **P**rogram a file.

   Q&A displays the file name of the database last accessed in the current session at the File to prompt.

3. If you just started Q&A or want to use a different file than the one indicated, enter the file's name at the prompt.

For this example, if your prompt does not show `BUDGET.DTF`, type this name at the prompt.

4. Press ⏎Enter to accept the file name.

You are now at the **Programming** menu.

5

Programming statements are stored in the **Program** form option on this menu.

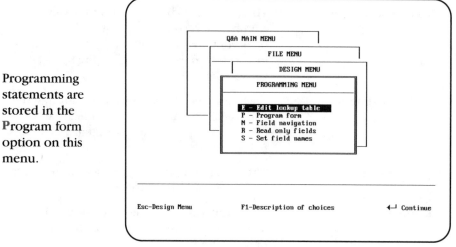

5. Select **Program** form.

The Program Spec appears on-screen.

Because of the variety of available programming statements, Q&A has extensive Help screens for this feature. Following Steps 6 through 8, briefly review the Help screens (to be aware of what is possible) and then begin your first programming statement.

6. Press F1 to view the first Help screen.

```
                              BUDGET

Check Number:                      Date of Expense:
Payee:
Amount:
Description:
Type:
Check Cleared?:
Service Charge:
Total Debit:
Dat
Tin  ┌──────────────────────────────────────────────────────┐
     │ 1) Type # and a unique number in each field that (a) you will │
     │    write a statement for or (b) you will refer to in another  │
     │    statement.                                                 │
     │                                                               │
     │ 2) Type the statement.  For example, to automatically calculate│
     │    BONUS as 10 percent of SALARY, you would type:             │
     │         Salary: #1        Bonus: #2 = #1/10                   │
     │                                                               │
     │            Press F1 for more explanation.                     │
     └──────────────────────────────────────────────────────┘
BUDGET.DTF              Program Spec              Page 1  of  1

Esc-Exit     F1-Help      F3-Clear Spec    F6-Program editor    F10-Continue
```

7. Press F1 to view additional Help screens.

```
┌────────────────────────────────────────────────────────────────┐
│              CREATING A PROGRAM SPEC          Pg. F-116           │
│                                                                  │
│ To program a form, you enter programming "statements" into the fields of the │
│ Program Spec.  Programming statements are executed when you add or update a   │
│ form.  See your manual for an in-depth discussion of programming.            │
│                                                                  │
│ 1) Enter a unique field identifier into each field which will contain a      │
│    programming statement or will be referenced by one.  A field identifier   │
│    consists of a # followed by a number.  Example: #1                        │
│                                                                  │
│    Statements will be executed in the order of their field identifiers       │
│    when you press CALC (F8) during add or update, unless you use < or >.      │
│    (Press PgDn for more details).                                            │
│                                                                  │
│ 2) Type a statement after the field identifier.                              │
│    Example:  #1 = #12 / 2   (to divide the value of field #12 by 2 and        │
│                              put the result into field #1)                    │
│                                                                  │
│    Use F6 to enter a statement that is longer than the field.                │
│                                                                  │
│ 3) When you have finished entering statements, press F10.                    │
│                                                                  │
│ Esc-Exit                    → PgDn-More ←                                     │
└────────────────────────────────────────────────────────────────┘
```

If more information is available than fits on your screen, the PgDn-More message flashes at the bottom of the screen. To access additional information, press the [PgDn] key. [PgUp] moves to the preceding screen.

8. Press [Esc] when you are ready to return to the Program Spec.

Assigning Field Identifiers

You enter each programming statement in a field in the database. Q&A then recognizes that the field is programmed and interprets the statement when you position the cursor in that field. Because most statements refer to other fields in their instructions to Q&A, you must provide positive identification for the referenced fields. A simple way to identify each field (the method that you have seen in previous chapters) is to assign a unique number to each field. *Field identifiers* number the fields that you use in programming statements. You select the number for each field and precede each number with a pound sign (#). For example, #1, #2, or #3. Q&A recognizes the pound sign (#) as the beginning of a field identifier.

When programming, first assign all fields their own field identifiers, then write the programming statements. In most cases you use successive identifiers, but you also can change the identifiers in increments of 10 or 100. (Q&A looks for the next higher number rather than the next number.) If you have databases with multiple pages, you can use the 100 number series for page 1; 200 for page 2; and 300 for page 3. When you review your programming statements, you can identify the field's page by the digit in the 100's position. Q&A does not specify the 100-per-page increment, however; you as easily can indicate a page by changing the identifiers by increments of 10 (10, 20, 30). The key to choosing identifiers is knowing that programming statements are executed according to the sequence of the field identifiers.

Before you begin to program, assign field identifier numbers to all fields in the database. For this example, use the BUDGET.DTF database. To assign field identifier numbers, follow these steps:

1. Press [Esc] to clear the small Help screen if necessary.

2. Enter field identifier numbers in the fields.

   For this example, enter these identifier numbers in the following fields:

Fields	*Identifier #*
Check Number	#1
Date of Expense	#2
Payee	#3
Amount	#4
Description	#5
Type	#6
Check Cleared?	#7
Service Charge	#8
Total Debit	#9
Date Entered	#10
Time Entered	#11

5

Typing Your Programming Statement

You can type programming statements many different ways. Q&A is not case-specific, so you can use all uppercase letters, all lowercase letters, or a combination of both when completing a statement; Q&A executes the statements without regard to capitalization. When entering statements, you can type the statements in all lowercase letters and the FILE NAMES and FIELD NAMES in all capital letters. This method enables you to read your file names and field names more easily when you review your statement. Some people prefer to start important command words with a capital letter. Use the method that works best for you.

Writing Calculation Statements

The first programming statement example is a *calculation statement*. It calculates the sum of the contents of the Amount field and the contents of the Service Charge field and places the result in the Total Debit field. In this exercise, you will write the programming statement to compute this arithmetic answer.

This programming statement involves three fields: Amount (#4), Service Charge (#8), and Total Debit (#9). Fields #4 and #8 contain information that is added and subsequently entered into field #9. Before Q&A can add fields

#4 and #8, however, Q&A must know the fields' values. Because the programming statement that adds the values is in field #9, you must enter values in fields #4 and #8 before the arithmetic is performed by the statement in field #9. Also, the Total Debit field (#9) executes its statement when you move the cursor to the field. The statement for the field is *on-entry* if a self-activation symbol—the less-than (<) symbol—precedes the field number. Q&A executes programming statements beginning with the less-than (<) symbol as soon as the cursor moves to the associated field.

To write a calculation statement, follow these steps:

1. Move the cursor to the field where you want Q&A to enter the calculated result. In this example, move to the Total Debit field.

   The length of the programming statement in this example is at least eight characters, so the Total Debit field is not large enough for this entry.

2. Press F6 to expand the size of a field to accommodate a long entry.

F6 initiates the field editing box. The cursor moves to the editing box, and Q&A displays the field's current contents, if any, in the editing box.

```
                                    BUDGET
         _____

         Check Number: #1              Date of Expense: #2
         Payee: #3
         Amount: #4
         Description: #5
         Type: #6
         Check Cleared?: #7
         Service Charge: #8
         Total Debit: #9
         ┌─────────────────────────────────────────────────────────┐
         │ #9                                                        │
         │                                                          │
         │                                                          │
         │                                                          │
         │                                                          │
         │                                                          │
         └─────────────────────────────────────────────────────────┘
         BUDGET                        0 %  1   Line 1 of 1
         BUDGET.DTF                    Program Spec              Page 1 of 1

         Esc-Exit    F1-Help   F2-Print   F7-Search   F8-Options   F10-Exit editor
```

3. Use the arrow keys to position the cursor over the # character. Press Ins (insert) and type the less-than (<) symbol. (The less-than (<) symbol tells Q&A to execute the statement as soon as you position the cursor in the field.) The field identifier moves to the right and then you can use the arrow keys to position the cursor in the first space to the right of the field identifier (in this example, #9).

5

110

4. Edit your statement to match the following figure.

```
                              BUDGET
    _____

    Check Number: #1                    Date of Expense: #2
    Payee: #3
    Amount: #4
    Description: #5
    Type: #6
    Check Cleared?: #7
    Service Charge: #8
    Total Debit: #9
    ┌─────────────────────────────────────────────────┐
    │ <#9 = #4 + #8                                   │
    │                                                 │
    │                                                 │
    │                                                 │
    │                                                 │
    │                                                 │
    └─────────────────────────────────────────────────┘
    BUDGET                        0 %  14  Line 1 of 1
    BUDGET.DTF              Program Spec            Page 1 of 1

    Esc-Exit     F1-Help    F2-Print    F7-Search    F8-Options    F10-Exit editor
```

This programming statement says that when the cursor enters field #9, Q&A adds field #4 (Amount) and field #8 (Service Charge) and enters the result in field #9 (Total Debit).

The calculation is executed when the cursor enters the Total Debit field because the less-than (<) symbol precedes the statement. Notice that an equal sign (=) follows the field identifier in this statement. Calculation statements use an equal (=) sign to begin the instructions.

5. Press F10 to exit the editor and add the programming statement.

Notice that the field display has changed. An arrow is now the last character in the Total Debit field, indicating that a Long Value exists for this field (that the statement contains more characters). To view the additional information in the Long Value, highlight that field and look at the line above the status line, where Q&A displays the additional contents. To move the cursor to an expanded field for editing, press F6.

In the preceding example, you used the plus sign (+) to indicate an addition of numbers. This symbol is an arithmetic operator. You can use a series of arithmetic operators to perform different types of numeric calculations.

111

Writing Conditional Statements

In programming, a condition is a decision point for subsequent action. As a real-life example, *if* you sink your putt, *then* you tee-off on the next hole; *else* (if you miss your putt), you must putt again. The condition is "if you sink your putt." Your action after the putting decision point is governed by whether or not you make the putt. The operative words in the example are *if*, *then*, and *else*. In programming, *if*, *then*, and *else* words state the framework of conditions. If/Then/Else statements are *conditional statements* because some condition (or conditions) must be evaluated to determine how to execute the statement.

The second programming statement example is a conditional statement. Because not all expenses are checks (some could be cash-out-of-pocket), not all records in the budget database contain an entry in the Service Charge field. The statement in this exercise tests whether a check number has been entered. If a check number has been entered, then the statement enters .15 in the Service Charge field; if not (the else condition), it leaves the field blank. This statement saves time when entering check expenses because Q&A fills in the Service Charge field. Because the statement is not a calculation, you do not use the = to begin the instructions; all noncalculation programming statements use a colon (:) to begin the program instructions.

When completing statements that enter a text value into a field (such as .15 as a text value), you must enclose that value in quotation marks (for example, ".15"). Using quotation marks guarantees that Q&A displays your field entries exactly as you specify.

To write a conditional statement, follow these steps:

1. Position the cursor in the field that you want to automate. In this example, move the cursor to the Service Charge field.

2. Press F6 to expand the size of this field in the editing box.

3. Enter the conditional statement. In this example, edit your statement to match the following figure.

112

```
                              BUDGET
   _____

   Check Number: #1              Date of Expense: #2
   Payee: #3
   Amount: #4
   Description: #5
   Type: #6
   Check Cleared?: #7
   Service Charge: #8
   Total Debit: <#9 = #4+

   ┌───────────────────────────────────────────────────────────────┐
   │ <#8: If #1 = "" then #8 = "" else #8 = ".15"                   │
   │                                                                 │
   │                                                                 │
   │                                                                 │
   │                                                                 │
   └───────────────────────────────────────────────────────────────┘

   BUDGET                            0 %  45  Line 1 of 1
   BUDGET.DTF                     Program Spec              Page 1 of 1

   Esc-Exit    F1-Help   F2-Print   F7-Search   F8-Options   F10-Exit editor
```

The statement in this example "translates" as follows:

If field #1 (Check Number) is equal to " " (blank), then field #8 will be equal to " " (blank); else (otherwise) field #8 is equal to .15 (decimal equivalent of 15 cents).

Because the less-than (<) symbol begins this statement, Q&A executes the statement when the cursor first enters the field.

Controlling Cursor Movement Using GoTo Statements

GoTo statements control cursor movement. Use these statements to move the cursor around the form, eliminating the need to press the Enter or Tab key to move to and from fields containing statements. If a field's value will be completed using some kind of statement, you do not need to move the cursor in and out of the field manually—you can program Q&A to move the cursor for you.

For example, in your BUDGET.DTF database, fields below the Check Cleared? field will be completed by programming statements. To execute the statements, however, the cursor does need to pass through these fields. You can add GoTo statements to these fields to make the cursor pass through the fields and execute the statements.

In this example, you will program fields #8 and #9. First, you add a GoTo statement to the Service Charge field; the GoTo statement then moves the cursor from the Service Charge field into the Total Debit field; finally, you add this statement at the end of the programming statement in the Service Charge field.

To add a GoTo statement, follow these steps:

1. In the Program Spec, move the cursor to the field where you want to add the GoTo statement. In this example, move the cursor to the Service Charge field.

2. If the field already contains a statement, move the cursor to the right of the existing text. In this example, move the cursor to the blank space after ".15".

3. Type a semicolon (;) to indicate an additional statement, then type the statement. For this example, type ;goto #9.

4. Press F10 to save this statement and move to the next field. In this example, field #9 (Total Debit) does not require a GoTo statement because it is the last field completed (Date Entered and Time Entered are already filled in by Set Initial values).

5. Repeat Steps 1 through 4 to add additional GoTo statements.

6. Press F10 to save all programming statements and return to the programming menu.

Retrieving Data Using Lookup Statements

A *lookup statement* is yet another kind of programming statement. A lookup statement retrieves information from a *lookup table* and enters that information into a field in your database.

For example, suppose that you have an address database. You are entering a series of addresses into your database and you want to insert the city based on the ZIP code information. To do this, you first store the city and ZIP code data in a table; then, when you type the ZIP code into your database field, Q&A accesses the table, looks-up the ZIP code, finds the correct city, and inserts the city into the appropriate field in the database.

The Type field in your BUDGET.DTF database also can use lookup statements and a lookup table. Rather than entering each expense type in the field, you then simply enter the first letter of the type. For example, you could enter F (food), U (utility), or R (rent). Your database reads the letter, accesses the lookup table, retrieves the full word, and enters the word into the Type field for you.

114

You must complete two steps to retrieve data using lookup statements:

1. Build the lookup table.
2. Write the programming statement that instructs Q&A to retrieve the value from the table and enter it into the field.

The first step is to build the lookup table.

When you build a lookup table, you type into a *Key* column the values that you or other users will enter into a field of the form during data entry. In the next column to the right, you type the values that you want Q&A to substitute for the key values that you entered in the first column. For more complex programming techniques, Q&A provides additional columns for other values; in this exercise, however, you will use only one substitute value for a given key.

For example, the lookup table for the BUDGET.DTF database contains the first letter of the Type and the full, spelled-out word of the Type (**F**=Food, **U**=Utility, **R**=Rent).

To build a lookup table, follow these steps:

1. From the **Programming** menu, select **E**dit lookup table.

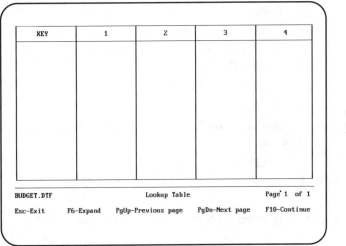

KEY	1	2	3	4

BUDGET.DTF   Lookup Table   Page 1 of 1

Esc-Exit   F6-Expand   PgUp-Previous page   PgDn-Next page   F10-Continue

Q&A displays a lookup table.

A lookup table consists of five columns. The leftmost column is the Key column, and in this example, it will contain the first letter of the type of expense. During data entry, when you enter the first letter of the type of expense (**F** for food, **U** for Utility, or **R** for Rent), Q&A looks for an exact match in this column. Columns 1 through 4 store the data you want Q&A to enter into the database. (You do not have to use all the columns; use only the columns you need for your programming technique. In most cases, you use only column 1.) In this example, Column 1 stores the entire word (**Food, Utility, Rent**) that will be transferred to the field in the database when the appropriate key letter is entered by a user.

Lookup tables can be very large. The tables look like they hold only 17 lines of information, but they can hold up to 64,000 characters. To access the additional table space, press the [PgDn] key. Also, each column in the table can be expanded to hold more characters than are visible. To expand the column capacity, press the [F6] key.

To build the table, position the cursor in the first space of the Key column of the lookup table.

1. In the Key column, enter the first *key value* that Q&A will check and press [Tab⇵].

   In this example, press **F** and then press [Tab⇵].

   The cursor moves to column 1.

2. In column 1, enter the value with which Q&A will replace the first key value.

   In this example, type **FOOD**.

3. Press [↵Enter] to move to the second line on the lookup table.

4. In the second line of the Key column, enter the second key value that Q&A will check and press [Tab⇵].

   In this example, press **U** and then press [Tab⇵].

   The cursor moves to column 1.

5. In the second line of column 1, enter the value with which Q&A will replace the second key value.

   In this example, type **UTILITIES**.

6. Continue entering key values and the values with which Q&A will replace them.

   In this example, finish by entering **R** in the Key column and **RENT** in column 1.

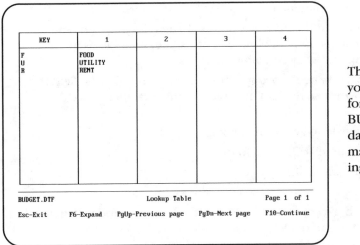

The lookup table you created for your BUDGET.DTF database should match the following figure.

7. To save your lookup table and return to the Programming menu, press F10.

Now that you have created the lookup table, you need to write a lookup statement that uses the table. The lookup statement tells Q&A that you have constructed a lookup table and what to do with the information in that table. Lookup statements require three types of information:

- Identification of the key field (the field that contains the entered value that matches a value in the Key column of the lookup table).

- Identification of the lookup table column from which to retrieve the corresponding values (the values that Q&A substitutes for the key values).

- Identification of the location in which to enter the corresponding value retrieved from the lookup table.

These critical items of information, called *arguments*, are contained in parentheses in the programming statement.

In this example, data in the lookup table pertains to the Type field, so the Type field will contain the programming statement which accesses the table. To complete the lookup statement, follow these steps:

1. From the **P**rogramming menu, select **P**rogram form.

   If you completed the exercises in this chapter for programming calculation and conditional statements, some of the fields in the Program Spec already contain statements.

2. In the Program Spec, move the cursor to the key field (the field that you want to access the lookup table). In this example, move the cursor to the Type field.

3. Modify the field to access the lookup table.

   The statement tells Q&A the following:

   - A lookup table exists.

   - When the user enters data, go to the lookup table.

   - Compare the contents of field #6 (the key field) and match it with the contents of the Key column.

   - When a match is found, go to column 1 (which contains the full name of the Type), retrieve that value, and enter the value into field #6.

   - Now you simply need to enter the first letter of the type of expense and move the cursor out of the field. The programming statement retrieves the complete word from the lookup table and inserts it into the Type field.

4. Press F10 to save your programming statements.

If you built a custom Help screen in the preceding chapter, you added help text that tells the user how to complete the Type field. Now that you have added a lookup table to the Type field, you need to modify that custom Help screen. In the Help screen, tell the user that only the first letter of the expense type must be entered.

To modify the Help screen, follow these steps:

1. From the **C**ustomize menu, select **D**efine custom help.

2. Press F8 to move the cursor to the key field. In this example, move the cursor to the Type field.

3. Use the arrow keys to position the cursor at the first entry. In this example, position the cursor on the first letter of the first type of expense.

4. Press the ⌊Ins⌋ key.

   You are now in insert mode and can edit the table without retyping it.

5. Type the first key value. In this example, type the first letter of the expense type followed by an equal sign (**F=Food**). Edit your Help screen, substituting your types of expenses.

6. Press ⌊F10⌋ to save the changes and return to the Customize menu.

Using @Functions in Programming Statements

The final programming statement you will learn uses *@functions*. These special programming statements are built into the software. You just press @ and the name of the function—Q&A does the rest. You can use @functions to perform commands using date fields; control when programming statements should execute (either in Add or Update mode); number items sequentially; and compute financial calculations such as growth rate, present value, loan payments, interest rates, and number rounding.

@function statements can do two things for your BUDGET.DTF database: display custom Help screens and display a special message on the message line. In the preceding chapter, you created a custom Help screen for the Check Cleared? field. This exercise teaches you how to make that Help screen appear automatically when the cursor is in that field.

Using the @HELP function you can display the Help screen when the cursor enters the Check Cleared? field. Use this function so that the user does not have to press F1 for help. Q&A displays the custom Help screen instantly to aid in the correct entry selection.

To begin your programming statement, follow these steps:

1. From the Programming menu, select Program form.

2. Move the cursor to the field for which you are providing help.

   In this example, move to the Check Cleared? field.

3. Press ⌊F6⌋ to expand the size of this field into the editing box.

4. Type the statement in the field as shown in the following figure.

   To make the statement execute when the cursor first enters the field, begin the statement with the less-than (<) symbol. Follow the less-than (<) symbol with the field identifiers and the function.

   In this example, the statement uses the @HELP function.

119

This statement tells Q&A to display the Help screen associated with field #7 when the cursor first enters that field.

```
                              BUDGET

Check Number: #1                    Date of Expense: #2
Payee: #3
Amount: #4
Description: #5
Type: >#6:Lookup (#6,1,#6)
Check Cleared?: #7
Service Charge: <#8:→
Total Debit: <#9 = #4→

<#7:@Help(#7)




BUDGET                        0 %  14  Line 1 of 1
BUDGET.DTF              Program Spec              Page 1  of 1

Esc-Exit      F1-Help    F2-Print    F7-Search    F8-Options   F10-Exit editor
```

5

Because Q&A assigns values to the time and date fields during data entry (with Set Initial values), the user probably finishes the form by completing the Total Debit field. Because the Total Debit field is the last field for data entry, it is a good place to include a message telling users not familiar with Q&A how to save the form and receive a new blank form (by pressing F10) or how to exit the Add mode. To add a message on the message line, which is between the status line and the key assignment line, use the function @MSG.

To display this message when the cursor moves to the Total Debit field, follow these steps:

1. In the Program Spec, move the cursor to the field with which you want to associate a message.

   In this example, move the cursor to the Total Debit field.

2. Press F6 to expand the field.

   In this example, the field already contains a calculation statement, but you are not limited to one statement per field.

3. Move the cursor to the end of any statement already in this field.

   Separate multiple statements with a semicolon (;); each statement is treated independently when executed.

120

4. Type a semicolon (;), then add the message as the argument of a @MSG function.

   In this example, type the following:

   ;@MSG ("* Press F10 to SAVE the form, Press Shift-F10 to SAVE the form and EXIT ***")**

5. To save your statements and return to the Programming menu, press F10.

To see whether all the statements work, you need to return to Add data on the File menu.

To return to Add data, follow these steps:

1. Press Esc to return to the Design menu.

2. Press Esc to return to the File menu.

3. From the File menu, select Add data for the BUDGET.DTF database.

4. In the Check Number field, enter 2000 (or any test number). Move to the next field.

5. In the Date of Expense field, type today's date. Move to the next field.

6. In the Payee field, enter the name of your grocery store (or any test name). Move to the next field.

7. In the Amount field, enter 73.54 (or any test amount). Move to the next field.

8. In the Description field, enter Weekly grocery shopping (or any test description). Move to the next field.

9. Press F1 to see the Help screen for Type.

10. Select one of the Types and enter it into the field. Move to the next field. Notice that the Help text displays automatically.

11. Press N for No in the Check Cleared? field. Move to the next field.

5

The remaining
fields are already
completed and
Q&A displays
your message to
the user on the
message line.

```
                              BUDGET

       Check Number: 1095                 Date of Expense: 08/17/90
       Payee: Grand Central Foods
       Amount: $56.73
       Description: Weekly grocery shopping
       Type: food
       Check Cleared?: N
       Service Charge: $0.15
       Total Debit: $56.88
       Date Entered: 08/23/90
       Time Entered: 1:23 pm




       F-Frmt  R-Rstrct  I-Initl  S-Spdup  P-Prgrm  L-Lkup  H-Help  C-Chng Paltte
```

12. Press ⇧Shift-F10 to save your new form and return to the File
    menu.

Printing from
the File Module

Chapter 2 taught you how to design and set up a
database in the File module of Q&A. In Chapter 3 you
learned how to enter and edit information in the database. This chapter teaches you how to print the information you need to the screen or on paper. You can print
any field or combination of fields.

When you print from Q&A File, you have several options. You can

- Use the DOS PrtSc, or Print Screen, facility to
  print a single record displayed on the screen.

- Print a single record with a Q&A print utility
  within File.

- Create a print specification—called a print
  spec—to print elaborate customized reports.

A print spec is a list of instructions that tell Q&A which
fields to print in what order. Designing a print spec
involves filling in a series of specification screens. You
can save the completed print spec for use again later,
and you can modify the saved specifications in order to
change the report before you print again.

Key Terms Used in This Chapter

Coordinate   A method of printing that prints customized reports so that you can use preprinted forms.

Free-form   A method of printing that prints a list of field contents down the left margin of a page.

Print spec   A list of instructions that tell Q&A which fields from your database to print and in what order.

Understanding the Print Menu

To print information from a single record or from a few selected records, simply display the record or records you want to print. You then press F2 and F10 to accept the default print specifications (see Retrieving Records in Chapter 3). If your printer is installed correctly, the contents of the current record are printed, together with the field names.

To print database information, follow these steps:

1. From the File menu, select Print.

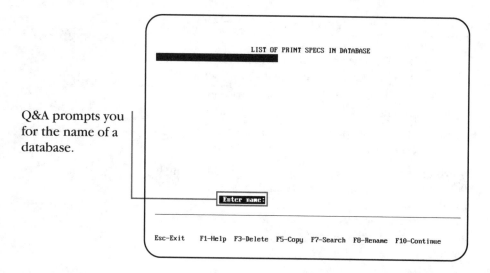

Q&A prompts you for the name of a database.

```
                    LIST OF PRINT SPECS IN DATABASE




                                      ┌Enter name:┐


    Esc-Exit    F1-Help  F3-Delete  F5-Copy  F7-Search  F8-Rename  F10-Continue
```

2. You now have three options. If a database name is displayed, you can accept the name by pressing ⏎Enter. You also can type a new name at the prompt (Q&A automatically erases the displayed name when you begin typing). Or, you can erase the displayed name and press ⏎Enter to display the List Files screen. From List Files, you can press the cursor-movement keys to highlight a file name and then press ⏎Enter.

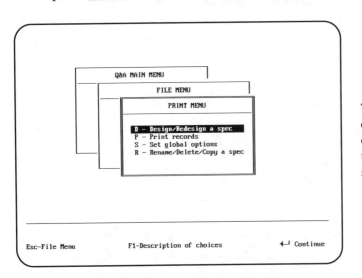

The Print menu is displayed and enables you to set up specific print specifications.

The Print menu contains the following choices:

- Use the **Design/Redesign a spec** option to design or redesign a print spec. After you design a print spec, the spec is saved for future use.

- Use the **Print records** option to print a designed print spec that does not require permanent modifications.

- Use **Set global options** to change print options, page defaults, and single form print defaults.

- Use the **Rename/Delete/Copy a spec** option to rename, delete, or copy print specs you designed and saved.

Designing a Print Spec

The **Design/Redesign a spec** option enables you to design a print spec and save it to memory for later use. You can design a print spec and then modify it whenever necessary.

From the Print menu, select Design/Redesign a spec. If you previously designed print specifications, a list of existing print spec names is displayed. If
you have not designed print specifications, this screen is blank.

Notice the large
bar in the upper
left of the screen.
The bar is used to
highlight the print
spec you want to
use.

```
                    LIST OF PRINT SPECS IN DATABASE
 ██████████████████████████████████




                    Enter name:


  Esc-Exit   F1-Help  F3-Delete  F5-Copy  F7-Search  F8-Rename  F10-Continue
```

The highlight bar shows you the amount of space available for the print
specification name. Print spec names can be up to 31 characters long. Be
specific as you select print spec names. As you develop more print specifications, you may be confused by all the names unless you choose descriptive
names.

To name a print spec, follow these steps:

1. Type a descriptive name for the print specification you want to
   design in response to the Enter name: prompt.

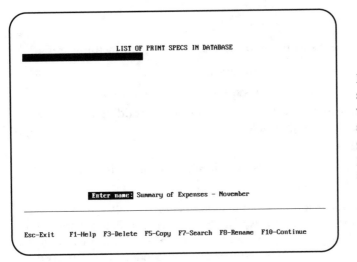

For example, suppose that you want a print specification that enables you to print a monthly summary report.

2. Press F10 to continue the design process.

Selecting Forms for the Print Spec

After you name a print specification, the Retrieve Spec screen is displayed. On this screen, you specify which forms you want included in the print spec. The process is the same as you used in Chapter 3 to retrieve forms. You can use wildcards, keywords, equal to matches, or any other criteria you choose. If you are not sure how to retrieve forms in a database, press F1 for help.

You can save the retrieve spec and use it again later without having to retype the field selection criteria. Before exiting the retrieve spec, press Alt-F8, give the spec a name, and press F10 to return to the Retrieve Spec screen. To retrieve a saved spec, press ⇧Shift-F8 at the Retrieve Spec screen and select the desired spec from the list that Q&A displays.

Suppose that you want to retrieve all forms for this print spec and sort them in ascending order by check number. To retrieve all forms at this point, press F10. Note that it is usually helpful to sort the selected records before you print them, however. Before leaving the Retrieve Spec screen, press F8 to access the Sort Spec screen.

Sorting Forms

To retrieve all forms and sort them in ascending order, follow these steps:

1. Press ⌈F1⌋ to get help setting up the sort.
2. Select the field on which you want to do the primary sort.

   Because you want to see all checks entered in ascending order, type **1AS** in the Check number field.
3. Press ⌈F10⌋ to continue.

You can specify up to 999 sort levels by entering the numerals 1 through 999 in the fields of the sort spec.

Just as you can save retrieve specs and use them later, you also can save the sort spec and use it later without retyping the sort criteria. Before exiting the Sort Spec screen, press ⌈Alt⌋-⌈F8⌋, type a name for the spec, and press ⌈F10⌋. To retrieve a spec, press ⌈⇧Shift⌋-⌈F8⌋ at the Sort Spec screen and select a saved spec from the list that Q&A displays.

Selecting a Print Style

Field specs contain information about which fields you want included and how you want them arranged when printed. To arrange the fields on a print-out, you can use the following methods:

- Free-form is used on mailing labels or other types of printouts that list all or part of specified fields consecutively down the left side of a page or across the page with a specified number of spaces between fields.
- Coordinate is used for preprinted forms or specially designed reports in which the fields may be positioned anywhere on the page.

128

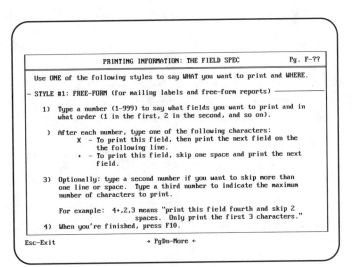

```
                          BUDGET

Check Number:                    Date of Expense:
Payee:
Amount:
Description:
Type:
Check Cleared?:
Service Charge:
Total Debit:
Date
Time    Use the Fields Spec to say what fields to print and where.

        If you want to print ALL the fields as they appear on the form,
        leave the Field Spec blank and press F10.

        If you want to print SELECTED fields or control where they get
        printed on the paper page, press F1 to find out how.


BUDGET.DTF              Fields Spec for Summary of Expense   Page 1  of 1

Esc-Exit            F1-Help           F6-Expand field        F10-Continue
```

If you want to print all the fields exactly as they appear on the screen, leave the field spec blank and press F10.

Setting Up Free-Form Style

The free-form style of printing uses the following two symbols to tell the print spec where to print the field:

- A plus (+) symbol tells the print spec to skip a space and then print the next field on the same line.

- An X tells the print spec to go to the next line before printing the next field.

```
            PRINTING INFORMATION: THE FIELD SPEC        Pg. F-??

Use ONE of the following styles to say WHAT you want to print and WHERE.

- STYLE #1: FREE-FORM (for mailing labels and free-form reports) ──────

    1)  Type a number (1-999) to say what fields you want to print and in
        what order (1 in the first, 2 in the second, and so on).

    )   After each number, type one of the following characters:
            X  - To print this field, then print the next field on the
                 the following line.
            +  - To print this field, skip one space and print the next
                 field.

    3)  Optionally: type a second number if you want to skip more than
        one line or space.  Type a third number to indicate the maximum
        number of characters to print.

        For example:  4+,2,3 means "print this field fourth and skip 2
                      spaces.  Only print the first 3 characters."
    4)  When you're finished, press F10.


Esc-Exit                    → PgDn-More ←
```

If you want to print selected fields, a Help screen is available to tell you how to complete this spec. Just press F1.

To use the free-form style of printing, follow these steps:

1. Press Esc to clear the Help screen from the monitor.
2. Place the cursor in the field you want to print first.

   For example, place the cursor in the Check Number field.

3. Enter the appropriate free-form symbol.

   Typing **1X** in the Check Number field causes that field to print first. The next field will print one line below the Check Number field.

4. Move the cursor to the field you want to print second.

   In the Payee field, type **2+**. The next field will print on the same line as Payee.

Continue to specify the order of the remaining fields.

```
                                    BUDGET


   Check Number: 1X                      Date of Expense:
   Payee: 2+
   Amount: 4X
   Description:
   Type: 3X
   Check Cleared?:
   Service Charge: 5X
   Total Debit: 6X
   Date Entered:
   Time Entered:




   BUDGET.DTF              Fields Spec for Summary of Expense   Page 1  of  1

   Esc-Exit          F1-Help            F6-Expand field         F10-Continue
```

5. To continue the process and go to the next screen, press F10.

With the free-form style of printing, you also can specify how many lines or spaces the program should insert between printed field data. For example,

If you enter	*Q&A prints*
1X,4	The field's contents in the first position, then moves the cursor down four lines
3+,5	The field third, then moves the cursor down five lines.

If the field's contents are larger than the space allowed, Q&A truncates (cuts short) the field's contents on the printout. To tell the program to print the entire contents of a field, type an E after the field position number on the print spec.

For example, if you type **2+,10,E**, Q&A prints the entire contents of the field, word-wrapping after the tenth character in the field.

On the print spec, which is explained later, you can indicate whether you want Q&A to print field labels (Name, Address, and so on). You also can have field labels printed selectively, on a field-by-field basis. To do so, at the end of the field type L. For example, typing **3+,15,L** causes Q&A to print the field, truncating it after the 15th character, and the field label.

To save a print spec for later use, at the Print Spec screen press Alt-F8.

Setting Up Coordinate Style

You use this method of printing when you want to complete a preprinted form with information in the database with fields printing anywhere on the form. Unlike the free-form style, which gives you the option of printing next to or below other fields of information, coordinate prints fields at the exact position on the page where you want them to appear. Coordinate is frequently used to complete preprinted forms, such as airbills and job applications.

From the Field Spec screen, you can continue to press F1 (Help) until you see information about the coordinate style of printing. This screen differs from the free-form Help screen. You must specify exactly where you want each field to print, including both the line on which it is to print and the space in which it will begin printing. You must measure the form to determine its dimensions and the location of the lines to receive the data.

For example, suppose that you have a form that goes to your accountant listing all check expenses and includes the same fields you used in the preceding free-form style report.

131

Checking Account Expense Form

Check#: _____   Amount: _____

Service Chg:_____

Total Debit:_____

Payee:_____

Type: _____

6

All dimensions translate to number of characters based on 10 characters per inch and number of lines based on six lines to an inch. The first field you want to print is Check #. This field is approximately one inch from the top of the form; therefore, its first coordinate is 6 (six lines per inch), assuming that most printers print six lines per inch. The first space for data entry is about an inch from the left side of the form. The second coordinate is 10. (10 characters per inch) horizontally.

To begin entering the coordinates, follow these steps:

1. Press Esc twice to cancel the help screens and return to the Field Spec screen.

2. With the cursor in the Check Number field, type the coordinates you want to use.

   For this example, type **6,10**. This setting causes the check number to print on the sixth line from the top of the form in the tenth character space from the left.

3. Move the cursor to the Amount field. Enter the coordinates.

   Because the Amount field is printed on the same line as Check # field, you know that the first coordinate will be the same. Data must print 30 character spaces to the left. Therefore, the coordinates are **6,30**.

4. Move the cursor to the Service Charge field. Service Charge is approximately one and one-fourth inches from the top of the form (line 8), and data prints 32 character spaces to the left. Therefore, the coordinates are **8,32**.

5. Move the cursor to the Total Debit field. Enter the coordinates **10,32**.

6. Move the cursor to the Payee field. Payee information should be about two and one-half inches from the top of the form or on line 14. Data should start printing in the 10th character position. The print coordinates are **14,10**.

7. Move the cursor to the Type field. Data information should be about two and three-quarters inches from the top of the form and in the tenth character position. The print coordinates are **16,10**.

```
                              BUDGET
                          _____

   Check Number: 6,10               Date of Expense:
   Payee: 14,10
   Amount: 6,30
   Description:
   Type: 16,10
   Check Cleared?:
   Service Charge: 8,32
   Total Debit: 10,32
   Date Entered:
   Time Entered:




   _____
   BUDGET.DTF            Fields Spec for Checking Account Exp   Page 1 of 1

   Esc-Exit   F1-Help  F6-Expand field  Shift+F6-Enhance F9-Goback   F10-Continue
```

This example shows what the screen should look like after you enter the coordinates.

8. Press F10 to continue.

You can improve the appearance of the printed output by applying boldface, underlining, italics, fonts, and other text enhancements to the codes on the Fields Spec screen. When you enter a code on the Fields Spec screen, simply apply the enhancement to the code.

To improve the appearance of the printed output, follow these steps:

1. On the Fields Spec screen, move the cursor to a field in which you want to enhance the printed data.

2. Press ⌂Shift-F6.

   Q&A displays the Text Enhancement and Fonts menu.

3. Press **B** (boldface), **U** (underline), or **I** (italic) to apply text enhancements. Press **R** to remove all enhancements previously applied. To apply a specific font, press one of the font keys (1 through 8) that you have assigned.

To assign fonts to the keys, press Ctrl-F9 to display the Font Assignment screen, or press **A** at the Text Enhancement and Fonts menu.

To improve the appearance of a coordinate print spec, apply enhancements to the page coordinates. To enhance a field label, apply the enhancement to the L code or to the text in parentheses following the L code.

Using File Print Options

Whether you used the free-form or coordinate style of printing, you must use the File print options to tell Q&A where and how to print the print spec. You can specify where you want the information to print, the kind of paper you want to use, and the positioning of the data on the paper. You also can set special commands for the printer and specify the number of forms, columns, and copies you want. Additionally, if your computer and display support graphics, you can preview your work on-screen. This option enables you to make any needed adjustments before you send your work to the printer.

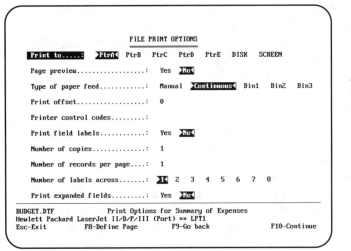

After you press
F10 from the
Fields Spec
screen, the File
Print Options
screen is dis-
played.

6

To set up the print options, follow these steps:

1. Press → to highlight the printer choice.

   The Print to option tells the computer where you want the print spec
   to print. You can select up to five printers. You also can choose just
   to print to screen. If you select to print to disk, Q&A creates an ASCII
   file, which any DOS-based computer can read.

   As you highlight printers A through E, look at the message line. Q&A
   displays the name of the printer assigned to that menu choice.

2. Press ↓ to move to the Page preview option. Then press → to select
   Yes or No.

   If your computer monitor supports graphics, the Page preview
   option enables you to specify whether you want to preview the
   report before you send it to the printer. At the File Print Options
   screen, set Page Preview to Yes and press F10 to display the page.
   Page preview is available from Q&A's print specs in File, Write,
   Report, and also can be displayed from the Intelligent Assistant.

After the Page Preview screen appears, press + and - to zoom in and out to enlarge and reduce the view of the printed data. Press F1 (Help) for the complete list of options, which include viewing side-by-side pages; normal, half-, and full-page views; scrolling up and down; and viewing next and previous pages. Press F2 to return to the File Print Options screen.

3. Press ⬇ to move to the Type of paper feed option.

This option describes the media that will hold the report. Choose Manual if you plan to insert each sheet of paper separately. Select Continuous if your printer has an automatic sheet feed. The remaining selections are used in combination with special bin feeders. For example, Bin1 may contain first-page letterhead, Bin2 may contain second-sheet letterhead, and Bin3 may contain legal-size paper. Note that if you select to print to the screen, this choice is nullified.

4. Press ⬇ to move to the Print offset option.

This option enables you to move the entire body of printed material to the right a specified number of spaces. Use this option to allow room for hole punching or binding. This option is not applicable if you chose to print to the screen.

5. Press ⬇ to move to the Printer control codes option.

Printer control codes specify how a printer should react to commands, such as type size or page length. Owners of PostScript printers can use this option to enter the names of files that contain special PostScript procedures. For example, use this option to print borders, shading, company logos, and so on. Consult your printer manual for these codes. Because most printers used with Q&A have print drivers that contain this information, this field usually should remain blank.

6. Press ⬇ to move to the Print field labels option.

Use this option to clarify what each piece of information is. If you want the field labels, as well as the data to print, select Yes.

7. Press ⬇ to move to the Number of copies field.

With this option, you can request multiple copies of the information.

8. Press ⬇ to move to the Number of records per page option.

Use this option when you want more than one form to print on the same page. Some forms may contain only a few lines. You save paper by choosing to print more than one form per page.

9. Press ⬇ to move to the Number of labels across option.

   This option enables you to print additional data to the right of the first column. You can print up to eight columns or labels on a sheet of paper. Q&A prints labels left to right across the page.

10. Press ⬇ to move to the Print expanded fields option.

    If the information contained in a field is longer than the space you allowed on the Field Spec, specify Yes. Information that does not fit in the allotted space word-wraps down to subsequent lines.

```
                          FILE PRINT OPTIONS
 Print to.....:     PtrA   PtrB   PtrC   PtrD   PtrE   DISK  ▶SCREEN◀

 Page preview.................:     Yes  ▶No◀

 Type of paper feed...........:     Manual  ▶Continuous◀  Bin1   Bin2   Bin3

 Print offset.................:     0

 Printer control codes........:

 Print field labels...........:     ▶Yes◀  No

 Number of copies.............:     1

 Number of records per page...:     10

 Number of labels across......:     ▶1◀  2   3   4   5   6   7   8

 Print expanded fields........:     Yes  ▶No◀
─────────────────────────────────────────────────────────────────────
 BUDGET.DTF              Print Options for Summary of Expenses
 Print to screen with page size adjusted to fit the screen.
 Esc-Exit          F8-Define Page          F9-Go back          F10-Continue
```

If you specify No, long data is shortened to fit within the specified length.

6

11. Press F10 to continue.

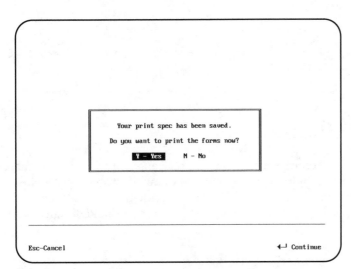

```
        ┌──────────────────────────────────────────┐
        │   Your print spec has been saved.        │
        │   Do you want to print the forms now?     │
        │        Y - Yes      N - No                │
        └──────────────────────────────────────────┘
```

You are asked whether you want to print now.

Esc-Cancel   ↵ Continue

6

This example
shows how the
screen looks
when you select
to preview a
printed copy of
the report in the
free-form style.

```
Check Number: 1095
Payee: Grand Central Foods Type: food
Amount: $56.73
Service Charge: $0.15
Total Debit: $56.88

Check Number: 1096
Payee: Great Lakes Gas & Electric Type: utility;gas/electric
Amount: $25.25
Service Charge: $0.15
Total Debit: $25.40

Check Number: 1097
Payee: Great Lakes Gas & Electric Type: utility;gas/electric
Amount: $23.78
Service Charge: $0.15
Total Debit: $23.93
```

Esc-Exit   F2-Reprint   {← →}-Scroll   Shift F9-Redesign   ↵ Continue

This example
shows what the
screen looks like
when you print in
the coordinate
style.

```
        1095              $56.73
                          $0.15
                          $56.88

        Grand Central Foods

        food
```

Esc-Exit   F2-Reprint   {← →}-Scroll   Shift F9-Redesign   ↵ Continue

Revising a Printout

After you see a form on-screen, you may want to rearrange information so that
it is easier to read. For example, suppose that you originally wanted two fields
of information to print on the same line. Now you decide that having the two
fields together is difficult to read. Press ⇧Shift-F9 to access the Redesign
menu.

```
Check Number: 1095
Payee: Grand Central Foods Type: food
Amount: $56.73
Service Charge: $0.15
Total Debit: $56.88

Check Number: 1096
Payee: Great Lakes Gas & Electric Type: utility;gas/electric
Amount: $25.25
Service Charge: $0.15
Total Debit: $25.40

Check Number: 1097
Payee: Great Lakes Gas & Electric Type: utility;gas/electric
Amount: $23.78
Service Charge: $0.15
Total Debit: $23.93



   Which spec?    R-Retrieve    S-Sort    F-Fields    P-Print    A-Page
```

For example, this form shows both the Payee and Type fields on the same line.

6

Changing a Field Spec

Changing a field spec is easy. A small menu appears across the bottom of the screen. You use this menu to jump to the spec you want to change, bypassing all other specs. Field location requirements are stored on the the Field Spec screen.

To change a field spec, follow these steps:

1. Type **F**.

    The Field Spec screen reappears.

2. Move the cursor to the Payee field. Change the criteria to **2X**.

    Make sure that you clear the rest of the information from the current line.

3. Press F10 to continue.

4. Press ↵Enter in response to the prompt.

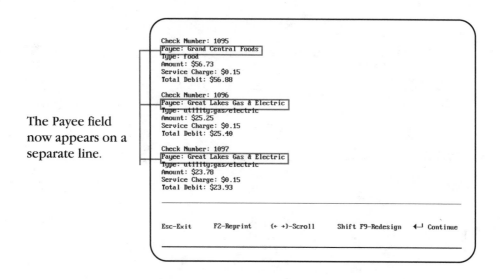

The Payee field now appears on a separate line.

Use the Redesign bypass keys to work with a design until you have it exactly as you want. Then print a paper copy if needed.

Use the ⏎Enter or PgDn keys to scroll to forms not displayed on this page. After all data has been displayed, you return to the Print menu.

Using the Define Page Screen

With the Define Page screen, you can change margins, page width, page length, and characters per inch. You also have an opportunity to set headers and footers from this screen.

Fields print to the screen in approximately the same location as they print on paper. You can adjust this space by using the Define Page screen. You can define the dimensions of the sheet of paper, margins, headers, and footers.

To access the Define Page screen, follow these steps:

1. Press ⇧Shift-F9.
2. Type A.

```
                        DEFINE PAGE

        Page width : 240        Page length..: 66

        Left margin: 0          Right margin : 240

        Top margin : 3          Bottom margin: 3

        Characters per inch:   ▶10◀  12   15   17
    ──────────────────── HEADER ────────────────────
    1:
    2:
    3:
    ──────────────────── FOOTER ────────────────────
    1:
    2:
    3:

    BUDGET.DTF            Define page for Checking Account Exp

    Esc-Exit      F1-Help      F9-Go Back to Print Options    F10-Continue
```

The Define Page screen is displayed.

6

The default setting for this screen is a page width of 85 characters and a page length of 66 lines. The right margin is set for 85 characters.

You change the default settings on the Define Page screen by highlighting the options you want to change and typing the new settings in the space after that option. You can enter the new settings in inches or as the number of rows or columns. For example, to specify dimensions in inches, you add the inch mark after each number.

The standard 8 1/2-by-11 inch paper has a page width of 85 characters and a page length of 66 lines. Margins are the blank spaces that are on either the right, left, top, or bottom of a printed page. Margins are expressed in characters. Q&A allows up to 240 characters across the page for print specs.

You also can change pitch, which is the number of characters per inch, with the Define Page screen. Ten characters per inch is used most often, but 12-pitch, which corresponds to a typewriter's elite type, is also popular. The third option, 15-pitch, may cause characters to overlap on some daisywheel or laser printers, unless you change the print wheel or font cartridge. The final option is 17-pitch, which produces condensed type on most printers. Some printers respond properly to this command only if they are set to print in draft mode.

You can use the Define Page option to customize your printouts by adding headers and footers to pages before printing. The procedure is simple. Just press Tab⇅ to move down to where the word HEADER is displayed. Position the cursor on the line below the word and type the text you want to appear at the top of each page of the printout. Handle bottom-of-page information in the same way by typing footer text below the FOOTER prompt. You can use any or all of the three available lines in the header and footer areas.

To automatically number the pages, place a pound sign (#) at the position on the line where you want the number to appear. If you put two pound signs together on a line in a header (page ##, for example), Q&A prints a pound sign with the page number. At the top of the third page, for example, you see

       page #3

Q&A interprets the first pound sign literally and computes and enters a page number to replace the second pound sign.

Through the settings on the Define Page screen, you can have Q&A read the date and time from the system clock and enter that data in a header or footer. Just type **@DATE***(n)* where you want the date to appear and **@TIME***(n)* where the time is to be displayed. The *n* stands for the date or time format.

You can separate the header and footer lines into three segments by placing an exclamation point between each section. For example, if you enter

       @DATE(1) !WEEKLY REPORT! Page #

Q&A prints the footer as

       August 12, 1988   WEEKLY REPORT   Page 6

Everything before the first exclamation point is left-justified, the section following is centered, and the final section is right-justified. Because Q&A treats spaces as characters, any spaces will be included in the formatting. Unnecessary spaces may throw off centering and justification. Without the second exclamation point, all text to the right of the first exclamation point is centered.

In the following header, all data will be right-justified because the header command is preceded by two exclamation points:

       !!@DATE @TIME Page ##

As a result, the header is printed as

       August 12, 1988 5:43 pm Page #6

6

Saving and Printing Specs

After you finish designing and customizing a print spec, you immediately can print information from the specifications you have entered, or you can save the spec and return to the Print menu without printing. In either case, the print spec you just designed is saved to disk. If you decide to print immediately, you return to the Print menu after the printing is complete. You can rename, copy, delete, or design a new spec after a spec is created. You also can make temporary changes to the print specification.

To use an existing print spec, select **P**rint from the File menu. Type the name of a database or erase the name that appears and press ⏎Enter to display a list of file names. To select a database file from the list, move the highlight to the database you want and press ⏎Enter. When the Print menu appears, select **P**rint Forms. A list of existing print spec names is displayed. Using the cursor-movement keys, highlight the spec you want to use and press ⏎Enter.

6

Before printing begins, a screen prompt asks whether you want to make any temporary changes to the design before you print.

When you elect to make temporary changes to a print spec, you are led through a series of screens that are identical to those you have seen before. On the Retrieve Spec screen, you specify the forms to be printed. If you want to enter sort specifications, you go to the Sort Spec screen by pressing F8. Then, from either the Retrieve or the Sort Spec screens, you can press F10 to get to the Fields Spec screen. After you specify the field arrangement on the Fields Spec screen, press F10 to access the Print Options screen. You then can press [F8] to go to the Define Page options screen. Then, from either the Print Options or Define Page screens, you can press [F10] to start the printing process.

If you select No and press [←Enter], the printing process begins. As the document is being printed, you may see that you need to change some of the specifications. To make changes, press [⇧Shift]-[F9] and printing will stop. Instead of going through all the specification screens, you can access the screen you want to change. Press [F2], choose the screen you want to edit, make the changes, and press [F10] to start the printing from the beginning of the print job.

Setting Global Options

If you use print specs frequently and must repeatedly change the same options on the Print Spec and Define Page Spec screens, you can change the default settings. The new global options you choose will affect every new print spec you develop. If most of your print specs are printed on 8 1/2-by-14-inch paper, for example, you can make this standard setting appear on the Define Page Spec.

To display the Global Options menu, follow these steps:

1. From the File menu, select Print.

2. Select Global Options.

The Global Options menu is displayed.

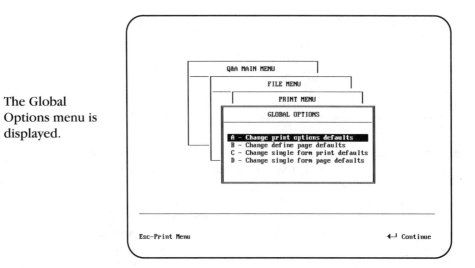

The screens that appear when you choose Change print options defaults or Change define page defaults are exactly the same as the Print Spec and Define Page Spec screens. The procedure for selecting items is the same as for a Print or Define Page Spec for an individual print spec.

This menu also contains the Change single form print defaults and Change single form page defaults. When you retrieve a form from a database, these two options enable you to print the form currently displayed on the screen. The screens displayed are exactly the same as the Print and Design Page spec screens. Changing an item on one of these menus affects every single form printout that you request.

Renaming, Deleting, or Copying a Print Spec

6

Not only can you create and modify an existing print spec, you can rename, delete, or copy a print specification.

To use these options, follow these steps:

1. From the File menu, select Print.

2. At the prompt, type the name of a database or erase the name displayed, if any, and press ⏎Enter to choose a name from a list.

3. From the Print menu, select Rename/Delete/Copy a spec.

```
                    LIST OF PRINT SPECS IN DATABASE
▀▀▀▀▀▀▀▀▀▀▀▀▀▀▀▀▀▀▀▀▀▀▀▀
Checking Account Expense Form
Summary of Expenses - November




                    Enter name:

Esc-Exit   F1-Help  F3-Delete  F5-Copy  F7-Search  F8-Rename  F10-Continue
```

You are prompted for the name of the spec you want to rename, delete, or copy. Type a name or press ⏎Enter to see a list of specs.

4. Press Esc to return to the Print menu.

Note that you can rename, delete, or copy a print spec by using the function keys. Highlight the desired print spec and press the appropriate function key. The following table lists the function keys and their uses.

Table 4.1
Print Spec Function Keys

Function Key	Use
F3	Deletes a specified print spec from memory.
F5	Copies an existing print spec and creates a new specification.
F8	Changes the name of an existing print spec.

6

Getting Started in the Report Module

7

After you enter data into the File module, the Report module enables you to print the data in columnar format. Database information is printed in columns, with each column capable of generating averages, totals, subtotals, maximum values, and a multitude of other mathematical functions. Not only can you include information from the database in which the report is written, but you also can extract information from other Q&A databases and include it in your report. You can save each report that you design and reprint it easily by following a few basic steps.

This chapter teaches you how to create reports from your databases. You learn how to change headings and formats and generate derived columns that perform calculations.

If you are not familiar with database concepts, read Chapter 2 to familiarize yourself with the basic procedures. The sample reports that you generate in this chapter print on-screen rather than on paper, so you do not need a printer to complete the steps in this chapter.

All exercises in this chapter use one of the sample databases that come with Q&A. The database is EMPLOYEE.DTF and is used by the Q&A tutorial. Make sure that this database is on your computer and that you know its location or drive path. Most likely, this database is resident in the same directory as the Q&A software. This chapter follows that assumption.

Key Terms Used in This Chapter

Columnar report	A report that arranges data in columns with the field labels at the top of each column. Each record or form takes up one line on this report.
Column heading	A description of the data that appears in the column. Headings usually are the field names, unless specified otherwise.
Column	Data that is arranged in a columnar or vertical manner with a description of the contents of the column appearing at the top of the column.
Crosstab report	A report that produces a summary of two fields and prints that summary in a third field. This report also follows a columnar format, but provides a look at relationships between database fields that might not be apparent in a columnar report.
Derived columns	A column of data that is a derivative of other fields in a database. Derived columns are not actual fields in a database, but their components are.
Footers	Information that is printed at the bottom of each page of a report. Footers can contain up to three lines of data.
Formatting code	Special codes that change the format of data within a column. Suppose, for example, that you have a number field that you want displayed as a money field. You can use a format code to make this change.

7

Global options	Options that affect all new reports that you design. By setting universal items that affect the entire database (such as type of paper feed, printer to use, and so on), you do not have to make selections for each report that you design.
Headers	Information that is printed at the top of each page of a report. Headers can contain up to three lines of data.
Operators	Symbols that perform basic mathematical tasks such as add, divide, multiply, or subtract. You can use four operator symbols: + (add), – (subtract), * (multiply), and / (divide).
Summary functions	Tasks or functions that Q&A can perform automatically. These functions always start with an @ symbol. They are used most frequently to perform mathematical calculations.

7

Understanding Report

The Report module enables you to print information from a database in a columnar format. Data is arranged in columns going across the page with headings at the top of each column. You can print any database field in a report.

If the data is numeric, you can perform calculations, such as totals, subtotals, averages, counts, minimum values, and maximum values. By using derived columns, you can create data from fields in a database, lookup tables, or external databases. As you design reports, you can save them to disk to print as needed. You also can customize headings and formats to improve the appearance and clarity of a report.

You can generate two types of reports within the Report module. Although both reports provide the same final information, one report gives a detailed presentation and the other provides summarized information.

A *Columnar Report* presents the information that you request in a series of columns.

```
Last name        First name      Department          Position
--------------   ------------    ----------   -----------------------
Abrams           Judy            OPS          Manager
Billingsgate     Rudy            ADMIN        Manager
Brothers         John            EXEC         President
Carter           James           SALES        Outside
Criswell         Ernest          ADMIN        Assistant
Darwin           Charles         R&D          Engineer
Dean             Sarah           SALES        Sales Administrator
Eisenstein       Joseph          LEGAL        Chief Counsel
Foobah           Dorian          PROMO        Manager
Fremont          Sam             SALES        Outside
Galluay          James           ADMIN        Manager
Guy              Mary            SALES        Regional Sales Manager
Gyorfi           Natalia         SALES        Outside
Jacobson         Will            SALES        Regional Sales Manager
Jeffers          David           SALES        Outside
Johnson          Charles         EXEC         Plant Manager
Johnson          Mildred         ADMIN        Secretary
Johnson          Nick            SALES        National Sales Manager
Jones            Jane            SALES        Sales Administrator

EMPLOYEE.DTF

Esc-Exit  F2-Reprint    { → ← ↑ ↓ }-Scroll    Shift+F9-Redesign    F10-Continue
```

A *Crosstab Report* summarizes the information that you request. The report uses three fields—the row field, the column field, and the summary field.

```
                        Sex
                 ------------------------       Total
Department        FEMALE         MALE           Salary
                 ============   ============   ==============
ACCNT            $35,000.00          $0.00      $35,000.00
ADMIN            $36,000.00    $102,000.00     $138,000.00
EXEC                  $0.00    $177,000.00     $177,000.00
LEGAL                 $0.00    $125,000.00     $125,000.00
OPS              $37,000.00          $0.00      $37,000.00
PROMO            $25,000.00          $0.00      $25,000.00
R&D                   $0.00    $143,000.00     $143,000.00
SALES           $232,000.00    $375,000.00     $607,000.00
                 ============   ============   ==============
Total Salary    $365,000.00    $922,000.00   $1,287,000.00

EMPLOYEE.DTF

Esc-Exit  F2-Reprint    { → ← ↑ ↓ }-Scroll    Shift+F9-Redesign    F10-Continue
```

In this chapter, you develop both types of reports using the EMPLOYEE.DTF database that is supplied with the Q&A software.

Using the Report Menu

You access the Report module from the Q&A Main menu. To select Report, highlight the option name and press ↵Enter.

```
┌──────────────────────────────────────────────────────────┐
│                                                            │
│    ┌─────────────────────────────┐                         │
│    │  Q&A MAIN MENU        │                               │
│    ├───┴─────────────────────────┤                         │
│    │       REPORT MENU           │                         │
│    │                             │                         │
│    │ █D - Design/Redesign a report█                        │
│    │  P - Print a report         │                         │
│    │  S - Set global options     │                         │
│    │  R - Rename/Delete/Copy     │                         │
│    │                             │                         │
│    │                             │                         │
│    └─────────────────────────────┘                         │
│                                                            │
│  ────────────────────────────────────────                 │
│                                                            │
│  Esc-Main Menu      F1-Description of choices    ← Continue│
│                                                            │
└──────────────────────────────────────────────────────────┘
```

The Report menu
appears.

7

The Report menu contains the following four options:

- **D**esign/Redesign a Report enables you to design a new report or change a previously developed report.

- **P**rint a Report enables you to print a report that you designed. You can make temporary or permanent changes to the report.

- **S**et Global Options enables you to change settings that affect all report designs. You can make modifications that affect such settings as column headings, format options, print options, and page options.

- **R**ename/Delete/Copy enables you to maintain a library of reports for a database.

Using these options, you can design a basic columnar report and then go back and add enhancements or use special features. You also can create a crosstab report and experiment with the available options.

Designing a Columnar Report

Designing a report is not a complex operation. You use the **D**esign/Redesign a Report option to create the report. Designs and modifications that you make using this feature are saved and apply to the report each time that you print it.

Because this example follows the sample database file that comes with the Q&A software, the report you are going to create will contain information about employees. This database is used by the personnel department of a fictitious company and contains employment information. The sections that follow provide information that you can use to create your own reports, whether you decide to follow the tutorial examples or not.

Suppose that you want to do a bonus factor analysis for each employee in your company. The report that you create should contain the last name and first name of each employee, review date, evaluation, bonus factor, salary, and bonus amount. This report will not include all fields in the database—only those needed for a bonus factor analysis.

To create a report, follow these steps:

1. From the Report menu, select Design/Redesign a Report.

A prompt appears at the bottom of the screen asking which database stores the information that you want to use for reports.

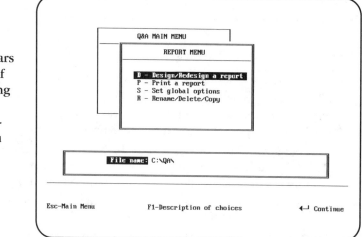

2. Type the drive path and directory of the database containing the information that you want to include in your report, or press the **space bar** and then press ↵Enter to choose a name from a list of database files in the current directory.

For this example, enter the drive path and directory for the EMPLOYEE.DTF database. Assuming that the database is stored on drive C in the same directory as the Q&A software, enter **C:\QA\EMPLOYEE.DTF.**

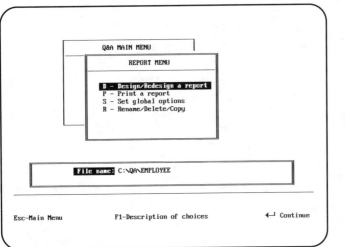

In this example, you see the drive path specified for the EMPLOYEE.DTF database.

3. Press ↵Enter to select the database.

Naming a Report

After you specify the database on which you want to base the report, the List of Reports In Database screen appears.

This screen contains a list of all the previously created reports for the database that you specified.

The cursor is located at the bottom of the screen next to the Enter Name field. You type all new report names in this field. Report names can be up to 31 spaces long, so you can make them very descriptive.

The example report will show all employees along with bonus information. Therefore, a logical name would be *Bonus Analysis*.

With your cursor located in the Enter Name field, type a name for the report and press ↵Enter. For this example, type **Bonus Analysis** and press ↵Enter.

Selecting the Report Type

After you name a new report, the Report Type screen appears.

153

You can generate
two types of
reports using
Q&A: columnar
and crosstab.

```
                           REPORT TYPE
                           ───────────

        Use → or ← to select the type of report you want to design:

                C - Columnar report      X - Crosstab report

        Press F1 if you need help deciding what kind of report you
        want to create.
        _____

   Esc-Exit                      F1-Help                  ←┘ Continue
```

7

Columnar Report

A columnar report presents the information requested in a series of columns. At the top of each
column is a heading (usually the name of the field)
that describes the data contained in the column. Each
row represents a record or form in your database with
the information requested going across the row.

X Crosstab Report

A crosstab report summarizes the requested information The report uses three fields: the row field, the
column field, and the summary field.

Because you are creating a Columnar report, select Columnar.

Using the Retrieve Spec to Select Forms

After you select the Columnar report type, a Retrieve Spec for Bonus Analysis
appears on-screen.

```
 ┌──────────────────────────────────────────────────────────┐
 │  Last name:▓▓▓▓▓▓▓▓▓▓▓▓▓▓▓     First name:                │
 │  Address:                                                 │
 │  City:                      State:       Zip:             │
 │                                                           │
 │  Sex:        Alma Mater:                                  │
 │  Hobbies:                                                 │
 │                                                           │
 │  Hired date:           Department:     Position:          │
 │  Classification:       Manager:                           │
 │                                                           │
 │  Review date:                                             │
 │  Review comments                                          │
 │                                                           │
 │                                                           │
 │  Evaluation:           Bonus factor:       Eligible:      │
 │  Salary:               Bonus:              Accrued Vacation: │
 │  Note:                                                    │
 │  Phone:                                                   │
 │  ──────────────────────────────────────────────────────  │
 │  EMPLOYEE.DTF         Retrieve Spec for Bonus Analysis   Page 1  of  1 │
 │                                                           │
 │  Esc-Exit  F1-Help  F3-Clear  F6-Expand  Alt+F8-List  ↑F8-Save   F10-Continue │
 └──────────────────────────────────────────────────────────┘
```

Use this Spec to tell Q&A which forms you want to include in the report.

To specify which forms you want included, review the help screen affiliated with the Retrieve Spec.

1. Press F1 for help.

```
 ┌──────────────────────────────────────────────────────────┐
 │  Last name:▓▓▓▓▓▓▓▓▓▓▓▓▓▓▓     First name:                │
 │  Address:                                                 │
 │  City:                      State:       Zip:             │
 │                                                           │
 │  Sex:        Alma Mater:                                  │
 │  Hobbies:                                                 │
 │                                                           │
 │  Hired date:           Department:     Position:          │
 │  Classification:       Manager:                           │
 │  ┌────────────────────────────────────────────────────┐  │
 │  R│  Use the Retrieve Spec to say what records you want to Retrieve. │  │
 │  R│                                                    │  │
 │   │  To retrieve ALL the records, leave the spec blank and press F10. │  │
 │   │                                                    │  │
 │  E│  To retrieve SELECTED records, enter restrictions into the fields. │  │
 │  S│  Press F1 for a summary of restrictions with examples. │  │
 │  N│                                                    │  │
 │  P└────────────────────────────────────────────────────┘  │
 │  ──────────────────────────────────────────────────────  │
 │  EMPLOYEE.DTF         Retrieve Spec for Bonus Analysis   Page 1  of  1 │
 │                                                           │
 │  Esc-Exit  F1-Help  F3-Clear  F6-Expand  Alt+F8-List  ↑F8-Save   F10-Continue │
 └──────────────────────────────────────────────────────────┘
```

The Help screen appears.

To retrieve all forms, leave the Retrieve Spec blank and press F10. Because this database does not contain many forms, you will use all of them in the example report.

2. Press F10 to continue.

Retrieving Selected Information

When you want to create a report based on only a selected portion of the information in your file, you fill out the desired data selection criteria on the Retrieve Spec screen.

To retrieve just one form, in the Retrieve Spec enter a piece of information that only that form contains—a customer's name, part number, or title of a report, for example. In the First name and Last name fields, you could type **Jennifer** and **Williams**, and then press ⏎Enter to retrieve a record for a single employee.

At other times, you may need to specify a range of values. Suppose that you need to see all employees hired after January 1, 1991 whose salary is greater than $10,000. In the Hired Date field, you would type **>1/1/91**, and you would type **>10000** in the Salary field. Press F10, and Q&A finds only those forms that meet the specified criteria.

For help setting up a retrieval, press F1 twice from the Retrieve Spec to view a table of retrieval criteria, complete with examples.

You also can tell Q&A to retrieve a group of forms that have values within a range of values. You can, for example, have Q&A display the records of employees whose ZIP codes fall within the range between and including 94086 and 95997. In the ZIP field, enter

94-86.. .95997

Notice that this request won't fit within the 10-character-long ZIP field. When there isn't room in a data field to enter the desired criteria, press F6 (Expand) to type your specification in an expanded entry line that can hold up to 254 characters.

When you specify a retrieval range, the range type can be money, numeric, text, keyword, date, or time. The Retrieve Spec help screen (F1) provides examples of formatting range retrievals for each of these data types.

Notice in our example that the high and low figures are separated by two dots. ZIP codes are text fields.

You can save the filled-in Retrieve Spec and run the same search again later, without having to retype the search restrictions. Follow these steps:

1. Fill in the Retrieve Spec, and then press [F8] (Save).

2. At the prompt, type a name for the saved spec and press [↵Enter] to return to the Retrieve Spec screen.

3. To recall the saved spec later, at the Retrieve Spec press [Alt]-[F8] to view the list of stored specs.

4. Move the cursor to the desired spec and press [↵Enter]. You are returned to the Retrieve Spec, which now shows the saved retrieval criteria in the appropriate fields.

You also can print the Retrieve Spec for reference purposes. At the Retrieve Spec screen, press [F2] to display the Spec Print Options screen. Be sure to set the Print Field Labels? option to Yes.

Q&A enables you to use calculations in a Retrieve Spec. If, for example, you want to retrieve records where salary is greater than 500 percent of bonus, you would enter the following in the salary field:

> **Salary: >{Bonus * 5}**

Notice that calculations and programming functions are contained {in braces}. If you make a mistake in formatting a calculated or programmed retrieval, Q&A displays an error message and positions the cursor at the mistake.

When you retrieve data stored with a template (phone numbers or part number codes, for example), you should be aware that Q&A stores the data without the template formatting characters. The phone number (415) 968-6502, for example, is stored as 4159686502. In the Retrieve Spec, you should type only the data itself, omitting the formatting characters. To retrieve records for the 415 area code region, for example, you would type 415.. in the Retrieve Spec. Q&A displays the retrieved records with formatting characters in place: (415) 968-6502.

You also can use programming expressions in a retrieval. Note, however, that you can use only those programming expressions that return a value. You cannot use summary functions, such as @MIN or @SUM, that require a range of values to produce a result. For help with entering programming functions, at the Retrieve Spec press [F1] twice and press [PgDn].

Programming statements, like calculations, must be enclosed in {braces}, and fields referred to in programming expressions must be referenced by name rather than field number (as is possible with some advanced Q&A programming techniques). To look up records for which Bonus factor is greater than 5 percent of salary plus bonus, for example, you would enter the following into the Bonus field:

> **>{@SUM(Salary + Bonus)}**

7

You may even perform retrievals based on data in external databases, using
Q&A's XLOOKUP functions. For further information on XLOOKUP, see
Chapter 5. To give you a hint of what you can do with XLOOKUP, you could
retrieve only those records where salary is greater than 110 percent of a salary
field for the corresponding employee name in an external file.

Indicating Columns and Sequence

After you use the Retrieve Spec to specify the forms that you want in your
report, the Column/Sort Spec appears. You use this Spec to indicate which
fields you want to include and in what sequence they should appear on the
report.

```
  Last name:▓▓▓▓▓▓▓▓▓▓▓▓▓▓▓  First name:
  Address:
  City:                        State:      Zip:

  Sex:        Alma Mater:
  Hobbies:


  Hired date:          Department:       Position:
  Classification:      Manager:

  Review date:
  Review comments


  Evaluation:          Bonus factor:         Eligible:
  Salary:              Bonus:                Accrued Vacation:
  Note:
  Phone:
  ─────────────────────────────────────────────────────────────
  EMPLOYEE.DTF        Column/Sort Spec for Bonus Analysis    Page 1  of 1

  Esc-Exit    F1-Help  F6-Expand  Shift+F6-Enhance  F8-Derived Cols  F10-Continue
```

Once again, a Help screen is available for this Spec. Press F1, and a help
screen appears at the bottom of the screen.

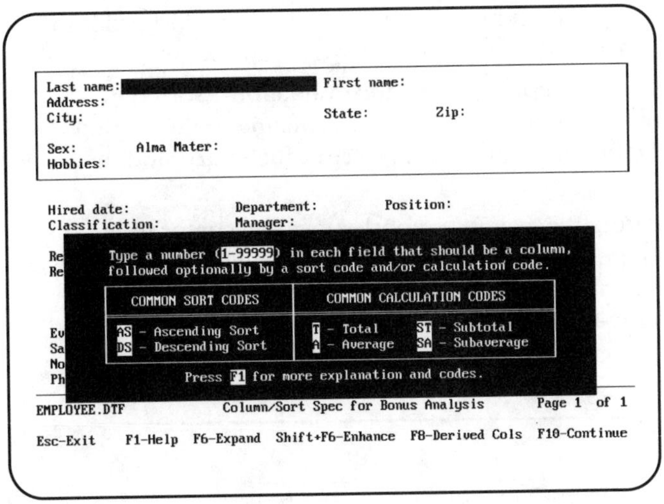
Last name: First name:
Address:
City: State: Zip:
Sex: Alma Mater:
Hobbies:
Hired date: Department: Position:
Classification: Manager:
Type a number (1-99999) in each field that should be a column, followed optionally by a sort code and/or calculation code.
COMMON SORT CODES
COMMON CALCULATION CODES
AS - Ascending Sort
DS - Descending Sort
T - Total
A - Average
ST - Subtotal
SA - Subaverage
Press F1 for more explanation and codes.
EMPLOYEE.DTF
Column/Sort Spec for Bonus Analysis
Page 1 of 1
Esc-Exit F1-Help F6-Expand Shift+F6-Enhance F8-Derived Cols F10-Continue

The Help screen contains common codes.

These codes are the most frequently used codes, but they are not the only ones that you can use. You can press F1 again to see more available codes. The first set of codes that you use contains the AS (ascending order) and DS (descending order) codes. As you proceed through this chapter, more of the calculation codes are explored in detail.

Each field that appears on the report needs a number indicating the column sequence. In addition, you need to indicate how you want the data sorted on the report. Use **AS** for ascending order (from A to Z or the lowest number to the highest number); use **DS** for descending order (from Z to A or the highest number to the lowest number).

To specify columns and sequence, follow these steps:

1. Move the cursor to the field that you want printed first on the report. Press **1** to indicate that this is the first column. If you want the column sorted, press the comma (,) and enter either AS or DS to indicate ascending or descending order.

   For this example, move the cursor to the Evaluation field and type **1,AS**. This code indicates that the Evaluation will be the first column of the report, and the column will be sorted in ascending order.

2. Continue assigning column numbers and, if you want, sort order to the database categories that will comprise your report.

   For this example, your report will list the evaluation—sorted in ascending order—in the first column, the last name in the second column, then the first name, the bonus factor, the salary, and the bonus.

   To continue creating the example report, move the cursor to the Last Name field and type 2. Move to the First Name field and type 3. Move to the Bonus Factor field and type 4. Move to the Salary field and type 5. Move to the Bonus field and type 6.

   Your Column/Sort Spec should look like the following figure.

In this example, you see the Column/Sort Spec for a report that is sorted by employee evaluation. The report also will contain the employee's last name, first name, bonus factor, salary, and bonus.

```
┌─────────────────────────────────────────────────────────────────┐
│                                                                   │
│   ┌─────────────────────────────────────────────────────────┐    │
│   │ Last name: 2                    First name: 3            │    │
│   │ Address:                                                 │    │
│   │ City:                          State:        Zip:        │    │
│   │                                                          │    │
│   │ Sex:         Alma Mater:                                 │    │
│   │ Hobbies:                                                 │    │
│   └─────────────────────────────────────────────────────────┘    │
│                                                                   │
│      Hired date:         Department:        Position:            │
│      Classification:     Manager:                                │
│                                                                   │
│      Review date:                                                │
│      Review comments                                             │
│                                                                   │
│                                                                   │
│      Evaluation: 1,AS    Bonus factor: 4      Eligible:          │
│      Salary: 5           Bonus: █6█████████    Accrued Vacation:  │
│      Note:                                                        │
│      Phone:                                                       │
│   ─────────────────────────────────────────────────────────────  │
│   EMPLOYEE.DTF          Column/Sort Spec for Bonus Analysis    Page 1  of 1 │
│                                                                   │
│   Esc-Exit    F1-Help  F6-Expand  Shift+F6-Enhance  F8-Derived Cols  F10-Continue │
└─────────────────────────────────────────────────────────────────┘
```

Notice the key assignment line on this screen. You will examine the functions of these keys as you proceed through this chapter.

3. Press F10 to continue.

Adding Derived Columns

Q&A Report has the capability of creating, or deriving, a column consisting of data calculated from figures in one or more fields in the report (which may or may not appear in the report itself). Each report can have up to 16 derived columns calculated from file fields or from other derived columns.

To add a derived column to a report, press F8 from the Column/Sort Spec to display the Derived Columns screen. On the Derived Columns screen, you type the heading, a formula, and a column location.

A column heading can be on one line only, but headings that have more than one word look better divided into two or three lines (three lines is the maximum). Use an exclamation mark to indicate where you want the heading to break. **Salary!Plus!Bonus**, for example, prints as:

    Salary
    Plus
    Bonus

At the `Formula` prompt, you enter a formula used to derive the column's data. A derived column formula uses a combination of column numbers or names, and arithmetic operators, such as #2 + #3, for example.

If column 2 is Salary and column 3 is Bonus, the formula creates a column of totals for the data in the Salary and Bonus fields. Note that if you use column numbers, the corresponding fields must be numbered on the Column/Sort Spec.

At the `Column Spec` prompt, you type a number indicating where the derived column should be printed in the report. In the figure, the derived column is the new fourth column. When the Derived Columns screen is complete, press F10 to go to the Report Print Options screen, or press F9 to return to the Column/Sort Spec.

You can used derived columns to compute summary information on data in other columns or in fields in the database. You can use summary functions to compute total, average, count, minimum, maximum, subtotal, subaverage, and subcount values. You also can use LOOKUP functions in derived columns. For further information, consult the Report section of the Q&A manual.

Making a Keyword Report

Keyword fields contain a variety of items separated by semicolons. The Hobbies field in the Employee database, for example is a keyword field. When you specify a keyword report type, Q&A knows that it will be dealing with multiple entries in the field, and searches for the keyword terms you specify.

This capability enables you to categorize report sections according to a single keyword field. When the report is printed, the first column will contain keyword data.

To produce a keyword report, on the Column/Sort Spec, assign the lowest column number to the keyword field, making it the leftmost column. After the column specification, type the letter **K**. Then add other columns and specifications to complete the report.

If you want to retrieve information based on a single keyword, that keyword must be entered in the appropriate field of the Retrieve Spec. If the report is to include only those employees whose hobby is sailing, for example, you must enter **sailing** in the Hobbies field on the Retrieve Spec. To retrieve information based on more than one keyword, enter the keywords in the field on the Retrieve Spec, preceding them with an ampersand (&) and separating them with semicolons. Do not put any spaces between the semicolons and the keyword entries:

&sailing;fishing;swimming

Formatting Report Columns

After you have filled in the Retrieve and Column/Sort Specs, you may want to consider adding special formatting instructions for your report. You do this before leaving the Column/Sort Spec. You can apply special character enhancements such as boldface, italics, and fonts; remove column breaks, insert page breaks, repeat a category, or make columns "invisible."

Formatting Column Contents

When you send your report to the printer, Q&A uses preset format settings that do a good job in most cases. Text in columns appears left-justified, numbers are right-justified, money is displayed in currency format, and dates and times are entered just as they appear in your database.

You can change these standard formats by entering the following special codes in the appropriate fields on the Column/Sort spec:

JR (Justify Right) All data in the column is aligned on the right. This is the default for numbers and money.

JL (Justify Left)	All data in the column is aligned on the left. This is the default for text.
JC (Justify Center)	All data in the column is centered.
U (Uppercase)	All text in the column is uppercase.
C (Comma)	Numbers print with commas. (Money values print with commas and currency symbols by default.)
WC (Without Comma)	Money values print without commas.
Dn (Date format n)	N is a number from 1 to 20, standing for 20 different date formats that you can view from the Column/Sort Spec by pressing ⌨F1⌨ (Help) twice, and then pressing ⌨PgDn⌨ twice.
Hn (Hour format n)	N is a number from 1 to 3, standing for one of the three time formats that you can view from the Column/Sort Spec by pressing ⌨F1⌨ (Help) twice, and then pressing ⌨PgDn⌨ twice.
TR (Truncate)	Truncate data that doesn't fit in the column width (instead of continuing the data on the next line of the column).
M (Money)	Treat a number as money.
Nn (Number format n)	N is a number from 1 to 7, standing for up to seven decimal places for a number. If n is not specified, Q&A uses default decimal place rules.
T (Text)	Treat a number as text. This is useful for derived columns that use certain advanced programming functions.

To specify a format for a column, type the word **Format** (or simply **F**) in the desired field followed by the code in parentheses. To sort column number 1, for example, in ascending order and display its values in uppercase letters centered in the column, enter

> **1,AS,FORMAT(U,JC)**

If you run out of room as you type format specifications, press the Expand Field key (⌨F6⌨).

Using Text Enhancements and Fonts

You can enhance column and derived column headings, calculated columns, and subcalculations with boldface, underline, super- or subscript, strikeout, or italics, as well as with any fonts that your printer supports. To apply a character enhancement, follow these steps:

1. At the Column/Sort or Derived Column Spec, move the cursor to the code that represents the text or calculations you want to enhance.

   To enhance totals generated by the following codes, for example, highlight the T and enter the following:

   2,AS,T

2. Press ⟨Shift⟩-⟨F6⟩ to display the Text Enhancements and Fonts menu.

3. Press ⟨B⟩, ⟨U⟩, ⟨P⟩, ⟨S⟩, ⟨I⟩, ⟨X⟩, or ⟨R⟩ to apply bold, underline, superscript, subscript, italics, strikeout, or regular (Roman) text.

   Note that pressing ⟨R⟩ removes any enhancements already in effect and applies the default regular (Roman) type.

4. To apply a font, press key ⟨1⟩ through ⟨8⟩.

5. Press ⟨F10⟩ to return to the Column/Sort Spec.

Before you can use fonts, you must install them. To assign fonts to items 1 through 8 on the Text Enhancements and Fonts menu:

1. Press ⟨A⟩.

Q&A displays a
Font Assignment
screen.

```
┌──────────────────────────────────────────────────────────┐
│ Last name:                                                │
│ Address:     ┌─────────────────────────────────┐         │
│ City:        │     TEXT ENHANCEMENTS AND FONTS  │         │
│              ├─────────────────────────────────┤         │
│ Sex:    Alma │ B - Bold                         │         │
│ Hobbies:     │ U - Underline                    │         │
│              │ P - Superscript                  │         │
│              │ S - Subscript                    │         │
│              │ I - Italics                      │         │
│ Hired date:  │ X - Strikeout                    │         │
│ Classification: R - Regular                     │         │
│              │ 1 - Font 1 (regular if not assigned) │      │
│ Review date: │ 2 - Font 2 (regular if not assigned) │      │
│ Review comments 3 - Font 3 (regular if not assigned) │      │
│              │ 4 - Font 4 (regular if not assigned) │      │
│              │ 5 - Font 5 (regular if not assigned) │      │
│              │ 6 - Font 6 (regular if not assigned) │      │
│ Evaluation:  │ 7 - Font 7 (regular if not assigned) │      │
│ Salary:      │ 8 - Font 8 (regular if not assigned) e: │   │
│ Note:        ├─────────────────────────────────┤ Vacation: │
│ Phone:       │ A - Assign fonts                 │         │
│              └─────────────────────────────────┘         │
│ EMPLOYEE.DTF                              Page 1 of 1     │
│                                                           │
│ Esc-Exit                                  ↵ Continue      │
└──────────────────────────────────────────────────────────┘
```

2. With the cursor at the `Font file name` prompt, press `⏎Enter` to display the list of printers you have installed for use with Q&A.

3. Move the cursor to a printer name and press `F10`. Q&A returns you to the Font Assignments screen.

4. Move the cursor to an empty line in the Font 1...8 section and press `F6` to display the List of Available Font Descriptions for the selected printer.

```
              LIST OF AVAILABLE FONT DESCRIPTIONS

 LJet-Courier 10 Med            Univers ItaBld
 LJet-Line Printer             Univers Med
 LJet IID/P/III Cour 12 Ita    Univers ItaMed
 LJet IID/P/III Cour 12 Bld    LaserJet-Courier 12 Med
 LJet IID/P/III Cour 12 Med    LaserJet-Courier 10 Ita
 LJet II/D/P/III Cour 10 Bld   LaserJet-Courier 10 Bld
 LJet II/D/P/III Cour 10 Ita   C01-CG Times 12 Bld
 LJet II/D/P/III Cour 10 Med   C01-CG Times 12 Ita
 LJet II/D/P/III Line Ptr 16   C01-CG Times 12 Med
 CG Times Bld                  C01-CG Times 13 Bld
 CG Times ItaBld           █   C01-CG Times 13 Ita
 CG Times Med                  C01-CG Times 13 Med
 CG Times ItaMed               C01-CG Times 18 Bld
 Univers Bld                   C01-CG Times 24 Bld

                               Press PgDn for more

        Font name: LJet-Courier 10 Med
_____


 Esc-Exit             F7-Search            F10-Continue
```

Highlight a font and press `F10` to assign it to Font 1...8.

Press `F10` to return to the Column/Sort Spec.

Setting Column Headings and Widths

As a final step in formatting your report, you can create your own column headings and adjust column widths. (Q&A normally uses field names for column headings.)

You enter column heading and width specifications on the Column/Sort Spec, or at the Heading prompt on the Derived Columns screen if you are printing a derived column. Suppose that a field is to be the first column, sorted in ascending order, assigned a column width of 6, and titled *1991 Bonus*. To make these settings, you enter

    1,AS,HEADING(6:1991!Bonus)

Be sure to include a colon after the column width, and don't insert any spaces before or after the colon. The exclamation mark (!) tells Q&A to print *Bonus* on the line below *1991*.

Removing Column Breaks

Q&A automatically inserts blank lines when a value changes in a sorted column. A blank line is inserted when, for example, the State value changes from *Arizona* to *California*. You can remove these blank lines (called column breaks) by entering the CS (cancel subcalculation) code as follows:

> State: 5,AS,CS

Inserting Page Breaks

To make reports easier to read, you can designate column breaks that cause the printer to skip to a new page every time a column break occurs. To do so, enter a page break code (**P**) in the desired field as follows:

> City: 4,AS,P

This code causes a new page to start when the values in the column change. Any headers and column headings are printed at the top of each page.

Repeating Values

When a sorted column is displayed in your report, each value in the sorted column is usually displayed just once. In a City column, for example, *Los Angeles* will print just once for each of many employees who live in Los Angeles. If you want, you can tell Q&A to print the field contents for each printed record. Just enter a repeat value code (**R**) in the appropriate field on the Column/Sort Spec as follows:

> City: 4,AS,P,R

Making Columns Invisible

You may want to "hide" columns because they contain confidential information (salaries, etc.), because they don't add to the usefulness of the report, or because they would make the report too wide. Even though hidden columns aren't printed, they can still be referenced by calculations, programming expressions, page breaks, or derived columns.

To create an invisible column, type an **I** in the desired field of the Column/ Sort Spec as follows:

> **Salary: 8,DS,I**

Specifying Calculated Columns

Reports that contain numerical data often are much more useful when they contain summary data, such as totals and subtotals. You can request these report embellishments on the Column/Sort or Derived Columns Spec.

To calculate a column, on the Column/Sort Spec, move the cursor to the desired field and type the calculation code. Be sure to separate codes with a space or comma:

T	Totals numerical columns
A	Averages numerical columns
C	Counts numerical or text values
MIN	Finds minimum numerical value
MAX	Finds maximum numerical values
ST	Subtotals numerical columns
SA	Subaverages numerical columns
SC	Subcounts numerical and text values
SMIN	Finds subminimum values in numerical columns
SMAX	Finds submaximum values in numerical columns
SSTD	Finds standard deviation for column segment
SVAR	Finds variance for column segment

The last seven calculations determine intermediate results. The answers for these calculations are displayed at column breaks. The results of the first six calculations are displayed at the end of the report.

When you perform a calculation on a column, every entry in the column is included. When you enter a Total code in the Salary field, for example, the column is added and the sum is displayed at the bottom of the column. Subcalculations are produced at column breaks.

In some reports, subcalculations produce too many column breaks. This happens when a sorted column breaks every time the value in the column changes. To eliminate this problem, cancel subcalculation for the sorted column by entering a cancel subcalculation code (**CS**) in the Column/Sort Spec.

Breaking on Year, Month, or Day

If you want to print a new page each time there is a change of year, month, or day in a column, enter the following codes:

YB	Yearly Break
MB	Monthly Break
DB	Daily Break

If you want the Hired date field to break on the year, for example, you could enter the following in the Hired date: field:

8,DS,YB

Breaking on Alphabetic Change

You also can break a column when the first character of a sorted field changes. Unlike a break on field value, an alphabetic break operates on only the first letter of the field contents. This feature is useful for printing lists, such as telephone directories, bibliographies, and indexes.

To create an alphabetic break, insert the code **AB** in the appropriate field on the Column/Sort Spec. To break on the first character in the Last name field, for example, enter

1,AS,AB

Setting Global Options for Columnar Reports

If you use some report settings repeatedly, you can make them the defaults to avoid entering the settings every time you create a new report. These default values are called *global options*.

Report's Columnar Global Options screen is displayed when you choose Set Global Options from the Report menu and press Ⓒ at the Global Options Screen. From this menu, you can set all default options except those on the Retrieve Spec, which usually needs no defaults because it is specific to each report.

To set new defaults for column widths and headings, press Ⓒ at the Columnar Global Options screen to display the Column Headings/Width Spec.

The Column Headings/Width Spec is similar to the Column/Sort Spec. You can move from field to field on this Spec screen and enter column width and heading defaults. In each field for which you want to set a new default, type the column width and column heading, separated by a colon (:). For example, in the Last name field enter

      15:Last Name

This process is similar to filling out the Report Column/Sort Spec, except that you don't need to enclose the width and heading in parentheses or enter the word **HEADING**.

Press F10 and you are returned to the Columnar Global Options screen. The new settings will apply to all new reports that you create, but they will not apply to reports you have already created.

To set new global format options, select Set Format Options from the Columnar Global Options screen. Q&A displays the Set Global Format Options screen. Use the arrow keys to move through the options and set each choice. You can specify the number of spaces to insert between columns (up to nine), or keep the variable setting, which tells Q&A to make the determination. (The default is five spaces, but the program may choose a narrower column if space is limited.)

Other settings on this screen set new defaults for repeating values, printing blank values, and inserting a blank line between column breaks.

When you have finished setting format options, press F10 to return to the Columnar Global Options menu.

To set default page options, choose Set Page Options at the Columnar Global Options menu. This screen enables you to give Q&A a new default paper size and margins.

Page width is the number of characters that can fit on one page of paper; and page length is the number of lines that can fit on a page. The standard page length is 66 lines. You also can set left and right and top and bottom margins.

The Characters per Inch setting controls the number of printed characters per inch. The choice you make for this option depends on the font sizes available with your printer.

When you have finished specifying page formatting options, press F10 to return to the Columnar Global Options menu.

To set new printing defaults, choose Set Print Options at the Columnar Global Options menu. You might want to have all reports printed to the screen by default. To do so, you would select SCREEN as the Print to option. You also can choose to display a print preview of the report by default, specify a printer offset to match your standard printed report format, and set printer control codes. The Print Totals Only option enables you to tell Q&A to print calculated totals only for all reports, or print the entire body of each report by default. You use the last three options to tell Q&A how to position the report body on the printed page (left, centered, or right), whether you want single- or double-spacing, and whether to split long records across a page break or move them to the next page.

If you use more than one printer, be sure to set the Printer option to match the printer you use most often.

When you have finished setting print options, press F10 twice to return to the Report menu.

Renaming, Deleting, and Copying a Report

The Rename/Delete/Copy option on the Report menu enables you to perform useful housekeeping chores on existing reports. Rename changes only the report's name, but Delete erases the report, and Copy makes a duplicate copy of the report (which can save you time when you want to create a similar report without repeating all the steps).

To rename a report, choose Rename/Delete Copy from the Report menu and enter the name of a database at the prompt, or erase the prompt and press ⏎Enter to select a name from the List of Files screen. (Note that a file name prompt does not appear if you have been working with a file in the current Q&A session.)

The following options are displayed:

R	Rename a Report
D	Delete a Report
C	Copy a Report

Select Rename a Report and enter the name of the report you want to rename or press ⏎Enter to choose from a list of reports you have created for the current file. At the Rename To prompt, press ⏎Enter to see a list of the reports you have designed for the selected file, or enter a new name of up to 20 characters. Press ⏎Enter, and Report returns you to the Rename/Delete/Copy menu.

To delete a report, select the Delete a Report option, enter the name of the report or press ⏎Enter to select a report from a list, and press ⏎Enter. Q&A warns you that the report is about to be deleted and asks for confirmation. Press Y to delete the report or N to cancel the operation.

To copy a report, choose Copy a Report and at the Copy From prompt, enter the name of the report you want to copy, or press ⏎Enter to choose from a list of reports. At the Copy To prompt, enter the name of the new report. If the report is to be copied to another drive, enter the drive specification as follows:

`Copy To:` **A:New_Report**

Press ⏎Enter twice to return to the Report menu.

Defining Report Print Options

After you complete the Column/Sort Spec screen, the Report Print Options screen appears. Use this screen to specify how the final report should look and the type of paper you will use.

7

```
                        REPORT PRINT OPTIONS


     Print to.........:   ▶PtrA◀  PtrB   PtrC   PtrD   PtrE   DISK   SCREEN

     Page preview.............:   Yes  ▶No◀

     Type of paper feed.......:   Manual  ▶Continuous◀  Bin1   Bin2   Bin3

     Print offset..............:   0

     Printer control codes.....:

     Print totals only.........:   Yes  ▶No◀

     Justify report body.......:   ▶Left◀  Center   Right

     Line spacing..............:   ▶Single◀  Double

     Allow split records.......:   ▶Yes◀  No


EMPLOYEE.DTF              Print Options for Bonus Analysis
Hewlett Packard LaserJet II/D/P/III (Port) »» LPT1
Esc-Exit        F8-Define Page        F9-Go back              F10-Continue
```

The Report Print Options screen contains the following fields:

Print to

Use this selection to tell your computer where the report will print. You can select Printer A (PtrA) through Printer E (PtrE). You also can print Specs to disk. Anything that you print to disk is converted into an ASCII file before printing, which is a type of file that any PC running DOS can read. Something printed to the screen appears on the monitor instead of on a piece of paper.

Page preview

Use this setting to see a preview of your report on-screen before printing it on paper. The option generates a graphical representation of the report, including all headers, footers, and text enhancements.

Type of paper feed

Use this setting to describe the type of paper feed that will be used to print the report. Manual requests you to press ⏎Enter to proceed with printing. Continuous sequentially feeds sheets of paper into the printer. Bins 1, 2, and 3 are used for special bin feeders. Bin1 might be first-page letterhead, Bin2 might be second sheets for letterhead, and Bin3 might be legal-size paper.

Print offset	Use this setting to move the entire body of the printed material to the right a specified number of spaces. You can use Print offset to allow space for hole punching or bindery.
Printer control codes	Use these settings to specify how a printer should react to commands sent to it regarding type size, page length, and so on. Most printers that you can use with Q&A have "print drivers" that already contain this information so that the codes are not necessary. See your printer manual for these codes.
Print totals only	Use this setting to indicate that you want totals—not detail—to print. If you request totals on the Column/Sort Spec, only the totals print, which creates a summary type of report.
Justify report body	Use this option to select the report positioning that you want. Reports can be flush with the left margin, flush with the right margin, or centered on the page.
Line spacing	Use this option to select the line spacing for the report. Reports can be printed single line or double line (a blank line between each row) spacing.
Allow split records	Sometimes a form or record can fit partially on a page, but will need to have some of the information carried to the next page of the report. To prevent records or forms from being split (part printed on one page and part on another), select No.

Generally, you will want to print data to the screen first to see how closely the format is going to match your requirements. Rarely are reports defined perfectly the first time; you usually need to make some modifications. When printing to the screen, you can make the modifications before generating a paper copy of the information.

To define Report Print Options, follow these steps:

1. With the highlight bar on Print to in the Report Print Options screen, select the place to which you want the report printed.

   For this example, select Screen.

2. Move to Page Preview and select Yes or No.

   Page preview generates a graphic representation of the report before you print it on paper. To use Page Preview, your computer must be equipped with a graphics card and monitor. This representation shows you any font assignments, text enhancements, headers, footers, and so on, as well as the placement of the page on paper. With Page Preview, you see more of the actual page than when you print to screen.

   For this example, select No because you are printing to Screen.

3. Move the cursor to Type of paper feed and select the type of paper feed that you are using.

   Because you are printing to Screen, this setting is nullified; however, if you were generating a piece of paper, use it to describe what kind of paper you will use.

4. Move the cursor to Printer Offset.

   You use this option to move the body of the entire printed area to the right the number of spaces that you specify. You can reposition printed information for appearance reasons or for bindery requirements.

   For this example, you are printing to Screen. Therefore, this setting is not functional.

5. Move the cursor to Printer Control Codes.

   Because you are printing to Screen, you do not need to specify any special instructions for the printer.

6. Move the cursor to Print Totals Only.

   Use this option to request a summary type of report, which does not print detail. Summary reports are useful for budgeting and related tasks where the final figures, not the detail, is needed.

   For this example, you only have a few forms in the database. Therefore, a summary report is not appropriate. Specify No in the blank.

7. Move the cursor to Justify report body and select the type of justification that you want in the report.

You can position the body of the report on the paper to the right, to the left, or centered. Most reports are centered on the page.

For this example, you will center the report. Select Center.

8. Move the cursor to Line spacing.

Line spacing controls whether the printed report is single- or double-spaced.

For this example, you are printing the report to the screen. Therefore, you do not need to adjust this setting.

9. Move the cursor to allow split records.

You can request that records not be split, thereby forcing a record to the next page if it does not fit entirely on the current page. Most often, you use this setting if you are printing fields that are too wide to fit in the width of a column.

For this example, all fields should fit in a column. Therefore, you do not need to adjust this setting. Do not make a change to this option.

You are now ready to run the report and see what type of document your specifications will generate.

10. After you specify the Report Print Options, press F10.

A small box appears in the center of the screen, indicating that Q&A has saved the report design, and you must select whether you want to print the report hold.

To run a report, refer to "Running a Report" later in this chapter.

11. Choose No to return to the Report menu, or choose Yes to begin printing the report.

Designing a Crosstab Report

In addition to a columnar style format for reports, you also can generate a crosstab report. A *Crosstab Report* uses information from two fields in your database and produces summary data that reveals relationships between those two fields.

Suppose that you are working with the EMPLOYEE.DTF database, which is included with the Q&A software and is used by the tutorial, and you want to know the average bonus for men and women, based on job classification.

```
                         Sex
                 ---------------------
                                      Average
       Classification   FEMALE    MALE    Bonus
       --------------   --------  -------- =========
       2                          $7,347.50 $7,347.50
       3                $4,200.00           $4,200.00
       4                   $0.00 $13,240.00 $8,826.67
       5                $6,700.00 $7,000.00 $6,820.00
       6                $5,550.00 $3,936.25 $4,115.56
       7                $3,200.00 $2,680.00 $2,940.00
       8                $2,070.00 $1,800.00 $1,980.00
       9                $1,440.00 $1,380.00 $1,400.00
       ==============  ========= ========= =========
       Average Bonus    $3,802.73 $5,299.05 $4,784.69




       EMPLOYEE.DTF

       Esc-Exit  F2-Reprint   { → ← ↑ ↓ }-Scroll   Shift+F9-Redesign   F10-Continue
```

Your crosstab report would look like this figure.

A crosstab report summarizes information into three types of data:

Column field
: The column determines the column headings for the report. Column headings go across the top of the report. In the preceding example, the column headings are MALE and FEMALE.

Row field
: The row field is each form or record's data that applies to the column headings. In the preceding example, the row data indicates the employees' job classification and breaks their bonus information into separate columns based on gender.

Summary field
: The summary field presents the summary information that you request in the format you specify. The preceding example shows the average bonus for each job classification regardless of gender. The summary information appears on the last line of the report.

To create a crosstab report, follow these steps:

1. From the Report menu, select **D**esign/Redesign a report.

2. Type the drive path and directory of the database containing the information that you want to include in your report, or press ⏎Enter to choose a name from a list.

   For this example, enter the drive path and directory for the EMPLOYEE.DTF database. Assuming that the database is stored on drive C in the same directory as the Q&A software, enter **C:\QA\EMPLOYEE.DTF**.

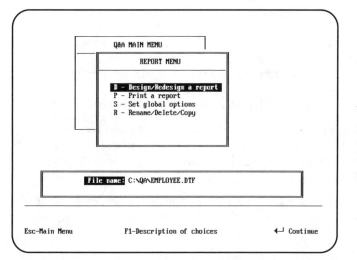

In this example, you see the drive path specified for the EMPLOYEE.DTF database.

3. Press ⏎Enter to select the database.

Naming a Report

After you specify the database on which you want to base a report, the List of Reports in Database screen appears.

177

```
                    LIST OF REPORTS IN DATABASE

Activities
Bonus Analysis
Employee Directory
keyword
Xtab Salary/Sex/Dept







              Enter name:



Esc-Exit    F1-Help  F3-Delete  F5-Copy  F7-Search  F8-Rename  F10-Continue
```

7

In this example, you see the list of reports for the EMPLOYEE.DTF database.

Some of these reports are columnar reports and some of them may be crosstab reports. When you name a report, you also should indicate whether it is a columnar or crosstab report. In the preceding figure, crosstab report names are preceded by an X.

You can select reports that are already developed from this list, or you can add a new report by typing a new name of up to 50 characters in the Enter Name field.

For this example, the crosstab report presents the average bonus for men and women based on job classification. Therefore, you can name the report *Average Bonus By Job Class*.

The cursor is located in the Enter Name field at the bottom of the screen. Type the report name—preceded by an X—and press ⏎Enter). For this example, type **XAverage Bonus by Job Class** and press ⏎Enter).

Selecting the Report Type

```
                    REPORT TYPE


    Use → or ← to select the type of report you want to design:

            C - Columnar report      X - Crosstab report

    Press F1 if you need help deciding what kind of report you
    want to create.




    _____

    Esc-Exit                 F1-Help                ←┘ Continue
```

After you name a new report, the Report Type screen appears.

Remember that you can generate two types of reports using Q&A: columnar and crosstab.

Columnar Report	A columnar report presents the information requested in a series of columns. At the top of each column is a heading (usually the name of the field) that describes the data contained in the column. Each row represents a record or form in your database with the information requested going across the row.
X Crosstab Report	A crosstab report presents the information requested in a summary manner. The report uses three fields: the row field, the column field, and the summary field.

Because you are creating a crosstab report, select XCrosstab.

Using The Retrieve Spec To Select Forms

A Retrieve Spec for XAverage Bonus By Class appears on-screen. You use this screen to tell Q&A which forms you want to include in the report.

To specify which forms you want included, review the help screen that is affiliated with the Retrieve Spec.

1. Press F1 for help.

   The help screen appears.

   To retrieve all records, leave this screen blank and press F10. For this example, leave this spec blank.

2. Press F10 to continue.

If you want to retrieve only those records that meet a narrower set of retrieval criteria, review the section "Retrieving Selective Data for a Columnar Report" that appears earlier in this chapter. The process of filling in a Retrieve Spec for crosstab reports is exactly the same as for columnar reports.

The Crosstab Spec tells Q&A which columns to display in the report. In the Crosstab Spec you also can specify calculated and derived fields, field groupings to make the printout more readable, and character and label enhancements and fonts.

In the Crosstab Spec, you must specify a column field, a row field, and a summary field. As with columnar reports, you also can create derived fields for crosstab reports.

To set up a crosstab report, follow these steps:

1. Move the cursor to the field that contains the information you want in the column field and type COL.

   For this example, column headings divide the data into MALE and FEMALE. The Sex field contains this information. Move the cursor to the Sex field and type COL.

   Note that you can name the same field as a summary and row or column field. Type COL,SUM or ROW,SUM in the field. You also can suppress the display of the summary column, summary row, or both, by typing NS in the ROW or COL fields, separated from the other codes by a comma.

   If you are using a keyword field as part of a crosstab report, it's best to specify it as the row field because Q&A automatically groups the data in a key field, but only if it's named as a row.

2. Move the cursor to the field that contains the information that you want in the Row field and type ROW.

   For this example, each job classification should have an individual row that shows male and female bonus amounts. The Classification field contains this information. Move the cursor to the Classification field and type ROW.

3. Move the cursor to the field that contains the information you want in the Summary field and type SUM.

   For this example, you want the summary to show bonus amounts paid to employees, and you want the report to compute an average bonus. The Bonus field contains this information. Move the cursor to the Bonus field and type SUM. To tell Q&A to display the summary data as averages, type an A after SUM as follows:

   SUM,A

   Press F1 (Help) twice to view a list of summary codes that you can use with crosstab reports.

4. Press F10 to continue.

Using Calculations in a Crosstab Report

Q&A can perform calculations on data before displaying it in a crosstab report. You can have have columns that contain total, average, minimum, maximum, count, standard deviation, and variance. Even if you don't specify any of these summary calculations, however, Q&A uses the following defaults in a crosstab report:

Data Type	Default Calculation
Text	Count
Number	Total
Money	Total
Keyword	Count
Date	Count
Hours	Count
Yes/No	Count

181

The codes used to specify summary calculations are as follows:

Code	Command	Meaning
T	Total	Prints total of cell values
A	Average	Prints average of cell values
C	Count	Prints count of values in cell
MIN	Minimum	Prints the minimum value in a cell
MAX	Maximum	Prints the maximum value in a cell
STD	Standard deviation	Prints the standard deviation from the mean value of the values in the cells
VAR	Variance	Prints the variance of the values in the cells

You can specify more than one summary calculation for the summary field. SUMMARY,C,A, for example, displays a count and average in the summary area of the report.

Note that there is no Sort Spec for crosstab reports. Q&A, however, sorts row and column titles in ascending order by default. To change the sort order of headings, type a sort code in the row or column field. The code AS forces an ascending sort; DS forces a descending sort. If, for example, you wanted to sort Classification in descending order, you would enter

Classification: ROW,DS

When the codes in a field become too long for the space available, press F6 to continue typing in the 240-character Expand Field line at the bottom of the screen.

Formatting Crosstab Reports

Crosstab reports use the same formatting codes as columnar reports. To change the default formatting of a crosstab report, follow these steps:

1. At the Crosstab Spec, move the cursor to the field whose row, column, or summary values you want to format.

2. Move the cursor to the end of the field. Type a comma, followed by the letter **F**. In parentheses, type any formatting codes for the field.

You can include more than one formatting code, separated by commas. For example:

> **Classification: ROW,F(D6,U,JC)**

These codes tell Q&A to format classification values with date format number 6 (dd/mm/yy), and to print dates in uppercase and centered. Because the procedure for formatting and enhancing crosstab reports is identical to that for formatting columnar reports, see the sections on formatting columnar reports for further information.

Enhancing Headings

As with columnar reports, you can customize the titles that Q&A displays in a crosstab report. To apply character enhancements and fonts, enter the following special codes in the appropriate fields of the Crosstab Spec.

TL	Enhances the TOTAL label
AL	Enhances the AVERAGE label
CL	Enhances the COUNT label
MINL	Enhances the MIN label
MAXL	Enhances the MAX label
STDL	Enhances the STD label
VARL	Enhances the VAR label
H	Enhances the heading of the column, row, or summary field selected
SH	Enhances the subheading of the column or row field. This heading is derived from data; you cannot change the text of this heading.
HS	Enhances heading separator lines. To specify a separator character, place it in parentheses: HS(-). Q&A uses it to separate the heading from the column.
SL	Enhances the separator line when using subcalculations and breaks. To specify a separator character, place it in parentheses: SL(+-+).
DL	Enhances the separator line when printing subcalculations.

For example, at the end of a field that contains a T (total) code, type a comma and enter the code **TL**, then apply the boldface enhancement to the TL code, as described earlier in the section on using text enhancements and fonts in columnar reports.

Setting a Scale Factor

Large numbers can be scaled up or down in a crosstab report, to make them more readable. You can, for example, display millions in units of one million; thus, 1,000,000 becomes 1, 5,000,000 becomes 5, and so on. To enter a scaling factor, at the Crosstab Spec move the cursor to the row, column, or summary field. Move the cursor to the end of the field, type a comma, then type **SCALE(n)**, where n is the number of units for the scale. To represent 100,000's as 100, 200,000 as 200, and so forth, type **SCALE(1000)**.

Derived Fields in Crosstab Reports

Data for columns, rows, or summary columns in crosstab reports may be derived from calculations on database fields that aren't included in the report. A crosstab report may contain from one to three derived fields. Unlike columnar reports, you cannot use invisible columns in a crosstab report.

To create a derived field, you must either number the fields on which calculations are based or refer to them by their field names. Field numbers must be entered on the Crosstab Spec before you can use the Derived Fields Spec, because you need to refer to those numbers in the Derived Fields spec. Field numbers have no effect on the order in which columns are displayed on the report or on the sort order.

After numbering the fields or deciding to refer to fields by their field labels, perform the following steps:

1. At the Crosstab Spec, press [F8] to display the Derived Fields Spec.
2. Move the cursor to the first Heading prompt.
3. Type the heading for the derived field.
4. Move the cursor to the Formula field and enter the formula for the derived field.

   Remember, you can reference fields in the form that are not included in the Crosstab Spec. To refer to the fields, use field numbers or field names.

In the Formula field of the Derived Field Spec, you can use any of Q&A's advanced LOOKUP commands to retrieve data from the lookup table or from an external file. Because this procedure goes beyond the scope of a QuickStart, the procedure is not described here. To give you some idea of what is possible, you can match records in the current file with corresponding records in a second file based on a parts identification number, and then retrieve part prices into a column of your crosstab report.

5. Move the cursor to the Crosstab Spec field and type ROW, COL, or SUM. This tells Q&A which part of the crosstab report will be the derived field.

6. Enter a heading, formula, and Crosstab Spec entry for each derived column, and then press F9 to return to the Crosstab Spec.

Defining Crosstab Print Options

After you complete the Crosstab Column/Sort Spec screen, the Crosstab Print Options screen appears. Use this screen to send special instructions to your computer regarding printer location, paper position and feed, and data presentation.

The Crosstab Print Options screen contains the following fields:

Print to	Use this selection to tell your computer where the report will print. You can select Printer A (PtrA) through Printer E (PtrE). You also can print crosstab reports to disk. Anything that you print to disk is converted to an ASCII file before printing, which is a kind of file that any PC running DOS can read. A report that you print to the screen appears on the monitor instead of being sent to a printer.
Page preview	Use this setting to see a preview of your report on-screen before printing it on paper. This option generates a graphical representation of the report, including all headers, footers, and text enhancements.
Type of paper feed	Use this setting to describe the media that will hold the report. Manual requests you to press ⏎Enter to proceed with printing. Continuous sequentially feeds sheets of paper into the printer. Bins 1, 2, and 3 are used for special bin

	feeders. Bin1, for example, might be first-page letterhead, Bin2 might be second sheets for letterhead, and Bin3 might be legal-size paper.
Print offset	Use this option to move the entire body of the printed material to the right a specified number of spaces. Printer offset is helpful for allowing space for hole punching or bindery.
Printer control codes	Use this option to specify how a printer should react to commands sent to it requesting type size, page length, and so on. See your printer manual for these codes. Q&A's drivers for most printers already contain this information so that entering the codes is not necessary.
Show results as	Use this option to specify whether you want report results to appear as numbers, a percentage of the total, a percentage of the row, a percentage of the column, or normalized.
Justify report body	Use this option to select the positioning that you want for the report. Reports can be positioned at the left margin, the right margin, or centered on the page.
Line spacing	Use this option to select the line spacing for the report. Reports can be printed single line or double line (a blank line between each row) spacing.

For the example, all settings remain the same except the Print To option. Instead of generating a piece of paper, you first print the report to Screen to review its content and format.

To define Crosstab Print Options, follow these steps:

1. With the highlight bar on `Print to`, select the place to which you want the report printed. For this example, select Screen.

2. Use the arrow keys to move the cursor through the prompts options on the Crosstab Print Options screen.

3. At the Page preview prompt, you can select Yes to display a graphic preview image of the printout on your screen. Your computer and monitor must be capable of displaying graphics to make use of this option.

   For the present example, leave Page preview set to No, because you will be printing a copy of the report to the screen. Page preview differs from printing to screen in that page preview displays all page headers, footers, and page numbers in place, whereas printing to screen displays only the body of the report.

4. At the Type of paper feed prompt, you can select Manual or Continuous, depending on the type of paper feed your printer has, or you can choose Bin1, Bin2, or Bin3 to print on paper held in a sheet-fed printer that has multiple paper storage bins.

5. You can use Print offset to override the default settings for left and right margins. This is useful to create a wider than usual left margin to allow space for binding. To enter an offset, type a positive number representing the number of characters to offset. Entering 5, for example, moves the entire report five characters to the right.

   Printer control codes tell your printer to use special fonts or enhancements (boldface, italics, and so forth) to print the report. Because Q&A supports these features through its standard printer drivers for most printers, it's rarely necessary to use this option.

6. At the Show results as prompt, you can tell Q&A to display crosstab report results as numeric or percentage values. The default, Numbers, displays results as numbers. % Total displays results as a percent of the total value of all summary field values. % Row displays the results as a percentage of the total or count for that row. % Column displays the results as a percentage of the total or count for that column. Normalized displays the results as some amount above or below the average, where the average is represented as 100.

7. Press F10 to continue the process.

```
        Your design has been saved.
    Do you want to print this report now?
          Y - Yes     N - No
```

Esc-Cancel   ← Continue

A window appears on-screen that tells you that your report has been saved and asks whether you are ready to print the report.

8. Select Yes and press ⏎Enter to print the report.

The final
report appears
on-screen.

```
                          Sex
                   -----------------------    Average
     Classification  FEMALE      MALE          Bonus
     --------------  ---------   ---------     =========
          2                       $7,347.50   $7,347.50
          3          $4,200.00                $4,200.00
          4              $0.00   $13,240.00    $8,826.67
          5          $6,700.00    $7,000.00    $6,820.00
          6          $5,550.00    $3,936.25    $4,115.56
          7          $3,200.00    $2,680.00    $2,940.00
          8          $2,070.00    $1,800.00    $1,980.00
          9          $1,440.00    $1,380.00    $1,400.00
     ==============  =========   ==========   =========
     Average Bonus   $3,802.73    $5,299.05    $4,784.69




     _____
     EMPLOYEE.DTF

     Esc-Exit  F2-Reprint   { → ← ↑ ↓ }-Scroll    Shift+F9-Redesign    F10-Continue
```

9. Press Esc to return to the Report menu.

7

Printing
Reports

Printing a report is a natural extension of the report design process. To print a report from an existing database, you first designate the specifications for the report and then send the output to the printer. In this chapter you will learn how to make any needed changes to accommodate your printer and computer system before you print a report. You will also learn how to maintain a library of reports.

With one exception, the process of printing columnar and crosstab reports is the same. The difference involves the Number setting on the crosstab Print Options screen. This is discussed later in this chapter.

When you print a report you select from two general options. You can either make temporary modifications to the report settings prior to printing or you can permanently modify the print settings for your report.

Because this section is devoted primarily to printing with Report, making temporary changes to your print settings is discussed briefly. For a more detailed explanation of the report design process, refer to Chapter 7.

Printing existing
reports

Making changes to a
report

Setting print options

Handling wide
reports

> ## Key Terms Used in This Chapter
>
> *Derived column*   A column that includes information that is not included in a database. The column is created by calculating two or more existing columns.
>
> *Column/Sort spec*   Tells Q&A which fields you want to print as columns.

Printing Existing Reports

After you create a database to store and organize your information, you need to be able to combine the information in printed reports. You can use Q&A's Report module to arrange and print the data in a variety of ways.

After you create a database to organize and store your information and design the report(s) summarizing that information, you need the capability of printing those reports. You can use the Report module of Q&A to specify the records to print, and make temporary changes to the report that affect only the current printing. Chapter 7 provides details on designing a report.

If you don't want to make any changes to the report before printing, the printing procedure is simple. Follow these steps:

1. From the Main menu, select **R**eport.
2. Select **P**rint a report.

You are prompted to specify a database and the report you want to print.

```
                    Q&A MAIN MENU
                      REPORT MENU

              D - Design/Redesign a report
              P - Print a report
              S - Set global options
              R - Rename/Delete/Copy


        File name: C:\WP\QA4\EMPLOYEE.DTF


  Esc-Main Menu          F1-Description of choices      ←┘ Continue
```

3. Type a database name at the prompt or press ⏎Enter to select a
   name from a list.

```
                    LIST OF FILES IN D:\QA\WRITE\*.*

\..
AGMEMO.DOC
BUDGET.DOC
LINE-DOC.DOC
MEMO110.DOC
ROSA.DOC
RYAN.DOC
TEST.DOC



┌──────┐  ┌─────────────────────────────────────────────┐  ┌──────┐
│      │  │ File name: D:\QA4BETA\WRITE\BUDGET.DOC       │  │      │
└──────┘  └─────────────────────────────────────────────┘  └──────┘

BUDGET.DOC     Size: 636      Date edited: 02/15/91    Time edited: 14:30
No description available.  Press F6 to add one.
Esc-Exit   F1-Help   F3-Delete   F5-Copy   F7-Search   F8-Rename   F10-Continue
```

Q&A next displays
a list of all the
reports created
for the selected
database.

Q&A asks whether you want to make changes.

```



                  Do you want to make any temporary changes
                      to this design before printing?

                           Y - Yes    N - No




Esc-Cancel                                          ⏎ Continue
```

When you select
No, the report is
sent directly to
the screen or
printer.

8

191

Making Temporary Changes to a Report

At certain times you may want to make temporary changes to a report, print it, and not alter the report specifications. For example, you may want to invert the column order for a single printing, or modify the retrieve specs. If you are making temporary changes to a crosstab report, you can also change the Cross Tab Spec and Cross Tab Print Options screen. These options are discussed in the sections that follow.

Using the Retrieve Spec

When you make temporary changes to your report, Q&A displays the Retrieve Spec.

Use the Retrieve Spec to select the forms you want to print from the database.

```
┌─────────────────────────────────────────────────────────────────┐
│                   ══ EMPLOYEE DATABASE ══                          │
│      ┌── Personal Information ─────────────────────────────────┐  │
│      │Last Name:              First Name:                      │  │
│      │Address:                                                 │  │
│      │City:                   State:          Zip:             │  │
│      │Telephone:                                               │  │
│      │Sex:       Alma Mater:                                   │  │
│      │Hobbies:                                                 │  │
│      └─────────────────────────────────────────────────────────┘ │
│      ┌── Compensation Information ─────────────────────────────┐  │
│      │Eligible:               Salary:                          │  │
│      │Bonus Factor:           Bonus:                           │  │
│      │Evaluation:                                              │  │
│      └─────────────────────────────────────────────────────────┘ │
│      ┌── Departmental Information ─────────────────────────────┐  │
│      │Hired Date:             Department:                      │  │
│      │Position:               Manager:                         │  │
│      │Accrued Vacation:                                        │  │
│      └─────────────────────────────────────────────────────────┘ │
│      ┌─────────┐                                                  │
│      │Comments:│                                                  │
│      └─────────┘                                                  │
│ EMPLOYEE.DTF          Retrieve Spec for Salary by Sex and   Page 1  of 1 │
│                                                                   │
│ Esc-Exit  F1-Help   F3-Clear  F6-Expand  Alt+F8-List  ↑F8-Save   F10-Continue │
└─────────────────────────────────────────────────────────────────┘
```

Procedures for completing the Retrieve Spec are discussed in Chapter 7. To review the steps, press F1 to view the Help screens. You can change the settings to retrieve a different set of records than you specified when you originally designed the report. If you originally left the Retrieve Spec blank to retrieve all records for the database, you can now narrow the retrieval by entering new specifications. For example, to retrieve only those records for which the state is California, Washington, or Oregon, in the State field enter

     State: CA;WA;OR

Because this entry doesn't fit in the State field, Q&A tells you to press [F6] and type the entry on the expanded data entry line at the bottom of the screen. When you finish typing the entry, press [↵Enter] to return to the Retrieve Spec screen. You can enter up to 240 characters on the expanded entry line.

When you finish entering the necessary information in the Retrieve Spec, press [F10] to continue.

If you are printing a columnar report, Q&A displays the Column/Sort Spec. If you are printing a crosstab report, the Cross Tab Spec is displayed. These two screens are discussed next.

Using the Column/Sort Spec for Columnar Reports

Use the Column/Sort Spec to tell Q&A which fields you want to print as columns on a columnar report. At the same time, you can determine the sorting order for the records and specify which numeric fields you want to count, total, subtotal, or average. You can also change the column headings or column widths, and justify the data within a column.

If you press [F1] when the Column/Sort Spec is displayed, you will see a brief reminder of how to complete the screen. If you press [F1] again, a detailed Help screen appears. Pressing [PgDn] displays a second screen of information.

Determine the order in which you want the columns to print, and enter the corresponding numbers in the fields. For example, to print last names in the first column, enter

Last name: **1**

You can arrange the data in ascending (AS) or descending (DS) order. To sort last names in ascending order, enter

Last name: **1,AS**

If you enter an incorrect letter code in any field, the warning Not a valid Sort Spec displays. Before you can continue, you must correct the error by changing the letter code.

Using the Derived Columns Menu

When changing your report specs temporarily, you may decide you need a column that isn't included in a field of your database. For example, you may

8

want a field on the report that displays the effect of increasing the bonus factor by 3 percent for all employees. A derived column accomplishes this.

To design a derived column, press F8 from the Column/Sort Spec to display the Derived Columns screen.

You can view Help screens by pressing F1. For a more thorough account of how to use the Derived Columns screen, see Chapter 7.

Using the Cross Tab Spec

If you are redesigning a crosstab report temporarily, press F10 at the Retrieve Spec to bring up the Cross Tab Spec.

At the Cross Tab Spec you tell Q&A which data to display in columns, rows, and summary areas of a crosstab report. Here you can optionally specify summary calculations, derived columns, formatting options and alternate headings, data groupings, and a scale factor for repetitive field data. These options are detailed in Chapter 5.

Press F1 (Help) at the Cross Tab Spec to view a screen sort and the calculation codes used with the Cross Tab Spec. At the help screen, you may press PgDn repeatedly to review four additional help screens.

Decide which three fields you want to include in the crosstab report, and type ROW, COL, and SUMMARY in the appropriate columns, as Chapter 5 explains. For example, to include the fields Sex, Department, and Salary, type the appropriate code in each field.

From the Cross Tab Spec you may also temporarily change or add derived fields. Press F8 to display the Derived Fields Spec, and make any changes.

Press F10 to exit the Cross Tab Spec and display the Cross Tab Print Options screen, described in Chapter 5 and summarized below.

Setting Print Options for Columnar Reports

When you press F10 from either the Column/Sort Spec or Derived Columns screen, Q&A displays the Print Options screen.

```
                    REPORT PRINT OPTIONS

   Print to.........:   PtrA   PtrB   PtrC   PtrD   PtrE   DISK  ▶SCREEN◀

   Page preview.............:   Yes  ▶No◀

   Type of paper feed........:   Manual  ▶Continuous◀  Bin1   Bin2   Bin3

   Print offset.............:   0

   Printer control codes.....:

   Print totals only........:   Yes  ▶No◀

   Justify report body.......:  ▶Left◀  Center   Right

   Line spacing.............:  ▶Single◀  Double

   Allow split records.......:  ▶Yes◀  No


   EMPLOYEE.DTF          Print Options for (NEW)
   Print to screen.
   Esc-Exit     F1-Help      F8-Define Page      F9-Go back      F10-Continue
```

The Print Options screen.

The Print Options screen for crosstab reports is similar to the Print Options screen for columnar reports. The one exception is the Show Results As option on the crosstab screen, which allows you to affect the way numbers display in crosstab calculations. The following options are available:

Numbers	The default. Displays results as numbers.
% Total	Displays results as a percentage of the total value for all summary field values from all records retrieved.
% Row	Displays results as a percentage of the TOTAL or COUNT for the row based on all records retrieved.
% Column	Displays results as a percentage of the TOTAL or COUNT for the column based on all records retrieved.
Normal	"Normalized"; displays results as an amount above or below the average, where the average is represented as 100. (Numbers above 100 represent data above the crosstab average; those below 100 represent data below the average.)

Using the Define Page Menu

Similar to Define Page menus in other modules, Report's Define Page menu enables you to change the appearance and position of the text on your printout. By entering headers and footers and changing page length and margins, you can vary the look of your report. By widening the margins, you can print more information on one page. You don't have to worry about making your reports too wide, however. Q&A automatically prints wide reports on more than one page.

To access the Define Page screen, at the Print Options screen, press F8.

The Define Page screen is displayed.

```
                              DEFINE PAGE
                              ─────────

            Page width.: 85        Page length..: 66

            Left margin: 5         Right margin.: 80

            Top margin.: 3         Bottom margin: 3

            Characters per inch:   10   12   15   17
    ────────────────────────── HEADER ──────────────────────
    1:
    2:
    3:
    ────────────────────────── FOOTER ──────────────────────
    1:
    2:
    3:
    ──────────────────────────────────────────────────────
    EMPLOYEE.DTF            Define page for (NEW)

    Esc-Exit      F1-Help        F9-Go Back to Print Options        F10-Continue
```

When you finish making all your temporary changes, press F10 to begin printing, or press F9 to return from the Define Page menu to the Print Options screen and make further changes. While the report prints, you can press Esc to cancel the operation and return to the Report menu, or press F2 to cancel the operation and bring up the Print Options screen. You can then make additional changes, if necessary. When you press F10 again, the printing restarts from the beginning of the file.

Making Permanent Changes to an Existing Report

To make permanent modifications to the print specifications for your report, use the Design/Redesign option of the Report menu. When you choose this option, you will again see the Retrieve and Column/Sort Specs and can make your adjustments. After the Specs are filled, the Print Options screen is displayed, and you are asked whether you want to print the saved report. (For an in-depth discussion of creating Print Specs for Report, see Chapter 7.)

Printing a New Report

The procedures for printing a new report and designing a report are similar. If you want to create a temporary report, you first select Print a report from the Report menu. When the list of report names is displayed, press ⏎Enter to design a report without a name. Q&A will display each of the screens to complete when you design a permanent report. The name New appears on the status line, indicating the report will be temporary. After the report is printed, you return to the Report menu. The temporary report is not saved.

Checking a Report Before Printing

To see how your report looks prior to printing, choose Screen from the Print To line option of the Print Options screen. If your computer's monitor displays graphics, you can also set Page Preview to Yes to view an image of the report that is similar to the final, printed result.

If you choose Print to Screen, the report will be displayed on your monitor (without headers and footers), one screen at a time. You can check the whole report by using the cursor keys to scroll. The End key takes you to the right edge of the report if it's too wide for one screen; the Home key returns you to the left edge. The PgUp and PgDn keys move from the current screen to the previous or next screens. Pressing either ⏎Enter or F10 will also bring up the next screen.

If you choose Print Preview, the report displays as a graphic image. You can scroll between pages of the report with the PgUp and PgDn keys, or display the report in enlarged or reduced format. Press F1 (Help) at the Print Preview screen to display a list of available viewing commands. Press F2 to return to the Print Options screen, or press F10 or Esc to return to the Report menu.

When you are satisfied with the report, print it by specifying the printer port on the Print Options screen. As the report prints, however, if you see additional changes that should be made, press ⇧Shift-F9. After making the changes, press F10. The report starts printing from the beginning of the file.

8

A direct access
window allowing
you to go directly
to the spec you
need to change is
displayed.

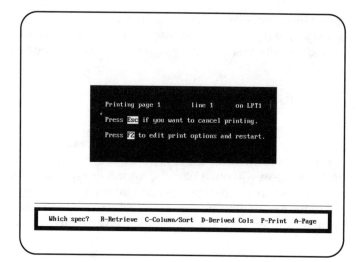

Handling Wide Reports

If the report is too wide for your page, a warning message displays before the
report is printed. You can ignore the warning and proceed; the data that is
beyond the edge of the page will be truncated. Rather than losing that part of
your printout, you can either return to the Print Options screen and correct
the problem or cancel printing.

Starting the
Write Module

9

This chapter teaches you the basics you need to
create a document in the Write module. Q&A Write is an
easy-to-use word processor that has all the features you
need for producing memos, letters, reports, and other
professional documents. If you have experience with
other word processing programs, you will find that Q&A
outperforms many of them.

This chapter teaches you how to enter text, move
around the screen, and make needed changes. You also
learn how to save your document for later use.

If you are new to Q&A and are not familiar with the
software package, please be sure to review Chapter 1
for menu navigation and option selection instructions. A
basic knowledge of these items is necessary to understand the information contained in this chapter. Not all
features available in the Write module are explored in
this chapter—only the key ones needed to begin the
learning process.

Understanding Write

Creating a new document

Saving a document

Clearing the screen

Key Terms Used in This Chapter

Default	A standard Q&A setting that is in effect unless you specify otherwise.
Document	A letter or other printed material produced with the Write module of Q&A.
Global setting	Settings that you use repeatedly and have stored as the default values.
Margin	Blank space bordering the sides and top and bottom of a document.
Word wrap	A feature that eliminates the need to press the Enter key each time you reach the right margin. You need to press Enter only when you come to the end of a paragraph.

Understanding Write

Write is Q&A's word processing module. Basically, a word processing package is a glorified typewriter that can store and print documents with the added benefits of typeface enhancement and a variety of other features. This module offers full service word processing functions and is easy to learn. You can produce any type of document from letters and reports to forms and books. In addition, information created in the File module can be included in Write documents. You can create term papers, reports, business letters, or pre-printed forms.

The Write module is the third selection on the Q&A Main menu and is easy to learn and intuitive. Menus guide you through the module offering options from which to select. Just as with other parts of Q&A, you can make menu selections by using the arrow keys to highlight the selection, typing the first letter of the selection, or entering the numeric sequence of the selection.

9

```
┌─────────────────────────────────────────────────────┐
│                                                       │
│  ▌                                                    │
│                                                       │
│               ┌─────────────────────────┐             │
│               │      Q&A MAIN MENU       │             │
│               ├─────────────────────────┤             │
│               │                          │             │
│               │    F - File              │             │
│               │    R - Report            │             │
│               │    W - Write             │             │
│               │    A - Assistant         │             │
│               │    U - Utilities         │             │
│               │    X - Exit Q&A          │             │
│               │                          │             │
│               └─────────────────────────┘             │
│                                                       │
│  ──────────────────────────────────────────────────  │
│  Q&A Version 4.0   125N  Copyright (C) 1985-1991, Symantec   All rights reserved. │
│                                                       │
│  X-Exit to DOS         F1-Description of choices      ◄┘ Continue │
└─────────────────────────────────────────────────────┘
```

To enter the Write module of Q&A, start from the Q&A Main menu and select Write.

```
┌─────────────────────────────────────────────────────┐
│                                                       │
│         ┌──────────────────────────┐                  │
│         │      Q&A MAIN MENU        │                  │
│         │     ┌───────────────────────────┐           │
│         │     │        WRITE MENU          │           │
│         │     ├───────────────────────────┤           │
│         │     │                            │           │
│         │     │   T - Type/Edit            │           │
│         │     │   D - Define page          │           │
│         │     │   P - Print                │           │
│         │     │   C - Clear                │           │
│         │     │   G - Get                  │           │
│         │     │   S - Save                 │           │
│         │     │                            │           │
│         │     │   U - Utilities            │           │
│         │     │   M - Mailing labels       │           │
│         │     │                            │           │
│         │     └───────────────────────────┘           │
│                                                       │
│  ──────────────────────────────────────────────────  │
│                                                       │
│  Esc-Main Menu        F1-Description of choices      ◄┘ Continue │
└─────────────────────────────────────────────────────┘
```

You see the Write menu.

This menu has the following eight options from which to choose:

- Use Type/Edit to type a new document or edit an existing document that you retrieved from storage.

- Use Define page to specify margins, tab settings, and number of characters per inch that the document will contain after it is in its final printed form.

- Use Print to generate a printed copy of a document.
- Use Clear to erase the screen of a displayed document so that you can create a new document.
- Use Get to retrieve or "get" a document that you created earlier and stored in the computer memory for reprinting, editing, or review.
- Use Save to store on disk a document you recently created or edited. Saved documents can be retrieved using the Get option.
- Use Utilities to determine global settings; export documents for use with other programs; recover deleted documents; and copy, rename, and delete document files.
- Use Mailing labels to generate mailing labels individually or as a group using data from the File module of Q&A.

You also can access some options from the Write menu from within a document by using function keys. Those options are Define page, Print, and Save.

Creating a New Document

Creating new documents in Q&A is easy. All you need to begin is a blank screen to receive your entry. From the Write menu, select Type/Edit. If a document is on-screen now, select Clear to remove the old document from the screen.

You see a new document form ready to receive input.

```
Lııııııııı1ıļııı7ıııı7ıııı7ıııııııı4ıııııııı5ıııııııı6ıııııııı7ıııı1ıııı
Working Copy                              0 %   Line 1 of Page 1 of 1

Esc-Exit  F1-Info  F2-Print  Ctrl+F6-Define Pg  F7-Search  F8-Options  ↑F8-Save
```

9

Important information appears at the bottom of the screen. This information helps you create a new document and use some of the special features Q&A offers. The following information is displayed:

- The key assignment line is the last line on the screen.

  This line shows frequently used function key assignments. Additional function key assignments can be viewed by pressing i.

- The line above the key assignment line is the message line.

  This line is blank now because Q&A does not have a message or instruction to give you at the moment. When you complete a process, this line tells you what is happening and may ask you for more information needed to complete the process.

- The third line from the bottom of the screen is the status line.

  This line tells you the name of the current document. If you have not yet named the document, you see Working Copy. Also displayed on this line are any special keys you are using (Caps Lock or Insert), as well as the percentage of memory used for the document, and the location of the cursor (Line 1 of Page 1 of 1).

- The line above the status line is the ruler line.

  This line shows the location of the cursor, left and right margins (shown with square brackets), and tabs that can be used.

Using Help

Before you get started, you may want to review the Help screen to familiarize yourself with the many features available in the Write module. Press F1 to see the help screen.

To view more key
assignments,
press PgDn.

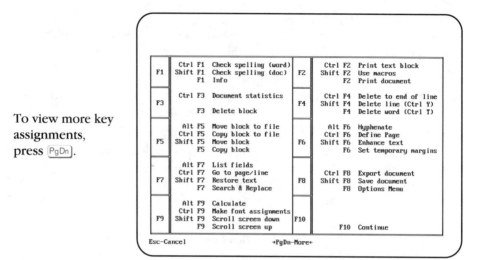

F1	Ctrl F1 Shift F1 F1	Check spelling (word) Check spelling (doc) Info	F2	Ctrl F2 Shift F2 F2	Print text block Use macros Print document
F3	Ctrl F3 F3	Document statistics Delete block	F4	Ctrl F4 Shift F4 F4	Delete to end of line Delete line (Ctrl Y) Delete word (Ctrl T)
F5	Alt F5 Ctrl F5 Shift F5 F5	Move block to file Copy block to file Move block Copy block	F6	Alt F6 Ctrl F6 Shift F6 F6	Hyphenate Define Page Enhance text Set temporary margins
F7	Alt F7 Ctrl F7 Shift F7 F7	List fields Go to page/line Restore text Search & Replace	F8	 Ctrl F8 Shift F8 F8	 Export document Save document Options Menu
F9	Alt F9 Ctrl F9 Shift F9 F9	Calculate Make font assignments Scroll screen down Scroll screen up	F10		
				F10	Continue

Esc-Cancel   ←PgDn-More→

Notice that Q&A has function key assignments in addition to the ones appearing on the key assignment line. To use a key combination, such as Ctrl-F6, press and hold down the Ctrl key and press F6. After you review the help screen, press Esc to return to the text entry screen. The top area of this screen is blank and will hold the document you create.

9

Entering Text

Entering text in the Write module is as easy as typing. The screen looks like a blank sheet of paper. The cursor is located in the first space available to accept an entry. Just start typing. Notice that as you type the cursor moves across the screen. If you type a sentence and all the words do not fit on one line, the cursor automatically moves to the next line. You do not have to press Enter. This feature is called word-wrapping. The only time you must press Enter is to end one paragraph and start a new paragraph.

You are now ready to create your document. Suppose that you want to write a memorandum thanking all department heads for their excellent work in preparing presentations for a quarterly meeting. Type the heading and press ↵Enter twice to move down two lines. Continue typing the memo heading segment and body. Do not be concerned with misspellings or typing errors now. You can do a spell check later. Q&A enables you to edit and revise the text later and even change the appearance of the text.

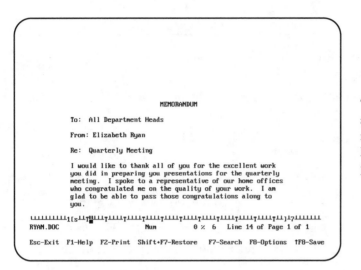

The memo appears on-screen much like it will look after it is printed.

Moving the Cursor

You can move the cursor through a document with the cursor-movement keys, which are located on the numeric keypad. Q&A also provides key combinations you can use to quickly move the cursor around the screen. The following table illustrates cursor movements in Q&A Write:

9

Table 9.1
Cursor Movement in the Write Module

Key	*Cursor Movement Function*
↑	Moves the cursor up one line.
↓	Moves the cursor down one line.
←	Moves the cursor left one position.
→	Moves the cursor right one position.
Ctrl-→	Moves the cursor right one word.
Ctrl-←	Moves the cursor left one word.
Home	Moves the cursor to the beginning of the line.
Home (two times)	Moves the cursor to the top of the screen.

continues

Table 9.1 *(continued)*

Key	Cursor Movement Function
[Home] (three times)	Moves the cursor to the top of the page.
[Home] (four times)	Moves the cursor to the beginning of the document.
[Ctrl]-[Home]	Moves the cursor to the beginning of the document.
[End]	Moves the cursor to the end of the line.
[End] (two times)	Moves the cursor to the bottom of the screen.
[End] (three times)	Moves the cursor to the bottom of the page.
[End] (four times)	Moves the cursor to the end of the document.
[Ctrl]-[End]	Moves the cursor to the end of the document.
[PgUp]	Moves the cursor to the top of the previous page.
[PgDn]	Moves the cursor to the top of the next screen.
[Ctrl]-[PgUp]	Moves the cursor to the top of the previous page.
[Ctrl]-[PgDn]	Moves the cursor to the top of the next page.

9

Working in Overwrite and Insert Modes

As you create a document, you can use two modes of text entry. Overwrite mode permits you to type over existing characters. Insert mode inserts new text at the cursor position. Existing text is moved to the right to make room for the added text. To move between Overwrite and Insert modes, press the Ins key. The letters Ins appear on the status bar near the bottom of the screen so that you know that Insert mode is operational. To turn off Insert mode, simply press Ins again.

You also can look at the cursor to tell which mode is active. If the cursor is a small rectangle, you are in Overwrite mode. If the cursor is a larger square, Insert mode is active. Overwrite mode is the default mode of operation.

Saving a Document

After you create a document, you should save it to insure against data loss. In fact, you should get into the habit of saving your work often. You never know when you may experience a power failure. Guard against lost data by saving frequently.

Saving to a Hard Disk

With Q&A, you can save your documents either from within the document or from the Write menu. To save from within the document, follow these steps:

1. Press ⌖Shift - F8 at any point during text entry.

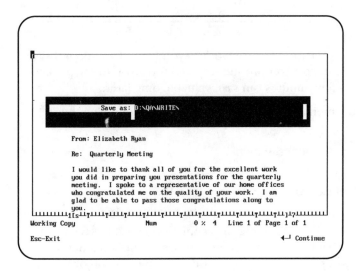

The first time you save a document, a dialog box appears and prompts you to name the document.

2. Type a name and press ↵Enter.

Subsequently, when you save from within that document, the dialog box displays this file name. You can press ⏎Enter to accept the name, or select a new name.

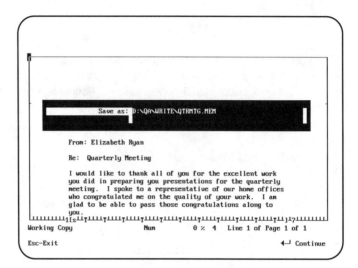

Use the Shift-F8 key combination to save work as you type. If you do not save often, a power failure can cost you productivity and force you to retype data. Pressing Shift-F8 every few minutes can save valuable time later.

You also can save documents through the Write menu by following these steps:

1. Press Esc to go to the Write menu.

2. Select Save.

    A dialog box appears and prompts you for a file name.

3. Type a name or press ⏎Enter to accept the existing name.

    The Save option on the Write menu is your last chance to save work before you exit Q&A or clear the screen to begin work on a new document. If you press Esc to exit to the Q&A Main menu or to clear the screen, you see a warning box.

```
! Warning !

Your latest changes to Working Copy
have NOT been saved. If you continue,
your changes will be lost PERMANENTLY.

Are you SURE you want to continue?

Y - Yes    N - No
```

Esc-Cancel   ←┘ Continue

Select No to
return to the
Write menu.

Saving to a Floppy Disk

Saving a document to a floppy disk is similar to the procedure you follow to
save documents to a hard disk. Follow these steps:

1. Press ⟨⇧Shift⟩-⟨F8⟩ or from the Write menu, select Save.

```
Save as:

From: Elizabeth Ryan

Re:  Quarterly Meeting

I would like to thank all of you for the excellent work
you did in preparing you presentations for the quarterly
meeting.  I spoke to a representative of our home offices
who congratulated me on the quality of your work.  I am
glad to be able to pass those congratulations along to
you.
```
Working Copy   Num   0 % 4   Line 1 of Page 1 of 1

Esc-Exit   ←┘ Continue

The Save As
dialog box is
displayed.

9

2. Press ⟨◆Backspace⟩ to delete the drive and directory name.

3. Enter the drive letter of the floppy drive (A: or B:) and the name of the document.

4. Press ⟨↵Enter⟩ to save.

Selecting a Name

Q&A follows DOS file naming conventions. You can select a name up to eight characters long. In addition, you can use a three character suffix, which is separated from the name by a period (.). Certain characters cannot be used in file names. Stick to the alphanumeric characters and the underscore character as you name documents.

Choose a name that reflects the contents of the document. JANMEMO.DOC is a good name for a memo to Jan, for example. An arbitrary name may be fine for now, but when you review file names six months from now you may find that you are unable to remember the contents of file with a name such as, QX124R.TXT. The extensions .DOC and .TXT are frequently used to indicate documents created by a word processor. Using a suffix is a handy way to indicate the date you created the document. Assigning a date makes house-keeping duties easier for you as your document list grows. By indicating a month and year of creation, you can archive old documents you no longer need based on the information provided in the suffix.

9

Clearing the Screen

As you type a document, the information is stored in the computer's memory, or RAM. RAM is a temporary storage area. When you save a document, you save it to a permanent storage on a disk. Even though the document is saved to disk, the document remains on the screen. You must clear the document from RAM and from the screen before you can begin another document.

To clear the screen, follow these steps:

1. Press **Esc** to return to the Write menu.

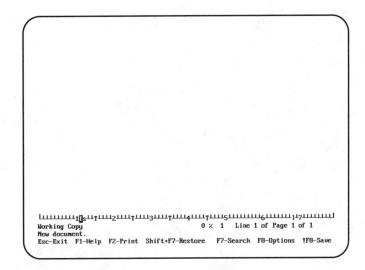

```
Lııııııı1ₒsıↄ1ₜıııı2ıııₜıııı3ıııↄ1ₜ4ııↄ1ₜıↄ15ıııııₜı6ıııↄ1ₜıↄ17ıııↄ1ₜıↄↄJ
Working Copy                        0 %  1   Line 1 of Page 1 of 1
New document.
Esc-Exit  F1-Help  F2-Print  Shift+F7-Restore   F7-Search  F8-Options  ↑F8-Save
```

2. Select **C**lear.

A new blank screen is displayed. You can tell that this is a new
document because the status and message lines indicate that this is a
Working Copy of a new document.

9

Retrieving and Editing Documents

Chapter 7 introduced you to Q&A's Write module. This chapter shows you how to retrieve documents that you previously saved so that you can edit and make any changes you need to make.

Making revisions is an important part of creating any polished document. After you retrieve the document, you learn how to add and delete text. With Q&A, you can delete a character or an entire block of text. You then can use the block functions to copy the text else where in the document. You can use Q&A's search-and-replace capabilities to quickly make editing changes. Then after you make the necessary changes, you can use the spelling checker to catch any spelling or typographical errors in your text. The spelling checker also searches for repeated words.

Key Terms Used in This Chapter

Special character   Characters that cannot be seen on-screen. These characters include font assignments, text enhancements, carriage returns, and character positioning commands that are given an alphabetic code.

Wild card   Characters, such as ? or .., that stand for any other character that may appear in the same place.

Retrieving a Document

After you save a document, you may want to return to it later to make needed changes. If you want to make further changes to a document, you must get the document from storage and display it on the screen. As you learned in Chapter 7, after you save a file and clear the screen, the only copy of the document that remains is on disk. Although you can save documents to a hard disk or to a floppy disk, the retrieval process is virtually the same for both.

Getting a Document from a Hard Disk

To retrieve a document you previously saved, follow these steps:

1. From the Write menu, select Get.

10

You are
prompted to
enter the name of
the document
you want to get.

```
                    Q&A MAIN MENU
                  ┌─────────────────────────┐
                  │      WRITE MENU         │
                  │                         │
                  │  T - Type/Edit          │
                  │  D - Define page        │
                  │  P - Print              │
                  │  C - Clear              │
                  │  G - Get                │
                  │  S - Save               │
                  │                         │
                  │  U - Utilities          │
                  │  M - Mailing labels     │
                  └─────────────────────────┘

        ┌──────────────────────────────────────┐
        │ Document: C:\QA\WRITE\                │
        └──────────────────────────────────────┘


    Esc-Main Menu          F1-Description of choices        ◄┘ Continue
```

At this point, you can type the exact name of the document, or you can ask Q&A to show you a list of stored documents from which you can select. Generally, selecting from a list of documents is faster. You may find that remembering exact names becomes difficult, especially as your library of saved documents grows. You also avoid making typing errors when you select from a list.

2. Press ⏎Enter to see a list of stored documents.

```
                 LIST OF FILES IN D:\QA\WRITE\*.*

  ▔▔▔▔▔▔▔▔▔▔▔
  \..
  AGMEMO.DOC
  BUDGET.DOC
  LINE-DOC.DOC
  MEMO110.DOC
  ROSA.DOC
  RYAN.DOC
  TEST.DOC



   ┌─┐    File name: D:\QA\WRITE\              ┌─┐
   └─┘    ▔▔▔▔▔▔▔▔▔▔▔▔▔▔▔▔▔▔▔▔▔▔▔▔▔▔▔▔         └─┘


  Esc-Exit  F1-Help  F3-Delete  F5-Copy  F7-Search  F8-Rename  F10-Continue
```

A list of files is displayed on the screen.

At the top of the screen, you see the directory in which Q&A is searching for the file. The list is arranged in alphabetical order by file name. To select a file in another directory, press Esc to back out of the documents list.

Press ⟨◆Backspace⟩ to delete the existing directory name and type the name of the directory you want to search. Then press ⟨⏎Enter⟩ to display the list of files found in that directory.

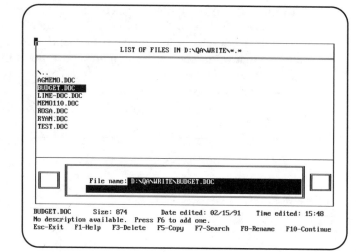

```
                         LIST OF FILES IN D:\QA\WRITE\*.*

 \..
 AGMEMO.DOC
 BUDGET.DOC
 LINE-DOC.DOC
 MEMO110.DOC
 ROSA.DOC
 RYAN.DOC
 TEST.DOC




             File name: D:\QA\WRITE\BUDGET.DOC

 BUDGET.DOC      Size: 874        Date edited: 02/15/91    Time edited: 15:48
 No description available.  Press F6 to add one.
 Esc-Exit   F1-Help   F3-Delete   F5-Copy   F7-Search   F8-Rename   F10-Continue
```

3. Press ⟨↑⟩ or ⟨↓⟩ to highlight your selection.

Notice that the status line provides you with information about the highlighted document. You see the name of the document, document size, date edited, and time edited.

If you are tying to locate a document but are not sure of the file name, all four pieces of information can be useful. You can use the time and date information to narrow the search.

Also notice the key assignment line. You can delete, copy, search for, or rename documents using the displayed function keys.

3. Press ⟨⏎Enter⟩ to retrieve the document.

The document you select appears on-screen.

Getting a Document from a Floppy Disk

If you saved a document to a floppy disk, the retrieval process is much the same. Just remember to insert the floppy disk that contains the document into the external disk drive. After you select the **G**et option, make sure that the prompt references the correct drive.

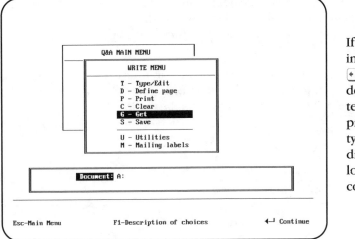

If the prompt is incorrect, press (+Backspace) to delete the contents of the prompt. Then type the external disk drive followed by a colon (:).

After you type the name of the document you want to retrieve and press (+Enter), the document is displayed on-screen.

Editing a Document

Editing is an important part of the creating process. With Q&A's editing features, you can fine tune your document. You do not have to fear making changes. You can delete a word or an entire block of text. You can use Q&A's block functions to move a block of text to a new location.

As you enter and edit text, you will need to move the cursor on the screen and around the document. When you need help, press (F1) to see the key usage help screen, which lists the actions related to the function keys. Return to the Type/Edit screen by pressing (Esc).

Deleting Text

After you create a document, you may decide that a portion of the text is not appropriate for one reason or another. With Q&A, you can use several methods to delete text within a document. The method you choose depends on how much text you want to delete.

10

You can delete a character, a word, an entire line, or an entire block of text. To delete a single character, position the cursor on the character you want to delete and press [Del]. You can continue this process until you remove all unwanted characters.

This process becomes tedious if you must delete large sections of text. In cases in which you want to remove more than one character, you may want to use Q&A's delete keys. The following table lists the choices from which you can choose:

Table 10.1
Text Deletion Keys in Q&A

Key(s)	Function
[Del]	Deletes one character at a time.
[F3]	Deletes a block of text.
[F4]	Deletes one word at a time.
[⇧Shift]-[F4]	Deletes an entire line of text.
[Ctrl]-[F4]	Deletes all characters beginning at the cursor and to the right of the cursor on the same line.

Deleting a Word

Deleting words with Q&A is simple. Suppose that after reviewing a letter, you decide that you can improve the readability by deleting a few words. The second sentence is a little wordy. You want to change the existing wording to delete the phrase "numbers were transposed and."

10

218

```
                                    Dear Account Manager,

                                         You have recently charged my checking account with the
                                    following incorrect check charges.  Evidently, when you
                                    entered the checks in your computer, numbers were
                                    transposed and my account was debited incorrect amounts.
                                    The amounts of the incorrect charges are shown on the
                                    attached page.

                                         Please correct these charges so that they will appear
                                    on my statement of the 5th of next month.

                                    Sincerely,
    llllllllll1[sllTlllllTlllllTlllllTlllllTlllllTllHlTlllllTlllllTllll]l7lllllllll
   Working Copy                      Num          0 x  38  Line 5 of Page 1 of 1

   Esc-Exit  F1-Help  F2-Print  Shift+F7-Restore   F7-Search  F8-Options  ↑F8-Save
```

Place the cursor on the first character of the first word you want to delete. In this case, the cursor is on the "n" in numbers.

```
                                    Dear Account Manager,

                                         You have recently charged my checking account with the
                                    following incorrect check charges.  Evidently, when you
                                    entered the checks in your computer, were transposed and
                                    my account was debited incorrect amounts.  The amounts of
                                    the incorrect charges are shown on the attached page.

                                         Please correct these charges so that they will appear
                                    on my statement of the 5th of next month.

                                    Sincerely,
   llllllllll1[sllTlllllTlllllTlllllTlllllTlllllTllHlTlllllTlllllTllll]l7lllllllll
   Working Copy                      Num          0 x  38  Line 5 of Page 1 of 1

   Esc-Exit  F1-Help  F2-Print  Shift+F7-Restore   F7-Search  F8-Options  ↑F8-Save
```

Press F4 to delete the first word. Notice that the word disappears and the balance of the sentence is adjusted to reflect the new placement.

10

Press F4 three
times to delete
the remaining
words.

```
Dear Account Manager,

       You have recently charged my checking account with the
following incorrect check charges.  Evidently, when you
entered the checks in your computer, my account was
debited incorrect amounts.  The amounts of the incorrect
charges are shown on the attached page.

       Please correct these charges so that they will appear
on my statement of the 5th of next month.

Sincerely,


Working Copy                    Num          0 %  38  Line 5 of Page 1 of 1
Esc-Exit  F1-Help  F2-Print  Shift+F7-Restore  F7-Search  F8-Options  ↑F8-Save
```

Deleting a Block of Text

You also can choose to delete more than one word at a time by using Q&A's
block deletion feature. Deleting blocks of text is useful when you want to
delete large amounts of text. You can delete sentences, paragraphs, or even an
entire document.

To delete a block of text, follow these steps:

1. Place the cursor on the first character of the first word of the section
   you want to delete.

In this example,
the cursor rests
on the first word
in the document.

```
Dear Account Manager,

       You have recently charged my checking account with the
following incorrect check charges.  Evidently, when you
entered the checks in your computer, numbers were
transposed and my account was debited incorrect amounts.
The amounts of the incorrect charges are shown on the
attached page.

       Please correct these charges so that they will appear
on my statement of the 20th of next month.

Sincerely,


Working Copy                    Num          0 %  1   Line 1 of Page 1 of 1
Use the arrow keys to select the text you want to copy, then press F10.
Esc-Exit                                                        F10-Continue
```

2. Press F3, which is the Delete Block key.

3. Press the cursor-movement keys to highlight the text you want to delete.

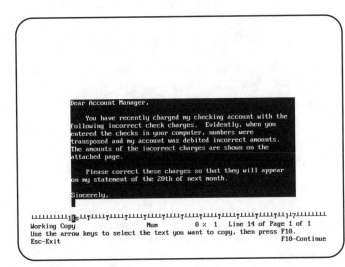

In this example, the entire document is highlighted.

4. Press F10 to delete the block.

With Q&A, you can use special keystrokes to select blocks of text. The following table illustrates these keystrokes.

Table 10.2
Text Selection Keys

Key	Function
Character key	Selects all text from the cursor to the next occurrence of that character.
Punctuation mark	Selects all text from the cursor to the next occurrence of that punctuation mark.
Carriage return	Selects all text from the cursor to the next carriage return.
Space bar	Selects the next word.
End	Selects all text from the cursor to the end of the line.

continues

10

221

Table 10.2 *(continued)*

Key	Function
End (two times)	Selects all text from the cursor to the end of the screen.
End (four times)	Selects all text to the end of the document.
Home	Selects all text from the cursor to the beginning of the line.
Home (two times)	Selects all text from the cursor to the beginning of the screen.
Home (four times)	Selects all text from the cursor to the beginning of the document.
Ctrl-End	Selects all text to the end of the document.
Ctrl-Home	Selects all text to the beginning of the document.
F3 (two times)	Selects the word.
F3 (three times)	Selects the sentence.
F3 (four times)	Selects the paragraph.
F3 (five times)	Selects the entire document.

Using Search-and-Replace Techniques

Often, after you create a document, some bit of information may change. Or you may find that you misspelled an individual's name throughout a document. You can read the document and make the necessary change as you go along, but this procedure can take a long time. With Q&A, you can search for the name and replace the name with the correct spelling.

Q&A's search-and-replace techniques make it easy for you to find specific information within a document. Use these techniques to find a word or a phrase or to locate special codes you added to a document.

Searching begins at the cursor location. You do not have to place the cursor at the beginning of the document. Once Q&A reaches the end of your document, the search resumes at the beginning of the document and continues until it reaches the cursor location.

Searching for Text

You need only tell Q&A the word or words you want to find. If you want to replace the word or phrase, just type the new word or phrase. To delete a word or phrase, you replace it with nothing, which removes the word or phrase.

To demonstrate how easy this search-and-replace process is, assume that you created a letter requesting that changes to your account appear on your statement on the fifth of the month. Now you want to change the date to the 20th.

To do a search-and-replace operation, follow these steps:

1. Press F7 .

```
 ┌─────────────────────────────────────────────────────────┐
 │                                                         │
 │                                                         │
 │    ┌─────────────┐                                      │
 │    │ Search for..:│                                     │
 │     Replace with:                                       │
 │     Method......: ▶Manual◀  Automatic   Fast automatic  │
 │                                                         │
 │    The amounts of the incorrect charges are shown on the│
 │    attached page.                                       │
 │                                                         │
 │         Please correct these charges so that they will appear│
 │    on my statement of the 5th of next month.            │
 │                                                         │
 │       Sincerely,                                        │
 │  ⊥⊥⊥⊥⊥⊥⊥⊥⊥⊥1[s⊥⊥⊥⊥⊥⊥⊥⊥⊥⊥⊥⊥⊥⊥⊥⊥⊥⊥⊥⊥⊥⊥⊥⊥⊥⊥⊥⊥⊥⊥⊥⊥⊥⊥⊥⊥⊥⊥ │
 │  Working Copy              Num      0 ％ 16  Line 4 of Page 1 of 1│
 │                                                         │
 │  Esc-Exit  PgDn-Advanced Options  F3-Clr  F8-Make Default  F7,F10-Begin Search│
 └─────────────────────────────────────────────────────────┘
```

You see the Search-and-Replace box on the screen. This box includes three options.

2. Type the text you want to find in the Search for field and press Enter . You are limited to a search string of 45 characters.

   In this example, type **5th**.

3. Type the replacement text in the Replace with field and press Enter .

   In this example, type **20th**.

4. Select the search-and-replace method you want to use by pressing the right-arrow key.

You can select from the following methods:

- Select Manual to view each possible match and confirm the replacement.

- Select Automatic to replace each match without confirmation. Each match is highlighted as it is replaced throughout the document.

- Select Fast Automatic to automatically replace all matches. This method, as with Automatic method, does not require you to confirm the replacement. However, it does not display each match as it is found.

In this example, the Manual option is selected.

```
Search for..: 5th

Replace with: 20th

Method......:  ▶Manual◀   Automatic   Fast automatic

The amounts of the incorrect charges are shown on the
attached page.

     Please correct these charges so that they will appear
on my statement of the 5th of next month.

     Sincerely,

Working Copy                    Num           0 %  16  Line 4 of Page 1 of 1

Esc-Exit   PgDn-Advanced Options   F3-Clr  F8-Make Default  F7,F10-Begin Search
```

5. Press F10 to begin the search.

10

224

```
┌─────────────────────────────────────────────────────────────────┐
│                                                                   │
│                                                                   │
│   Dear Account Manager,                                           │
│                                                                   │
│        You have recently charged my checking account with the     │
│   following incorrect check charges.  Evidently, when you         │
│   entered the checks in your computer, numbers were               │
│   transposed and my account was debited incorrect amounts.        │
│   The amounts of the incorrect charges are shown on the           │
│   attached page.                                                  │
│                                                                   │
│        Please correct these charges so that they will appear      │
│   on my statement of the 30th of next month.                      │
│                                                                   │
│   Sincerely,                                                      │
│ ⊥⊥⊥⊥⊥⊥⊥⊥⊥1[s⊥T⊥⊥⊥T⊥⊥⊥T⊥⊥⊥T⊥⊥⊥T⊥⊥⊥T⊥⊥⊥T⊥⊥⊥T⊥⊥⊥T⊥7⊥⊥⊥⊥⊥⊥⊥⊥       │
│ Working Copy            Num          0 ╱ 24  Line 11 of Page 1 of 1 │
│ FOUND!  Press F7 to search again, F10 to replace and continue, Esc to cancel. │
│ Esc-Exit  F1-Help  F2-Print  Shift+F7-Restore   F7-Search  F8-Options  ↑F8-Save │
└─────────────────────────────────────────────────────────────────┘
```

The message line informs you when the match is found and gives you instructions on what to do next.

6. After Q&A finds the text, you can do one of the following things:

- Press F10 to replace the text and continue the search.
- Press F7 to continue the search without replacing the text.
- Press Esc to cancel the search.

```
┌─────────────────────────────────────────────────────────────────┐
│                                                                   │
│                                                                   │
│   Dear Account Manager,                                           │
│                                                                   │
│        You have recently charged my checking account with the     │
│   following incorrect check charges.  Evidently, when you         │
│   entered the checks in your computer, numbers were               │
│   transposed and my account was debited incorrect amounts.        │
│   The amounts of the incorrect charges are shown on the           │
│   attached page.                                                  │
│                                                                   │
│        Please correct these charges so that they will appear      │
│   on my statement of the 20th of next month.                      │
│                                                                   │
│   Sincerely,                                                      │
│ ⊥⊥⊥⊥⊥⊥⊥⊥⊥1[s⊥T⊥⊥⊥T⊥⊥⊥T⊥⊥⊥T⊥⊥⊥T⊥⊥⊥T⊥⊥⊥T⊥⊥⊥T⊥⊥⊥T⊥7⊥⊥⊥⊥⊥⊥⊥        │
│ Working Copy            Num          0 ╱ 28  Line 11 of Page 1 of 1 │
│ Search and replace completed.                                     │
│ Esc-Exit  F1-Help  F2-Print  Shift+F7-Restore   F7-Search  F8-Options  ↑F8-Save │
└─────────────────────────────────────────────────────────────────┘
```

After Q&A finds all instances of the text, the message Search and replace completed. is displayed.

10

If you enter all lowercase letters when you ask Q&A to search, the program will find the item in any combination of lower- and uppercase letters. If you use uppercase letters when you enter the search string, however, Q&A finds the exact match only.

Searching with Wild Cards

You just learned how to use Q&A's search-and-replace feature to find an exact match. You knew what you were looking for and exactly how it was presented in the document. But what if you are unsure of the spelling of a word? You can use a wild-card search. You use wild cards, which are special symbols that take the place of other characters, when you aren't sure exactly where or how the match may occur.

Q&A Write has two wild-card characters you can use: . . (two periods) and ? (question mark). The ? character replaces one alphanumeric character. The . . wild card can be used to represent any number of characters. The following table provides examples of possible uses for wild-card searches.

Table 10.3
Sample Wild-Card Searches

Search String	Meaning	Examples
0?	Any two-letter word beginning with an o.	on, of, Or
o..	Any word beginning with an o.	on, onward, Offer, organic
..t	Any word ending in t.	cat, elephant, at
?le..	Any word with le as its second and third characters.	clever, elephant

You may want to search for a character that is itself a wild-card character. Q&A provides a special wild-card character for this type of search. When a backslash (\) is placed before a character, Q&A reads the character that follows literally. In other words, entering \.\. causes Q&A to search for two periods. To search for a questions mark, type \?.

You perform a wild-card search in the same manner as you perform a search-and-replace operation. Just enter the wild cards in the Search for field.

10

Using Advanced Search Features

At some point in your work with Q&A, you may need to replace one person's name with another. Or you may need to replace both the singular and the plural forms of a word. Q&A provides advanced search options that enable you to perform these operations.

To access the advanced level of search options, follow these steps:

1. Press F7.

   The Search-and-replace box appears.

2. Press PgDn.

```
 ┌──────────────────────┐
 │  Search for..:       │
 │  Replace with:       │
 │  Method......:  ▶Manual◀  Automatic   Fast automatic │
 │  Type........:  ▶Whole words◀  Text   Pattern │
 │  Case........:  ▶Insensitive◀  Sensitive │
 │  Range.......:  ▶All◀  To end   To beginning │
 │  Search Joins:  Yes  ▶No◀ │
 └──────────────────────┘
Lllllllll1[sLLTLLLLTLLLLTLLLLTLLLLTLLLLTLLLLTLLLLTLLTLj|7LLLLLLLL
Working Copy            Num        0 % 28  Line 11 of Page 1 of 1

Esc-Exit   PgUp-Reg Options   F3-Clear   F8-Make Default   F7,F10-Begin Search
```

The box now expands to offer the advanced search selections.

Notice that this box contains three additional criteria that you can specify for the search-and-replace operation.

You use the Type field to indicate whether you want to search for whole words, text, or a pattern. Replacing CAT with DOG is an example of a whole word search. This search finds CAT but does not find CATS. A text search looks for part of a word or a text fragment. For instance, a text search finds CATS if you search for CAT. A pattern search looks for patterns, such as numbers. For example, 999 looks for three numbers together, 999- looks for three numbers followed by a hyphen.

10

Use the Case field to ask Q&A to be selective based on capitalization. If you searched for CATS, for example, and selected case sensitive, the words cats and Cats would not be found.

Use the Range field to specify whether you want to search all of a document, only from the cursor location to the end of the document, or from the cursor location to the beginning of the document.

Use Search Joins to connect this search with other documents by using the JOIN, QUEUE, or QUEUP print commands.

Searching for Special Characters

Not only can you search for and replace text you want to change, but you also can use this powerful feature to find and change special characters. Special characters include font assignments, text enhancements, carriage returns, and centered text (see Chapter 11 for a complete discussion of special characters). Even though you cannot see these characters on the screen, you can search for them.

Each special character is given an alphabetic code. For example, bold text is coded BD. Table 10.4 shows some of the special characters for which you can search.

When you search for a special character, you enter an @ symbol before the alphabetic code. The @ symbol indicates that the character is a special character and performs a specific function within the software. You must include this symbol when you search for special characters.

An example of an advanced search-and-replace operation is changing bold text to underlined text. Instead of searching through the document for every occurrence of bold text, you can use the advanced search features to make this change for you. Follow these steps to use the advanced search-and-replace operation:

1. Press [F7].

2. Type the text you want to find in the Search for field and press [↵Enter].

   In this example, type @BD.

3. Type the replacement text in the Replace with: field and press [↵Enter].

   In this example, type @UL.

Table 10.4
Special Characters

Code	Special Character
Text Enhancement Codes	
@RG	Regular text
@BD	Bold text
@UL	Underlined text
@IT	Italic text
@SP	Superscript text
@SB	Subscript text
@XO	Strikeout text
Font Assignment Codes	
@F1	Font 1
@F2	Font 2
@F3	Font 3
@F4	Font 4
@F5	Font 5
@F6	Font 6
@F7	Font 7
@F8	Font 8
Options Menu Selections	
@CT	Centered text
@NP	New page break
@CR	Carriage return

10

4. Select the Automatic mode of replacement.

This screen shows the advanced options dialog box with the special character for which you are searching and the code you want to replace it with. Notice that Automatic mode is selected.

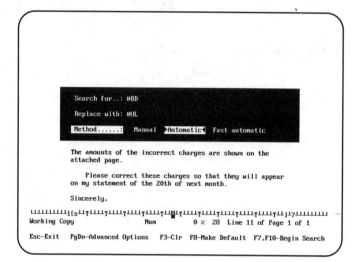

```
Search for..: @BD

Replace with: @UL

Method......:   Manual  ▶Automatic◀  Fast automatic

The amounts of the incorrect charges are shown on the
attached page.

      Please correct these charges so that they will appear
on my statement of the 20th of next month.

   Sincerely,

╙╨╨╨╨╨╨╨╨╨1ᴸˢ╨ᵀ╨╨╨ᵀ╨╨╨╨ᵀ╨╨╨╨ᵀ╨╨╨╨ᵀ╨╨╨╨ᵀ╨╨╨╨ᵀ╨╨╨╨ᵀ╨╨╨╨ᵀ╨╨╨╨ᵀ╨17╨╨╨╨╨╨╨
Working Copy              Num          0 ⁒  28  Line 11 of Page 1 of 1

Esc-Exit   PgDn-Advanced Options   F3-Clr  F8-Make Default  F7,F10-Begin Search
```

5. Press F10 to begin the search.

The message line tells you when the operation is complete.

Copying and Moving Text

You also use Q&A block functions to copy and move text. Copying and moving text are common editing functions. With Q&A, copying is not restricted to one word. You can copy an entire document if you choose.

When you copy text, you use the cursor-movement keys to select the text you want copied or moved. Copying text leaves the original selection in place and inserts the new copy at the cursor position. Moving text removes the text from its original location and inserts the text at the cursor location. The same methods can be used to copy and move text.

You can copy or move text by using the Options menu commands or by pressing F5. The following table lists the function key assignments for copying and moving text.

10

Table 10.5
Function Key Assignments for Copying and Moving Text

Key(s)	Function
F5	Copies a block of text.
⇧Shift-F5	Moves a block of text.
Alt-F5	Moves a block of text into another document.
Ctrl-F5	Copies a block of text into another document.

Using the Options Menu To Copy

To copy a block of text using the Options menu, follow these steps:

1. Press F8 to activate the Options menu.
2. Select Block Operations and press ⏎Enter.
3. Select Copy.
4. Use the cursor-movement keys to highlight the text you want to copy, or consult Table 10.2 for a detailed list of text selection keys.
5. Press F10.

Using F5 To Copy

To copy a block of text using the F5 key, follow these steps:

1. Move the cursor to the place you want the text copied.
2. Press F5 to copy.
   The message line tells you to highlight the text you want copied.
3. Press the ↓ key to highlight the text.
4. Press F10.

10

The message line indicates that you should move the cursor to the location in which you want the block of text copied.

```
Dear Account Manager,

    You have recently charged my checking account with the
following incorrect check charges.  Evidently, when you
entered the checks in your computer, numbers were
transposed and my account was debited incorrect amounts.
The amounts of the incorrect charges are shown on the
attached page.

    Please correct these charges so that they will appear
on my statement of the 20th of next month.

Sincerely,
```

```
Working Copy                    Num         0 %  1   Line 14 of Page 1 of 1
Move the cursor to the place you want the text copied, then press F10.
Esc-Exit                                                        F10-Continue
```

5. Move the cursor to the new location and press F10.

10

The text is copied to the new location.

```
        Dear Account Manager,

            You have recently charged my checking account with the
        following incorrect check charges.  Evidently, when you
        entered the checks in your computer, numbers were
        transposed and my account was debited incorrect amounts.
        The amounts of the incorrect charges are shown on the
        attached page.

            Please correct these charges so that they will appear
        on my statement of the 20th of next month.

        Sincerely,


        Dear Account Manager,

            You have recently charged my checking account with the
        following incorrect check charges.  Evidently, when you
        entered the checks in your computer, numbers were
```

```
Working Copy                    Num         1 %  1   Line 19 of Page 1 of 1

Esc-Exit  F1-Help  F2-Print  Shift+F7-Restore   F7-Search  F8-Options  ↑F8-Save
```

Using the Spelling Checker

No matter what type of document you are creating, you should proofread your work before you go much further. Proofreading used to be a time-consuming task, but with Q&A you can have the software check for typing errors, misspelled words, and repeated words. You can check one word or the entire document.

232

The spelling checker included with Q&A comes with two dictionaries. The main dictionary contains up to 100,000 words and is ready to use when you install Q&A. The personal dictionary is developed by you as you use the system. A personal dictionary can be developed with terms that are unique to your industry or profession.

Always place the cursor where you want the spelling check to begin. Spelling checks begin at the cursor location and go forward through the document. You also should note that header and footer text are not included in the spelling check.

The function keys assigned to the spelling checker are not displayed on the key assignment line. You must access the help screen by pressing F1 to see the spelling checker function key assignments.

To use the spelling checker, follow these steps:

1. Move the cursor to the beginning of the document.

   You can press Ctrl-Home to move quickly to the top of the document.

2. Press ⇧Shift-F1 to start the spelling check of the entire document. If you want to check the spelling of just one word, place the cursor at the start of the word and press Ctrl-F1.

```
          Please correct these charges so that they will appear
       on my statement of the 20th of next month.

       Sincere
              ┌─────────────────────────────────────┐
              │ L - List possible spellings          │
              │ I - Ignore word & continue           │
              │ A - Add to dictionary & continue     │
              │ S - Add to dictionary & stop         │
              │ E - Edit word & recheck              │
              └─────────────────────────────────────┘




       LLLLLLLLL1[sLL7LLLL7LLLL7LLLL7LLLL7LLLL7LLLL7LLLL7LLLL7LL7L7LLLLLLLL
       Working Copy          Num        0 % 26  Line 11 of Page 1 of 1

       Esc-Exit                                    ←┘ Continue
```

The document is scanned until Q&A finds a word that is unknown to the dictionary. When an unknown word is encountered, the Spelling menu appears.

10

The Spelling menu has the following choices:

- Use List possible spellings to show you alternative choices retrieved from the dictionaries.

- Use Ignore word & continue to bypass the word highlighted and not add it to your personal dictionary.

- Use Add to dictionary & continue to add the highlighted word to your personal dictionary and continue the spelling check.

- Use Add to dictionary & Stop to add the highlighted word to your personal dictionary and stop the spelling check.

- Use Edit word & recheck to change the spelling of the highlighted word and then recheck to verify that the edited version is correct. This option is used most frequently when no possible spellings for a word are found.

3. Press the cursor-movement keys to highlight a menu selection and press ⏎Enter

4. Continue through the document, responding to the prompts until the spelling check is completed.

10

When the spelling check is completed, you return to the starting location and a message appears on the message line.

```
Dear Account Manager,

    You have recently charged my checking account with the
following incorrect check charges.  Evidently, when you
entered the checks in your computer, numbers were
transposed and my account was debited incorrect amounts.
The amounts of the incorrect charges are shown on the
attached page.

    Please correct these charges so that they will appear
on my statement of the 20th of next month.

    Sincerely,

Working Copy              Num          0 %  1    Line 1 of Page 1 of 1
Spelling check completed.
Esc-Exit  F1-Help  F2-Print  Shift+F7-Restore   F7-Search  F8-Options  ↑F8-Save
```

Using the Personal Dictionary

You cannot edit the main dictionary, but you can put special terms, personal names, geographical names, or any words you choose into the personal dictionary. You can add words to your personal dictionary

- By adding the words as you perform the spell check of the document.

- By entering the words into the personal dictionary file, which is called QAPERS.DCT.

234

As you use the spelling checker in a normal document, you can add a high-lighted word that the main dictionary does not contain.

```
     Please correct these charges so that they will appear
on my statement of the 20th of next month.

Sincere┌─────────────────────────────────────┐
        │ L - List possible spellings         │
        │ I - Ignore word & continue          │
        │ A - Add to dictionary & continue    │
        │ S - Add to dictionary & stop        │
        │ E - Edit word & recheck             │
        └─────────────────────────────────────┘




⊔⊔⊔⊔⊔⊔⊔1[s⊔T⊔⊔⊔T⊔⊔⊔T⊔⊔⊔T⊔⊔⊔T⊔⊔⊔T⊔⊔⊔T⊔⊔⊔T]⊔7⊔⊔⊔⊔⊔⊔⊔
BADDEBIT.DOC              Num        0 % 26  Line 11 of Page 1 of 1

Esc-Exit                                        ←┘ Continue
```

To add a word to the dictionary, select Add to dictionary & continue or Add to dictionary & Stop.

The second method is more complex, but useful when your writing contains many acronyms, technical terms, or abbreviations that would not appear in the main dictionary. You can enter these words into the personal dictionary file.

The personal dictionary is saved under the name QAPERS.DCT. To add words to the personal dictionary, follow these steps:

1. From the Write menu, select Get.

   A dialog box is displayed.

2. Select the file format and press ⌨Enter

10

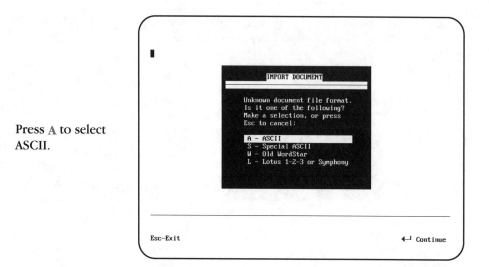

Press **A** to select
ASCII.

3. When the file is open, add your list of words exactly as you want
   them to appear in your documents. The list must be in alphabetical
   order.

4. Press Ctrl-F8 to save the file in the ASCII file format.

10

Remember that
the words listed
must be in
alphabetical order
and that
QAPERS.DCT
must be saved in
ASCII file format.

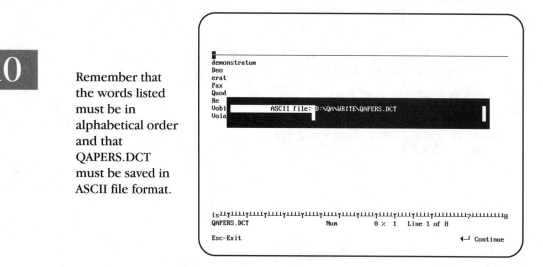

If these two conditions are not met, the spelling checker does not function
properly.

Using the Thesaurus

A thesaurus permits you to add spice to your writing by varying your choice of words. Q&A has its own electronic thesaurus, which you can consult as you write documents. As you compose your work, you can replace a selected word with one of the list of synonyms Q&A provides.

To use the thesaurus, follow these steps:

1. Highlight a word in the document for which you want to see a list of synonyms.
2. Press Alt-F1.

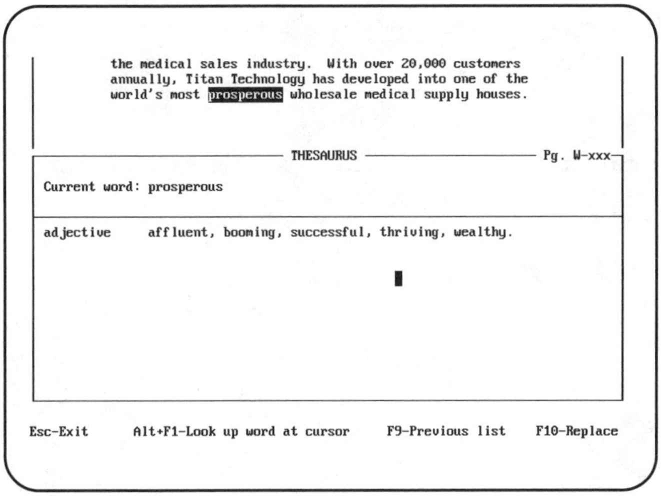

```
                the medical sales industry.  With over 20,000 customers
                annually, Titan Technology has developed into one of the
                world's most  prosperous  wholesale medical supply houses.



    ─────────────────────── THESAURUS ──────────────── Pg. W-xxx─┐

    Current word: prosperous

    adjective      affluent, booming, successful, thriving, wealthy.


                                    █





    Esc-Exit      Alt+F1-Look up word at cursor     F9-Previous list    F10-Replace
```

The word you selected appears at the cursor. A list of possible replacement words is displayed below.

10

2. To replace the selected word with one of the synonyms, move the cursor to the desired replacement and press F10.

The word will be
replaced by the
suggested word.

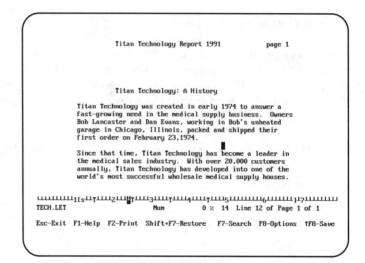

3. To exit the Thesaurus screen without selecting a replacement word,
   press Esc.

Formatting and Enhancing

In the last two chapters you learned the basic fundamentals of Q&A's Write module. You learned how to create and save documents and how to enter and search for text. Chapter 10 taught you how to retrieve and edit a document. Specifically, you learned how to insert, delete, copy, move, and edit text.

This chapter shows you how to enhance your documents. Text enhancements enable you to add a polished touch to your documents, thus ensuring greater readability. This chapter teaches you how to create columns, headings, and custom margins. You also learn to use the Line Draw feature of Q&A. In addition, this chapter covers the special text features such as boldface, underline, and text alignment. You also learn how to install and apply fonts.

Setting tabs

Drawing lines

Setting margins

Using text enhancements

Justifying text

Using the asterisk commands

11

Formatting a Document

Q&A provides many formatting options that enable you to make your documents more interesting. Formatting adds style, emphasis, and clarity to your documents; it makes documents easy to read; and it gives documents a professional appearance. These formatting characteristics reside in the document file with the text. When you save a document, you save not only the text but all the formatting information as well.

You can set tabs, draw lines, center text, and use other options to further enhance the looks of a document, and creating pleasant-looking documents increases readability.

Understanding the Options Menu

Most of the formatting commands appear on the Options menu. You can access the Options menu from anywhere in Q&A Write by pressing F8.

The Options menu is displayed.

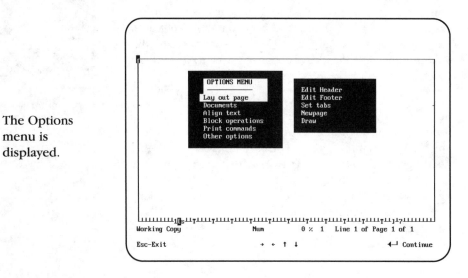

The Options menu includes the following features:

- Lay Out Page, which enables you to develop headers and footers, change tab settings, indicate page breaks, and draw rules.

- Documents, which enables you to retrieve a new document or insert a document into the on-screen document.

11

- **Align Text**, which enables you to specify whether text is left-, center-, or right-justified. You also can use this option to set temporary margins and control line spacing within a document.

- **Block Operations**, which enables you to copy, move, and delete blocks of copy. This option also controls text enhancements.

- **Print Commands**, which enables you to insert special print commands within a document.

- **Other options** enables you to do editing tasks, file management tasks, and math calculations.

Setting Up Columns

Tabs are settings that move the cursor a designated amount of spaces with one keystroke. When doing columnar entry, you can use tabs to make cursor movement faster and more consistent.

You can use the following types of tabs:

- Standard tabs move the cursor to the space in which you want to begin typing. Standard tabs are shown on the ruler line with a T in the space where the tab occurs.

- Decimal tabs align the decimals in the numbers regardless of the size of the numbers. Use these tabs when you must enter numbers that involve decimal places. Decimal tabs are shown on the ruler line with a D in the space where the tab occurs.

Because of standard settings that come with Q&A, all documents have preset tabs. These settings, however, may not meet your needs. You can change these tab settings using the Options menu.

Setting Standard and Decimal Tabs

To set up columnar text entry, follow these steps:

1. From the Options menu, select Lay out page.

2. Select Set tabs from the Lay out page submenu that appears to the right of the Options menu.

   The cursor disappears from the text part of the screen and appears on the ruler line.

3. Press the space bar until the cursor is on the position where you want the first tab. Any old tab settings that were located before the first new tab are deleted.

4. Type ⊤ to set a standard tab; type a Ⓓ to set a decimal tab.

241

11

For this example, type T to indicate a standard tab.

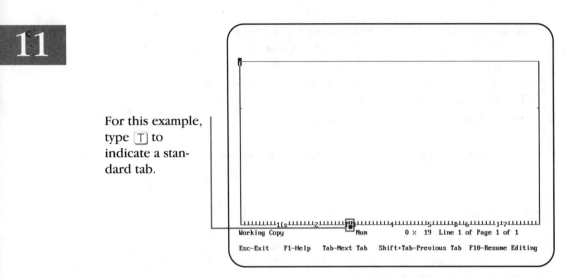

```
Working Copy                        Num           0 %  19  Line 1 of Page 1 of 1

Esc-Exit    F1-Help    Tab-Next Tab    Shift+Tab-Previous Tab  F10-Resume Editing
```

5. Continue pressing the space bar to position the cursor where you want tabs and pressing D or T to indicate the type of tab.

6. Press F10 when you finish adding tabs.

    Corrected tab settings are saved and the cursor reappears on-screen. You can resume editing the document; the tabs that you just created are now in effect.

In addition to using the space bar to move around the ruler line, Q&A Write also supports several keyboard shortcuts. These keys are shown in Table 11.1.

Table 11.1
Ruler Movement Keyboard Shortcuts

Key	Moves cursor to
Tab⇆	Next tab marker, which may be standard or decimal.
⇧Shift-Tab⇆	Previous tab marker.
Ctrl-←	Five spaces to the left of the cursor position.
Ctrl-→	Five spaces to the right of the cursor position.
Home	Left margin.
End	Right margin.

Entering Tabular Information

11

Now that you know how to set up tabs, entering the columns of data is simple. Tab columns are the quickest and easiest way to create columns for simple lists, such as telephone lists or lists containing items and prices.

To type tabular data, follow these steps:

1. Create tab settings for the number of columns in the list. Each column of information should have one tab stop. Dollar amounts or other numeric entries with decimal points should be set up as decimal tabs.

2. Beginning at the left margin of the document, type the entry for the first column on the first line.

3. Press [Tab⇄] once.

   The cursor moves to the next tab stop you created.

4. Type the entry for the second column on the first line.

5. Press [Tab⇄].

   The cursor moves to the next tab stop that you created.

6. Continue entering information and pressing the Tab key until all the entries for the first line are complete.

7. Press [⏎Enter].

   The cursor moves to the next line.

8. Repeat Steps 2 through 7 until you have entered all data.

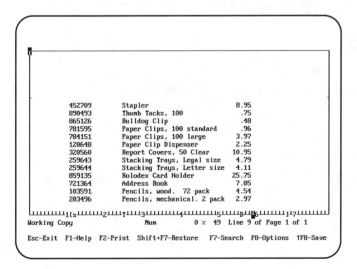

In this example, you see three columns of data. Two columns are entered as standard tabs and one column is entered as a decimal tab.

11

Adding Column Headings

After you create columns of information, you may want to add headings to describe the data in each column. Although columns align data and present the information in a balanced, easy-to-read format, headings provide a description for each column. You know what the data in each column represents, but your reader may not. You can use the Draw feature, which is located on the Options menu, to add column headings.

You must first insert a blank line to hold the column headings. To insert a blank line, follow these steps:

1. Press the cursor-movement keys or Home to move the cursor to the first space on the blank line before the first column entry.
2. If you are not in the Insert mode, press Ins.

   If Insert mode is active, the status line displays Ins and the cursor is a large, blinking square.
3. Press ↵Enter once to insert a blank line.

Now you can insert the column headings. To enter the column headings, follow these steps:

1. Make sure that the cursor is in the far left position on the line before you begin.
2. Type the first column heading.
3. Press Tab↹ once.
4. Continue entering column headings. Press Tab↹ to separate headings.

   To center headings over the decimal point on a decimal tab, press Tab↹ and then press ←Backspace to move the cursor where you want to begin the column heading.
5. Press ↵Enter after you enter all column headings.

244

11

```
 Item No.     Item Name              Price

 452709       Stapler                 8.95
 890493       Thumb Tacks, 100         .75
 865126       Bulldog Clip             .48
 781595       Paper Clips, 100 standard .96
 784151       Paper Clips, 100 large   3.97
 120648       Paper Clip Dispenser     2.25
 320560       Report Covers, 50 Clear 10.95
 259643       Stacking Trays, Legal size  4.79
 259644       Stacking Trays, Letter size 4.11
 859135       Rolodex Card Holder     25.75
 721364       Address Book             7.05
 103591       Pencils, wood. 72 pack   4.54
```

```
OFFLIST.DOC            Num         0 % 1   Line 3 of Page 1 of 1

Esc-Exit  F1-Help  F2-Print  Shift+F7-Restore   F7-Search  F8-Options  ↑F8-Save
```

In this example, you see the column headings and the blank line that separates the data from the headings.

Using Line Draw

The Draw feature, which is located on the Options menu, enables you to place lines, boxes, and graphics in your documents. For the example, you can use the Draw function to add a line under the headings of columnar data entry.

To use the Draw feature, follow these steps:

1. Press F8 to access the Options menu.
2. Select Lay out page.
3. From the Lay out page submenu, select Draw. Then press ↵Enter.

11

Notice that the message line now contains instructions on how to use the cursor-movement keys to draw.

```
           Item No.        Item Name                Price

           452709          Stapler                  8.95
           890493          Thumb Tacks, 100           .75
           865126          Bulldog Clip               .48
           781595          Paper Clips, 100 standard  .96
           784151          Paper Clips, 100 large    3.97
           120648          Paper Clip Dispenser      2.25
           320560          Report Covers, 50 Clear  10.95
           259643          Stacking Trays, Legal size 4.79
           259644          Stacking Trays, Letter size 4.11
           859135          Rolodex Card Holder      25.75
           721364          Address Book              7.05
           103591          Pencils, wood.  72 pack   4.54
OFFLIST.DOC                    Num        0 % 1   Line 2 of Page 1 of 1
Use the cursor keypad to draw.  Press F8 to erase.  Press F10 when done.
Esc-Exit   → ← ↓ ↑   Shift →←↑↓     F6-Pen up    F8-Erase    F10-Resume editing
```

4. Use the arrow keys to draw a single line up, down, left, or to the right of the cursor position. You cannot draw a diagonal line.

   To draw a double line, press and hold ⇧Shift and then press an arrow key on the numeric keypad. Note that Number Lock must be off.

5. Press F6 to lift the pen.

   A new message appears on the message line, stating that the pen is now up. You can move the cursor freely throughout the document now.

6. Reposition the cursor where you want to begin drawing the next line.

7. Press F6 again to put down the pen.

   To erase lines, use the arrow keys just as you do to draw lines. After you erase the lines you want, press F8 to resume drawing.

8. Press F10 to save the drawings and resume editing.

```
‖

     Item No.     Item Name             Price

     452709       Stapler                8.95
     890493       Thumb Tacks, 100        .75
     865126       Bulldog Clip            .48
     781595       Paper Clips, 100 standard    .96
     784151       Paper Clips, 100 large  3.97
     120648       Paper Clip Dispenser    2.25
     320560       Report Covers, 50 Clear 10.95
     259643       Stacking Trays, Legal size   4.79
     259644       Stacking Trays, Letter size  4.11
     859135       Rolodex Card Holder    25.75
     721364       Address Book            7.05
     103591       Pencils, wood.  72 pack 4.54
     203496       Pencils, mechanical. 2 pack  2.97

└┴┴┴┴┴┴┴┴┴1[s┴┴┴┴┴┴2┴┴┴T┴┴┴3┴┴┴┴┴┴4┴┴┴┴┴5┴┴┴D┴┴6┴┴┴┴┴7┴┴┴┴┴
OFFLIST.DOC              Num        0 %  48  Line 15 of Page 1 of 1

Esc-Exit  F1-Help  F2-Print  Shift+F7-Restore   F7-Search  F8-Options  ↑F8-Save
```

In this example, you see the column headings with rules.

The following table explains the function key assignments for the Draw feature.

Table 11.2
Function Key Assignments for Draw

Key	Function
Esc (Cancel)	Cancels Draw mode and returns to Edit mode.
→, ←, ↑, ↓	Draws a single solid line in the direction of the arrow.
⇧Shift-→, ←, ↑, ↓	Draws a double line in the direction of the arrow.
F6 (Pen up)	Lifts the pen up to enable you to move to another location to continue drawing.
F8 (Erase)	Erases lines.
F10 (Resume editing)	Saves the drawing and returns you to Edit mode.

11 Setting Margins

Not all documents you create with Q&A Write require the same formatting. Some documents are correspondence—letters or memos—some documents are much longer, such as reports or presentations. Each document has its own unique formatting needs.

Left and right margins are displayed on-screen exactly as they appear when printed. Two methods are available for changing margins. You can change margins for the whole document by using the Define Page screen options, or you can temporarily change margins for a part of a document.

Setting Document Margins

To set margins for your entire document, follow these steps:

1. From the Write menu, select Define Page.

   If you are in the document, press Ctrl-F6.

The Define Page screen is displayed.

```
                              DEFINE PAGE


         Left margin: 10               Right margin : 68

         Top margin : 6                Bottom margin: 6

         Page width : 78               Page length  : 66

         Characters per inch............:  10◄  12   15   17

         Begin header/footer on page #...:  1

         Begin page numbering with page #:  1

         _____

                     Page Options for Working Copy

    Esc-Exit         F1-Help         F2-Print Options      F10-Continue
```

You can enter margin settings in inches, centimeters, character columns (for left and right margins), or lines (for top and bottom margins). Select the unit of measurement best suited to your needs. The default unit is characters.

11

To enter margin settings in inches, type the number followed by the inches symbol ("). Enter fractions of an inch in decimal numbers, such as **1.25"**.

To enter margin settings in centimeters, type the number followed by the letter **c**, as in **3c**. Fractions of a centimeter should be entered as decimal numbers.

To enter margin settings in characters, type the number of characters. Note that setting margins in characters requires these considerations:

- The left margin is the number of characters from the left edge of the paper.
- The right margin is the number of characters from the right edge of the paper.
- The top margin is the number of lines from the top of the paper.
- The bottom margin is the number of lines up from the bottom of the paper.

In general, six lines of text equal a vertical inch on paper. You can mix units of measurement within a document. You can have the top and bottom margins of a document measured in inches, for example, and the right and left margins measured in characters.

Entering the settings on the Define Page screen is simple. Press ⬅, ➡, ⬆, ⬇, or ⎋Tab⎋ to highlight the settings you want to change. Then enter the setting and press F10 to save the change.

Setting Temporary Margins

Temporary margins cause your text to appear differently depending on when and where you use them. When you enter new text, a temporary left margin affects the line below the cursor but does not affect the line in which the cursor is positioned. A temporary right margin affects the line in which the cursor is positioned when you enter new text.

Temporary margins come in handy when you want to indent a long quotation or create a bulleted or numbered list within a larger document. Try to plan in advance, however, because temporary margins affect new text only. You can add temporary margins to existing text, but the margin setting must be set for each individual paragraph.

11

To set temporary margins with the F6 key, follow these steps:

1. Place the cursor where you want the left temporary margin to begin.
2. Press F6.

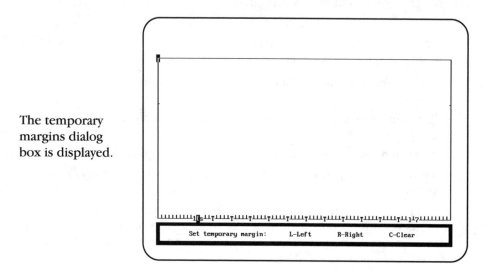

The temporary
margins dialog
box is displayed.

3. Press L to set the left temporary margin.

   A left angle bracket (<) appears on the ruler line.
4. Move the cursor where you want the right temporary margin to begin.
5. Press F6 again.

   The temporary margins dialog box reappears.
6. Press R to set the right temporary margin.

   A right angle bracket (>) appears on the ruler line.

11

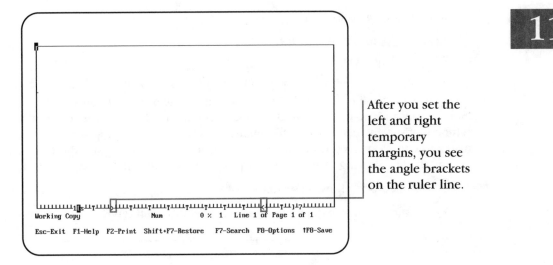

After you set the left and right temporary margins, you see the angle brackets on the ruler line.

7. Type the text and press ⏎Enter.

8. Press F6.

    The temporary margins dialog box reappears.

9. Press C to clear the temporary margins.

To set temporary options from the Options menu, follow these steps:

1. Press F8.

2. Select Align text.

3. Select Temporary margins from the Align text submenu.

    The temporary margins dialog box appears.

4. Set the margins you want to use and press F10.

Setting Line Spacing

Q&A Write documents can be single-, double-, or triple-spaced. You have two methods you can use to set line spacing on documents. With the first method, you set line spacing on-screen. The second method affects line spacing on the printed document only.

251

11

To set line spacing, follow these steps:

1. Press [F8] to access the Options menu.

2. Select **A**lign text.

3. Select Single space, Double space, or Triple space and press [↵Enter].

Changes made to line spacing from the Options menu are visible on-screen immediately and are reflected in the printed document. The other method of setting line spacing becomes useful when you must print a draft for others to read and edit. You can set the document to print double-spaced and then change the line spacing to single-spaced on the final printout.

To use this method, follow these steps:

1. Press [F2] from the document, or select **P**rint from the Write menu.

The Print Options
screen is dis-
played.

```
                              PRINT OPTIONS
■
      From page.............:   1              To page............:   END

      Number of copies......:   1              Print offset.......:   0

      Line spacing..........:  ▶Single◀    Double      Envelope

      Justify...............:   Yes  ▶No◀  Space justify

      Print to..............:  ▶PtrA◀  PtrB   PtrC   PtrD   PtrE   DISK

      Page preview..........:   Yes  ▶No◀

      Type of paper feed....:   Manual  ▶Continuous◀  Bin1   Bin2   Bin3   Lhd

      Number of columns.....:  ▶1◀   2    3    4    5    6    7    8

      Printer control codes.:

      Name of merge file....:

      _____

      Esc-Exit    F1-Help   Ctrl+F6-Def Pg   F9-Save changes & go back   F10-Continue
```

2. Highlight the line spacing option you want.

3. Press [F10] to print the document.

Creating Headers and Footers

Headers appear at the top of each page of a document; footers appear at the bottom of each page. Header options are activated using the Options menu. Headers and footers usually contain information such as page numbers and titles.

11

Write prints the header or footer at the top and bottom margin respectively. The top and bottom margins must be large enough to accommodate this text. If you plan to have a six-line header at the top of a document and the top margin is six lines, the margin will be completely covered by the header. You always should leave some space around the header or footer so that your readers can distinguish the main part of the text from the header or footer.

The Edit Header and Edit Footer commands operate similarly. To create a header or footer, follow these steps:

1. Press F8 to access the Options menu.

2. Select **L**ay out page.

3. Select Edit **H**eader (or Edit **F**ooter) from the Lay out page submenu.

    The cursor moves to the top (or bottom) of the page.

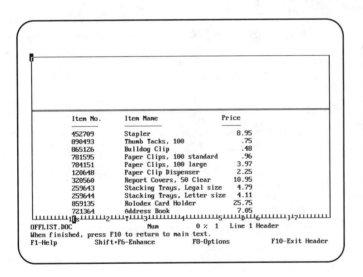

The area inside the box is the area available for the header. The size of this area varies, depending on the top margin setting. The cursor is on the first space available for text entry.

4. Type the text you want to appear in the header.

5. Press F10 to return to your document.

Headers and footers often contain page numbers. To insert a page number, you enter the pound sign (#). Use one pound sign for each digit of the page number. If your document will contain at least 100 pages, for example, enter three pound signs in the header. If the page number does not fill all three digits, Q&A converts the pound signs to spaces.

11

When you print a document that contains headers and footers, you must set the Begin Header/Footer and the Begin Page Numbering options on the Define Page screen. The Begin Header/Footer option enables you to specify on which page you want the headers and footers to begin. You usually do not want a header and footer on the title page, for example. This option enables you to specify that headers and footers should begin on page two.

The Begin Page Numbering option indicates the page number that Q&A should print on the first page. The default setting is one. This setting is useful when you must print sections of a larger document, such as chapters of a book.

Q&A has special commands that can be embedded in documents to perform particular tasks. These commands are typed in the body of the document and enclosed in asterisks. When the computer encounters these commands, it performs the functions as requested.

Headers and Footers can utilize the following asterisk commands when used in the Write module of Q&A:

@DATE	Prints the current date read from the computer's internal calendar.
@DATE(n)	Prints the current date read from the computer's internal calendar and places the date in the requested format.
@TIME	Prints the current time read from the computer's internal clock.
@TIME(n)	Prints the current time read from the computer's internal clock and places the time in the requested format.

Aligning Text

With Q&A, you can choose left, right, or center alignment for text. The default setting is for left-aligned text. To select text alignment, follow these steps:

1. Press ⌜F8⌝ to access the Options menu.
2. Select Align text.

   The Align text submenu is displayed.
3. Select the alignment you want. You can choose left, right, or center. Then press ⌜⏎Enter⌝.

   You are returned to the document.
4. Type the text.

To align existing text, select the text before opening the Options menu. If you align text in this manner, only the selected text is aligned. Note that you can align header and footer text in the same manner.

Using the Justify Command

Documents can be justified with one of two methods. Justification refers to the alignment of text along both margins. The first method requires that you select Justify=Yes on the Print Options screen. This method justifies the entire document. To justify a portion of a document, use the Justify command. Just embed the command in asterisks. To justify text within a document, for example, type *JUSTIFY YES*. Type *JUSTIFY NO* to turn off justification.

Suppose that you want to justify a long quotation but want to leave the rest of the document unjustified. Follow these steps:

1. Place the cursor where you want to begin justifying text.
2. Make sure that you are in Insert mode.

   The status line displays Ins when Insert mode is active.
3. Type *JUSTIFY YES*.
4. Move the cursor where you want the justified text to end.

   The cursor should be outside the ending punctuation mark.
5. Type *JUSTIFY NO* to turn off justification.

11

ou can preview the document by following these steps:

1. Press F2 from within the document.

The Print Options
screen is dis-
played.

```
                            PRINT OPTIONS

From page.............:  1              To page.............:  END

Number of copies......:  1             Print offset........:  0

Line spacing..........:  ▶Single◀    Double      Envelope

Justify...............:  Yes  ▶No◀  Space justify

Print to..............:  ▶PtrA◀  PtrB   PtrC   PtrD   PtrE   DISK

Page preview..........:  ▶Yes◀  No

Type of paper feed....:  Manual  ▶Continuous◀  Bin1   Bin2   Bin3   Lhd

Number of columns.....:  ▶1◀  2   3   4   5   6   7   8

Printer control codes.:

Name of merge file....:


Esc-Exit    F1-Help   Ctrl+F6-Def Pg   F9-Save changes & go back   F10-Continue
```

2. Set the Page Preview option to Yes.
3. Press F10.

Your document
appears on-screen
with the justified
text visible.

```
      In his famous treatise on politics, Machiavelli discusses
      the qualities that a ruler must have.  The most well-known
      passage is the following:

           Continuing now with our list of
           qualities, let me say that every
           prince   should   prefer   to   be
           considered   merciful   rather  than
           cruel, yet he should be careful not
           to   mismanage   this   clemency   of
           his...No  Prince  should  mind being
           called  cruel  for what  he  does to
           keep his subjects  united and loyal:
           he may make examples of a few...



   Esc-Exit    F1-Help    F-Full Page    + Zoom in    - Zoom out    Length =66
```

Using the Linespace Command

You use the Linespacing command to specify the space you want between lines of text. You can set line spacing for an entire document or just a portion of a document. With this command, you can specify from one to nine spaces between lines. Note that line spacing must be in whole numbers. You cannot request line spacing of one-and-one-half spaces, for example.

The Linespacing command works on the same premise as the Justify command. The command must be embedded between two asterisks; turned on where the special spacing requirements are needed; and turned off when the requirements are no longer needed.

You can use the Linespacing command from the Options menu or at the beginning of a document. Type *LINESPACING 2* at the beginning of a document, for example, to double-space a document. To insert a single-spaced paragraph in a double-spaced document, type *LINESPACING 1* before the paragraph. To return to double-spacing, at the end of the single-spaced paragraph type *LINESPACING 2*

```
 In his famous treatise on politics, Machiavelli discusses
 the qualities that a ruler must have.  The most well-known
 passage is the following:


    *LINESPACE 1*
    Continuing now with our list of
    qualities, let me say that every
    prince should prefer to be
    considered merciful rather than
    cruel, yet he should be careful not

MACHI.DOC              Num        0 %  46  Line 7 of Page 1 of 1
Esc-Exit  F1-Help  F2-Print  Shift+F7-Restore   F7-Search  F8-Options  ↑F8-Save
```

In this example, you see a single-spaced paragraph within a double-spaced document.

Note that line spacing is not visible on-screen. Proper line spacing appears only after the document is printed.

11 Using Text Enhancements

You can enhance text within a document to make it more attractive or to add emphasis to the text. Text enhancements are additions to a font—eye-catching tricks such as bold text, italics, or underlining. Fonts are typefaces, such as Courier or Helvetica. A font is the complete collection of letters, punctuation marks, numbers, and special characters to which enhancements can be added.

Before you can begin using text enhancements, you must make sure that your printer is installed properly. If you have not installed your printer, refer to the "Q&A User's Manual" for detailed instructions. You do not have to install the enhancements or the fonts.

Applying Text Enhancements

Text enhancements are applied from the Text Enhancements and Fonts menu. The menu offers the following text enhancement choices:

- Bold displays type in a **bold** style.
- Underline displays a <u>rule</u> under type in a document.
- Italic displays type in *italics* (some printers do not print italics; check your printer's manual).
- Subscript prints a subscript. Subscript characters print below the line. The formula H_2O uses a subscript to lower the position of the number 2.
- Superscript prints a superscript character. Superscript characters print above the line. Footnotes are an example of superscripts.
- Strikeout prints a dash (–) over a letter or word. Strikeout text is commonly used in the legal field for contract editing.
- Regular cancels any of the preceding text enhancements and returns the text to a regular style of printing.

To add text enhancements to a document, follow these steps:

1. Move the cursor to the beginning of the text you want to enhance.
2. Press `⇧Shift`-`F6`.

11

```
             Office S┌─────────────────────────────────────┐
                     │    TEXT ENHANCEMENTS AND FONTS        │
                     ├───────────────────────────────────────┤
                     │ B - Bold                              │
                     │ U - Underline                         │
                     │ P - Superscript                       │
             Item No.│ S - Subscript                         │
             ────────│ I - Italics                           │
             452709  │ X - Strikeout                         │
             890493  │ R - Regular                           │
             865126  │ 1 - Font 1 (regular if not assigned)  │
             781595  │ 2 - Font 2 (regular if not assigned)  │
             784151  │ 3 - Font 3 (regular if not assigned)  │
             120648  │ 4 - Font 4 (regular if not assigned)  │
             320560  │ 5 - Font 5 (regular if not assigned)  │
             259643  │ 6 - Font 6 (regular if not assigned)  │
             259644  │ 7 - Font 7 (regular if not assigned)  │
             859135  │ 8 - Font 8 (regular if not assigned)  │
             721364  │                                       │
             103591  │ A - Assign fonts                      │
     └─────1[s──────└───────────────────────────────────────┘    ────1₁7─────
     OFFLIST.DOC                                        Page 1 of 1

     Esc-Exit                                           ↵ Continue
```

The Text Enhancements and Fonts menu is displayed.

3. Type the letter or number that appears next to the selection you want to use.

   Press B to select bold or I to select Italic, for example.

```
             Office Supply Price List        Page 1



             ▯tem No.      Item Name              Price
             ───────       ─────────              ─────
             452709        Stapler                 8.95
             890493        Thumb Tacks, 100          .75
             865126        Bulldog Clip              .48
             781595        Paper Clips, 100 standard .96
             784151        Paper Clips, 100 large   3.97
             120648        Paper Clip Dispenser     2.25
             320560        Report Covers, 50 Clear 10.95
             259643        Stacking Trays, Legal size  4.79
             259644        Stacking Trays, Letter size 4.11
             859135        Rolodex Card Holder     25.75
             721364        Address Book             7.05
             103591        Pencils, wood. 72 pack   4.54
     ─────1[s───2───7───3───4───5───6───17─────
     OFFLIST.DOC            Num        0 % 1   Line 1 of Page 1 of 1
     Use the arrow keys to select the text you want to embolden, then press F10.
     Esc-Exit                                           F10-Continue
```

The message line provides further instructions.

11

4. Highlight the text you want to enhance.

5. Press [F10] to save the text enhancement and continue.

```
          Office Supply Price List              Page 1


          Item No.      Item Name              Price
          _____      _____              _____
          452709        Stapler                 8.95
          890493        Thumb Tacks, 100          .75
          865126        Bulldog Clip              .48
          781595        Paper Clips, 100 standard .96
          784151        Paper Clips, 100 large   3.97
          120648        Paper Clip Dispenser     2.25
          320560        Report Covers, 50 Clear 10.95
          259643        Stacking Trays, Legal size 4.79
          259644        Stacking Trays, Letter size 4.11
          859135        Rolodex Card Holder     25.75
          721364        Address Book             7.05
          103591        Pencils, wood. 72 pack   4.54

  OFFLIST.DOC   [Bold]           Num      0 ½ 1   Line 1 of Page 1 of 1

  Esc-Exit  F1-Help  F2-Print  Shift+F7-Restore  F7-Search  F8-Options  ↑F8-Save
```

Notice that the status line reflects any text enhancement made.

If you have a color monitor, you can see that enhanced text appears in a different color. If you have a monochrome monitor, enhanced text appears in a brighter intensity. Both color and monochrome monitors indicate any text enhancements on the status line.

Assigning and Applying Fonts

Fonts must be purchased separately. All printers come with at least one font (commonly Courier). Preinstalled fonts are called internal fonts. Some printers, such as PostScript-compatible laser printers, have many internal fonts. A dot-matrix printer usually does not contain as many internal fonts as a laser printer. Internal fonts do not require additional hardware or software.

Some printers, most notably Hewlett-Packard laser printers, accept font cartridges. These small, hard plastic cases plug into the printer and supply additional fonts without taking up the printer's internal memory. The cartridges can be purchased from your printer manufacturer.

Soft fonts are stored on the hard disk of the computer and are transmitted, or downloaded, into the printer's memory. These fonts may require large amounts of printer memory and can take up to 10 minutes to load into the printer. Q&A takes care of downloading these fonts for you, bypassing the need for special utilities.

Q&A interacts with the various types of fonts by means of font description files. A font description file provides details about the font, such as spacing and size, but does not contain the font itself. You must install the font description file before you can use the font.

Installing Fonts

You use the Font Assignment screen to install fonts. You must be in a document to access this menu. To assign a font, follow these steps:

1. Start a new document or retrieve an existing document.

2. Press Ctrl-F9 to activate the Font Assignment screen, or select Assign Fonts from the Text Enhancements and Fonts menu.

```
                        FONT ASSIGNMENTS              Pg. U-???

   Font file name:

          Font name              Abbr. Point Pitch    Comments
Regular:

   Font 1:
   Font 2:
   Font 3:
   Font 4:
   Font 5:
   Font 6:
   Font 7:
   Font 8:


OFFLIST.DOC

Esc-Exit      F1-Help      F6-List fonts     F8-Make default    F10-Continue
```

The Font Assignment screen is displayed.

3. Press ⏎Enter.

A list of available
font files is
displayed.

```
┌─────────────────────────────────────────────────────────┐
│                                                          │
│ ▌       LIST OF FILES IN D:\QA\WRITE\*.FNT                │
│                                                          │
│  \..          CIT124.FNT                                 │
│  $LOCK1.FNT    CIT180.FNT                                 │
│  $LPS200.FNT   CITMSP.FNT                                 │
│  ALPS200.FNT   EPSOMEX.FNT                                │
│  BLOCK1.FNT    EPSOMFX.FNT                                │
│  BROHL8.FNT    EPSONGQ.FNT                                │
│  BROTHER.FNT   EPSONLQ.FNT                                │
│  CANON.FNT     EPSOMMRX.FNT                               │
│  CANON10E.FNT  FUJ2000.FNT                                │
│  CANON8.FNT    HPDESKJ.FNT                                │
│  CAPAC25.FNT   HPDJ500.FNT                                │
│                                                          │
│  ┌──┐        File name: D:\QA\WRITE\             ┌──┐    │
│  └──┘                                            └──┘    │
│                                                          │
│ Esc-Exit  F1-Help  F3-Delete  F5-Copy  F7-Search  F8-Rename  F10-Continue │
└─────────────────────────────────────────────────────────┘
```

You must select a file from this list. If you are unsure which file is
best suited for your printer, press Esc to quit and consult your
documentation.

4. Press the cursor-movement keys to highlight the file you want to use
and press ⏎Enter.

You return to the Font Assignment screen.

5. Press F6.

A list of available
fonts is displayed.

```
┌─────────────────────────────────────────────────────────┐
│ ▌            LIST OF AVAILABLE FONT DESCRIPTIONS          │
│                                                          │
│ Internal-Courier 10 Bld       7L-Courier 12 20p Bld      │
│ Internal-Courier 10 Med       7L-Courier 12 20p Med      │
│ Internal-Courier 16 Bld       7L-Courier 24 10p Bld      │
│ Internal-Courier 16 Med       7L-Courier 24 10p Med      │
│ Internal-Courier 20 Bld       7L-Courier 6 20p Bld       │
│ Internal-Courier 20 Med       7L-Courier 6 20p Med       │
│ Internal-Courier 5 Bld        7L-L.Gothic 12 12p Bld     │
│ Internal-Courier 5 Med        7L-L.Gothic 12 12p Ita     │
│ 7K-Courier 12 16p Bld         7L-L.Gothic 12 12p Ita Bld │
│ 7K-Courier 12 16p Med         7L-L.Gothic 12 12p Med     │
│ 7K-Courier 24 16p Bld         7L-L.Gothic 12 24p Bld     │
│ 7K-Courier 24 16p Med         7L-L.Gothic 12 24p Ita     │
│ 7L-Courier 12 10p Bld         7L-L.Gothic 12 24p Ita Bld │
│ 7L-Courier 12 10p Med         7L-L.Gothic 12 24p Med     │
│                                                          │
│                               Press PgDn for more        │
│                                                          │
│       Font name:  Internal-Courier 10 Bld                │
│ ─────────────────────────────────────────────────────── │
│ OFFLIST.DOC                                              │
│                                                          │
│ Esc-Exit                  F7-Search            F10-Continue │
└─────────────────────────────────────────────────────────┘
```

6. Select the font you want as the regular text font and press ⏎Enter.

You return to the Font Assignment screen. Several columns of information now appear. These columns are as follows:

- The Font name column shows the name of the font. These names can be rather cryptic, but usually indicate the name of the font, its size, and any enhancements. Thus, TmsRmn, 10 Bld, Itl is Times Roman 10 point Bold Italic. The font name can be up to 20 characters long.

- The Abbr column is the abbreviated font name, an even more cryptic version. The abbreviation can contain no more than four characters.

- Point is the point size of the font.

- Pitch is the number of characters per horizontal inch. A 10 pitch font has ten characters per horizontal inch of text. Proportionally-spaced fonts display a P in this field.

- The Comments column contains additional information about the font, such as whether it is a cartridge or soft font.

7. Press the cursor-movement keys to move the highlight bar to the Font 1 field. Select an additional font. Continue the selection process.

```
┌─────────────────────────────────────────────────────────────┐
│ ▌                                                            │
│              FONT ASSIGNMENTS              Pg. U-???         │
│                                                              │
│   Font file name: D:\QA\WRITE\HPDESKJ.FNT                   │
│                                                              │
│   ┌──────────────────────────┬─────┬─────┬─────┬──────────┐ │
│   │        Font name         │Abbr.│Point│Pitch│ Comments │ │
│   │Regular: Internal-Courier 10 Med│C10m│12│10│HP DeskJet Internal Fo│
│   │                          │     │     │     │          │ │
│   │Font 1: Internal-Courier 10 Bld│C10b│12│10│HP DeskJet Internal Fo│
│   │Font 2: 7L-L.Gothic 12 12p Med│L12m│12│12│HP DeskJet Cartridge:│
│   │Font 3: 7L-L.Gothic 12 24p Ita Bld│L12i│12│24│HP DeskJet Cartridge:│
│   │Font 4: 7L-L.Gothic 24 12p Ita│L24i│12│12│HP DeskJet Cartridge:│
│   │Font 5: 8D-Univers Cnd 12 Med│U12m│12│P│HP DeskJet Soft Font:8│
│   │Font 6: B-Prestige 12 Med│P12m│12│12│HP DeskJet Cartridge:│
│   │Font 7: B-Prestige 12 Ita│P12i│12│12│HP DeskJet Cartridge:│
│   │Font 8: D-TmsRmn 10 Ita Bld│T10ib│12│P│HP DeskJet Cartridge:│
│   └──────────────────────────┴─────┴─────┴─────┴──────────┘ │
│                                                              │
│ OFFLIST.DOC                                                  │
│                                                              │
│ Esc-Exit      F1-Help     F6-List fonts   F8-Make default   F10-Continue │
└─────────────────────────────────────────────────────────────┘
```

You see the completed Font Assignment screen.

8. Press F10 to save the font assignments and return to your document.

11 Applying Fonts

You apply fonts in the same manner as you apply text enhancements. Simply press ⟨Shift⟩-⟨F6⟩ to display the Text Enhancements and Fonts menu.

The available fonts are displayed.

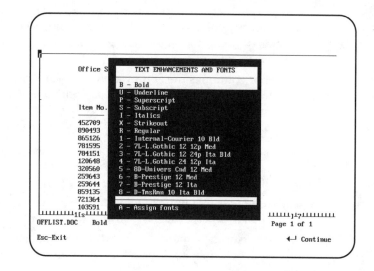

Select the font you want to use by highlighting it or pressing the number key assigned to the font. You can apply text enhancements to fonts. If your default font is Helvetica, for example, you can use the bold text enhancement to create Helvetica bold. Some combinations of fonts and enhancements are not suported by certain printers. Trial and error or careful examination of your printer's documentation will tell you what your printer can do.

12

Printing a Document

After you complete all text enhancements, spell checking, and editing, the next logical step is to print the document. You either print a hard copy of your document on paper or print an electronic copy to disk. If a printer is attached to your computer, you can print the document on paper. If a printer is not attached to your computer, you can print, or send, the document to disk instead.

This chapter teaches you how to set the print options, such as the page span you want to print, number of copies, and the printer you want to use. You also learn how to set up the physical dimensions of the printed page.

Q&A has the capacity to line up print jobs so that you do not have to retrieve each document individually for printing. You also can use Q&A's mail merge to transfer information from a database to a Write document so that you can create form letters and mailing labels.

Printing from the Type/Edit screen

Printing from the Write menu

Setting print options

Defining the page

Printing on paper

Printing to disk

Using the print queue

Creating form letters

12

Key Terms Used in This Chapter

Justification   The alignment of text so that the lines of type are flush with both the left and right margins.

Mail merge   The process of combining information contained in a database with documents contained in the Write module.

Print to disk   Sending a document to print on a disk instead of paper. Q&A generates the text in ASCII format, which most computers can read.

Understanding the Printing Process

When you are ready to make a printed copy of a document you have created with Write, you have several options. One option is to print the document as soon as you have entered it—without leaving Type/Edit mode. Plain and simple reports are easy to print with this option. If you require more elaborate printouts, Q&A provides the Print Options settings. With these settings, you indicate your printer and paper type, how you want the document spaced, and a number of other options. Use the Print Options selection from the Write menu to specify these settings. Then use the Define Page options to describe to the software the physical dimensions of the paper on which the document will be printed.

To print a document, you must install your printer using the Utilities module of Q&A. Your Q&A Instruction Manual contains installation instructions. Your printer should be turned on and ready to print.

Printing from the Type/Edit Screen

If you just finished typing a document, you can order printing without leaving the Edit mode. Just press ⌨F2 to begin the printing process. This key and its function are listed on the key assignment line at the bottom of the screen. The Print Options screen, which is discussed later in this chapter, is displayed. You can bypass this menu by pressing ⌨F10.

You can print any portion of a document quickly without displaying the Print Options screen. Press Ctrl-F2 and then highlight the block to be printed using the cursor-movement keys. Then press F10. The block is printed immediately.

You can press Esc to cancel the print operation. Q&A returns you to the Type/Edit screen. Printing stops if you press F2, and the Print Options screen is displayed again. You then can modify the settings and press F10. If your printer has a buffer that stores input from your computer, however, printing does not stop immediately when you press F2. If the buffer is large, you may want to turn off the printer and reset the top of the form when you cancel printing to avoid printing large amounts of unwanted text.

Printing from the Write Menu

To print a document from the Write menu, the document must be on the editing screen. Return to the Write menu, select **P**rint, and press F10. Before you can print a file that you are not working on currently, you must load the file into memory by selecting the **G**et option from the Write menu.

Q&A displays the name of the most recently used file as the default in the document line. If you cannot remember the name of the file you want to print, press the space bar to clear the default name and press ↵Enter. A list of available document files is displayed.

Highlight the file you want to print and press ↵Enter. The file is displayed on the Type/Edit screen. You then can press F2 to print.

Determining Print Options

The Print Options menu enables you to select the line spacing, justification, and number of columns, as well as other settings, for a document. Although you probably will use the default settings for most of these options, it is a good idea to check the settings each time you print a document.

Display the Print
Options menu by
selecting **P**rint
from the Write
menu or by
pressing $\boxed{F2}$ from
within the
document.

```
                              PRINT OPTIONS

       From page.............:   1           To page...........:  1
       Number of copies......:   1           Print offset........:  0
       Line spacing..........: Single  Double     Envelope
       Justify...............:  Yes  No
       Print to..............: PtrA  PtrB   PtrC   PtrD   PtrE    DISK
       Type of paper feed....: Manual  Continuous  Bin1  Bin2   Bin3   Lhd
       Number of columns.....:  1   2    3    4    5    6    7    8
       Printer control codes.:
       Name of Merge File....:
       ───────────────────────────────────────────────────────────────
                      Print Options for BADDEBIT.110
       Reminder:  Make sure fonts are installed in the printer before printing.
       Esc-Cancel   F1-Info   Ctrl F6-Def Pg   F9-Save changes & go back  F10-Continue
```

Use this screen to indicate the following printing specifications to Q&A:

- Use the From page, To page option to specify which pages of the document you want to print. You can print an entire document or only a portion of it.

- Use the Number of copies option to specify the number of copies you want to print, up to 99,999 copies.

- Use the Print offset option to position the printed material on the page. For example, you may need to three-hole punch a copy of the letter to be filed in a ring binder. To allow extra room for the holes, specify how many characters you need for the left margin. If you type 10 in this field, the body of the letter moves to the right 10 spaces.

- Use the Line spacing option to change the line spacing of a document. Documents can be single- or double-spaced. You also can choose an option for envelope printing. When selecting Envelope, the first left block address of the letter is printed on an envelope.

- Use the Justify option to align text so that the right margin is even, not jagged. Extra spaces are inserted in the line so that it begins in the first space on the left margin and ends in the last space on the right margin.

- Use the Print to option to indicate where you want the document printed. You can select one of five printers (PtrA, PtrB, PtrC, PtrD, or PtrE) or disk. When printing to disk, the document is translated into ASCII, which is a standard code that most computers can read.

- Use Page Preview to preview a document as it will appear when printed.

- Use the Type of paper feed option to choose the type of paper you want to use to print the document. Paper can be manual feed (one sheet at a time manually inserted into the printer), continuous (a stack of paper in a continuous form, with individual pages separated by perforation), Bin 1-3 (special bins or feeders that may be attached to your printer), or Lhd (the first sheet taken from Bin1, with all following sheets taken from Bin2).

- Use the Number of columns option to request up to eight printed columns on a sheet of paper. Use this setting if you do not have much data to print and want more than one column of information printed.

- Use the Printer control codes option to indicate any special control codes that must be sent to the printer to activate specific features. Most of these codes are included in the print driver when you install your printers, but this option is available if it is needed for special effects. You can leave this field blank.

- Use the Name of Merge File option to indicate which database should be combined with the document for mail merge. You can leave this field blank.

Setting Print Options

To set the print options, follow these steps:

1. In the From Page and To Page fields, enter the beginning and ending page of the range that you want to print.

   The Q&A default is to print the entire document (From Page 1 and To Page END). To print a single page of a longer document, press Tab or the cursor-movement keys to move between the fields. Entering 1 in the From Page field and 1 in the To Page field, for example, prints only page one of a document.

2. Press ⌨Tab⇅ or ↵Enter to move to the Number of Copies field. Type the number of copies you want printed. You can print up to 99999 copies of a document.

   For this example, the Number of Copies field is set to **1**.

3. Press ⌨Tab⇅ to move to the Print Offset field. Enter the number of spaces to the right where the document will be positioned on the page. If you want the document to print normally, enter **0**.

   For this example, the Print Offset is set to **0**.

12

4. Press [Tab⇲] or [↵Enter] to move to the Line Spacing field. Enter whether you want the document single- or double-spaced or printed on an envelope.

   For this example, the Line Spacing is set to **Single**.

5. Press [Tab⇲] or [↵Enter] to move to the Justify field. Select whether you want justifications turned on in the Justification field.

   For this example, Justification is set to **Yes**.

6. Press [Tab⇲] or [↵Enter] to move to the Print To field. Highlight the printer you are using. Generally, you set this field to PtrA.

   For this example, **PtrA** is the printer.

7. Press [Tab⇲] or [↵Enter] to move to the Page preview field. Select whether you want to preview your work.

   For this example, **No** is selected.

8. Press [Tab⇲] or [↵Enter] to move to the Type of paper feed field. Select the type of paper you are using with your printer.

   For this example, **Continuous** is selected.

9. Press [Tab⇲] or [↵Enter] to move to the Number of Columns field. Enter the number of columns that you want your document to print.

   In this example, the Number of Columns selected is **1**.

10. Press [Tab⇲] or [↵Enter] to move to the Printer control codes. Printer control codes are special codes that are sent to the printer to enable it to print bold, underline, or other type styles. In most cases, you will not use these codes. You should use the font enhancements (discussed in Chapter 11) to create special effects rather than using the control codes.

11. You use the Name of merge file field to enter the name of the database file you are using to merge print your document. For this example, the field should be blank.

```
                        PRINT OPTIONS

    From page...........:   1            To page............:   1

    Number of copies.....:   1            Print offset.......:   0

    Line spacing.........: █Single◄  Double    Envelope

    Justify..............:   Yes  ►No◄

    █Print to...........:  ►PtrA◄  PtrB   PtrC   PtrD   PtrE   DISK

    Type of paper feed...:   Manual  ►Continuous◄  Bin1   Bin2   Bin3   Lhd

    Number of columns....:  █1█   2    3    4    5    6    7    8

    Printer control codes.:

    Name of Merge File....:
  _____
                    Print Options for BADDEBIT.110
  HP LaserJet (Portrait) »» LPT1
  Esc-Cancel    F1-Info    Ctrl F6-Def Pg    F9-Save changes & go back    F10-Continue
```

For the example, your selections should look like this screen. Your screen may differ some if you are not using PtrA or Continuous paper.

12

Determining Define Page Options

The second step in the printing process is to describe the dimensions of the paper on which you want to print the document. These dimensions are determined using Define Page. You can access the Define Page menu from the Print Options screen by pressing the Ctrl - F6 key combination that you see on the key assignment line.

```
                        DEFINE PAGE


    █Left margin: █ 10            Right margin : 68

    Top margin : 6               Bottom margin: 6

    Page width : 78              Page length  : 66

    Characters per inch..........:  ►10◄   12    15    17

    Begin header/footer on page #...:   1

    Begin page numbering with page #:   1

  _____
                    Page Options for BADDEBIT.110

  Esc-Cancel       F1-Info      F2-Print Options            F10-Continue
```

Press Ctrl - F6; the Define Page Options screen appears.

12

The settings displayed in the preceding figure are the standard settings used by Q&A for most letters. The settings allow for approximately a one-inch margin on both sides of the document and a one-inch margin on the top and bottom of the document.

Characteristics that you select here describe the physical dimensions of the paper on which you will print your document. You can define dimensions in two ways: by specifying the number of character spaces or by using inches. Most screens are preset to follow the number of characters. For most print-ings, this setting is sufficient. If you use proportional fonts for your docu-ments, however, you need to change these settings to inches instead of number of characters. When you specify inch dimensions, express the size of the sheet of paper in decimals, not fractions. For instance, to specify an 8 1/2-inch sheet of paper, enter **8.5"**.

The following options are available on the Define Page menu:

- Use the Left/Right Margin option to determine the amount of blank space to the left and right of the paper. Margins help increase the readability of the document and allow extra blank space before the edge of the sheet.

- Use the Top/Bottom Margin option to determine the blank space at the top and bottom of the paper. These margins are used for headers and footers and are usually expressed in lines per inch. An average 11-inch sheet will print six lines per inch, which equals 66 lines per sheet. To achieve a top and bottom margin of one inch, both settings should be 6 (six lines equal one inch).

- Use the Page Width/Length option to describe the dimensions of the paper. Width should be between 78 and 85 characters if you are using the standard of 10 characters per inch. Page length should be 66, indicating 6 lines per inch for 11 inches of length (6 X 11 = 66).

- Use the Characters Per Inch option to determine the width of the character when printed. Standard width is 10 characters per inch and allows a maximum of 85 characters per line (10 X 8.5" width = 85). Frequently, a selection of 12 characters per inch is used. This setting allows for a maximum of 102 characters per line (12 X 8.5" = 102). The size of the type is a little smaller than 10 characters per inch. Use 15 characters per inch for even smaller type size. This setting allows for 127 characters per line. The smallest and most condensed type size is 17 characters per inch, which allows up to 144 characters per line (17 X 8.5" = 144).

12

- Use the Begin Header/Footer on Page # option to tell Q&A on which page you want the first header or footer to appear. Headers print at the top of each page, and footers print at the bottom of each page. You may not want the header or footer to print on the first page—especially if you are printing a multiple-page letter. Set this option to **2** to begin printing headers and footers on the second page.

- Use the Begin Page Numbering With Page # option to determine the first page number that is printed if you requested page numbers (in the header or footer). If you start your headers on page 2, you may also want to begin numbering on 2 by setting this option to 2.

Printing on Paper

You can print a document on paper if you have a printer connected to the computer and have installed the printer in Q&A. You must specify which printer you are using before you can send any data to the printer. If you have more than one printer installed, you can redirect the output to a different printer port. Q&A displays the name of the printer that is currently installed.

```
                        James T. Ryan
                    1234 East South Avenue
                    San Francisco, CA. 94090




    Dear Sirs:

    You have recently charged my checking account with the
    following incorrect check charges.  Evidently, when you
    entered the checks in your computer, my account was
    debited incorrect amounts.  The amounts are as shown
    below:

    Check#| Payee               | Amount  | Debit
    ======+=====================+=========+========
    1095  | Grand Central Foods | $56.73  | $65.73
    1096  | Great Lakes Electric| $25.25  | $152.52

    Please make these corrections to my account so they
    appear on my statement for the 5th of next month.

    Sincerely,

    Your Name
```

This document was printed on a dot matrix printer.

12

This document
was printed on a
laser printer.

```
                              James T. Ryan
                           1234 East South Avenue
                           San Francisco, CA. 94090




Dear Sirs:

You have recently charged my checking account with the following incorrect check
charges.  Evidently, when you entered the checks in your computer, my account was
debited incorrect amounts.  The amounts are as shown below:

Check#| Payee                    |  Amount  |  Debit
======+==========================+==========+=========
1095  | Grand Central Foods      |  $56.73  |  $65.73
1096  | Great Lakes Electric     |  $25.25  |  $152.52

Please make these corrections to my account so they appear on my statement for the 5th
of next month.

Sincerely,

Your Name
```

When you are ready to print, follow these steps:

1. Make sure that the settings shown on the Define Page screen and the Print Options screen are correct for the document you want to print.

2. From the Print Options screen, press `F10` to print the document.

   A small box appears, which shows you the progress of printing as the computer goes through the document one line at a time and sends it to the printer. After the printing is completed, you are returned to your document.

Printing To Disk

You can choose to print a document to a disk rather than on paper. Suppose, for example, that you do not have a printer connected to your computer or that you want to print a document on another computer that does not have Q&A. A standard ASCII file is created. The file includes the same margins and page breaks as the Q&A file, and headers and footers are preserved.

To print a document to disk, follow these steps:

1. Make sure that the settings on the Define Page screen are correct for the document you want to print. Use the settings that you would select for your own printer.

2. Press F2 or select Print Options from the Write menu to access the Print Options screen.

3. If you want to print to a floppy disk, make sure that the disk is in the disk drive.

```
                        PRINT OPTIONS

From page............:   1          To page............:  1
Number of copies.....:   1          Print offset........:  0
Line spacing.........:  Single◀  Double    Envelope
Justify..............:  Yes  No◀
Print to.............:  PtrA  PtrB  PtrC  PtrD  PtrE  DISK◀
Type of paper feed...:  Manual  Continuous◀  Bin1  Bin2  Bin3  Lhd
Number of columns....:  1◀  2   3   4   5   6   7   8
Printer control codes.:
Name of Merge File...:
_____
                 Print Options for BADDEBIT.110
Print plain text to disk file.
Esc-Cancel   F1-Info   Ctrl F6-Def Pg   F9-Save changes & go back   F10-Continue
```

Select **DISK** as the destination for the Print To option.

4. Press F10 to continue.

   The Disk Print menu appears.

```
                    DISK PRINT MENU

            I - IBM ASCII format
            M - Macintosh ASCII format

_____
            Print Options for BADDEBIT.110
Esc-Cancel                                    ↵ Continue
```

The Disk Print menu asks whether you want to print based on an IBM computer or an Apple Macintosh computer.

6. Select **I** to print the file on an IBM computer or **M** on a Macintosh computer.

   In this example, **I**-IBM ASCII format is selected.

7. Press ⏎Enter to continue.

A dialog box appears at the bottom of the screen and requests the name of the disk file in which you want to store the printed copy of the document.

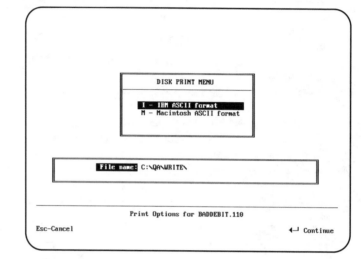

8. Make sure that the file name reflects the appropriate disk drive and directory.

If the file name is incorrect, press ◂Backspace until the name is deleted. Then type the correct file name, including the drive and directory, if necessary.

276

Make sure that you do not use the same file name as the original document file. Using the same file name can cause you to lose the original document. Selecting a different extension can eliminate this problem.

9. Press ⏎Enter to print the document to disk.

A small box is displayed to show you the progress of the print process. After printing to disk is completed, you are returned to the document.

Using the Print Queue

As you can see, printing documents is easy, and it only requires two keystrokes. To print a document, you simply retrieve the document and then press F2. This procedure works well when you print only one document at a time. If you are printing a series of documents, however, retrieving each document before printing can be a time-consuming process. You can use an easier procedure to print the documents at the same time without having to retrieve each document separately. You can use this method to print all the documents you have worked on in one day all at one time, such as at the end of the day. You can organize all the print jobs into one file, called a Queue document, that you can print later.

A Queue document contains nothing but the Queue command enclosed in asterisks and the names of the documents you want printed. Q&A retrieves the first document, sends it to the printer, then retrieves the next document listed and sends it to the printer. The program continues to work through the list, printing in the sequence that you request. Each document is printed as if it were individually retrieved and printed using F2. Headers and footers contained in any of the documents are printed as they were set up, each following its own format.

To create a Queue document to hold the Queue command, follow these steps:

1. From the Write menu, select Type/Edit.

2. Type the Queue command followed by the name of the document file you want to print first.

12

```
                           *Queue BADDEBIT.110*
```

For this example,
type *Queue
BADDEBIT.110*.

```
|||||||||1|||T|||||T||||T|||T▮||||||||4||||||||5||||||||6|||||||||7||||||||
Working Copy                          0 %   Line 1 of Page 1 of 1

Esc-Exit  F1-Info  F2-Print  Ctrl+F6-Define Pg  F7-Search  F8-Options  ↑F8-Save
```

If you want to print additional documents in this Queue document, add them
to the document on successive lines. Be sure to include the asterisk, queue
command, and the name of the document followed by another asterisk.

To print the Queue document, follow these steps:

1. Press F2 to access the Print Options menu.

2. Press F10 to begin printing.

   Your Queue document finds the document(s) you requested and
   sends them to the printer. After all documents in the Queue document are printed, you return to the working copy of the document.

3. Press ⇧Shift-F8 to save and name the document.

The Queue command prints a series of documents, each with its own page
numbers. When one document finishes printing, Q&A begins printing the next
document with page number 1. You can print the documents with continuous
page numbers. Suppose that you have three parts of one report in three
different files. The QUEUE command gives all documents in the queue
continuous page numbers. You follow the same procedure to use the QUEUE
command as you follow to use the Queue command.

Using Mail Merge

With Q&A's mail merge option, you can create form letters. You first create a Q&A File database that contains the information you want to merge into a document. (For information on how to create a database, see Chapter 2.) Create a Write document that contains the text of the form letter and the names of the fields in the database that contain the information you want to insert. You then print the document using the Print Options screen.

An example of a mail merge operation is a letter informing all clients of the new address of your business. The database for this example contains the names and addresses of clients in the following fields: First Name, Last Name, Address, City, State, and Zip.

To create a mail merge document, follow these steps:

1. From the Write menu, select Type/Edit to create a new document.

2. To enter the merge fields, type the names of the database fields that contain the information you want to merge.

   Make sure that you place an asterisk before and after the name of the field. Note that the field name you enter must match the field name in the database.

   For this example, type

   First Name *Last Name*
   Address
   City, *State*, *Zip*

   The asterisks tell Q&A that the information between them is a database field name and not document text. The asterisks do not print when the documents are merged.

3. Type the text of the document, inserting the merge field names as needed.

   You can use the same merge field name more than once.

12

You can, for
example, use the
First Name field
once in the inside
address and once
in the salutation.

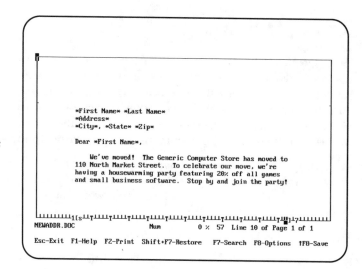

```
  *First Name* *Last Name*
  *Address*
  *City*, *State* *Zip*

  Dear *First Name*,

      We've moved!  The Generic Computer Store has moved to
  110 North Market Street.  To celebrate our move, we're
  having a housewarming party featuring 20% off all games
  and small business software.  Stop by and join the party!
```

NEWADDR.DOC   Num   0 % 57 Line 10 of Page 1 of 1

Esc-Exit F1-Help F2-Print Shift+F7-Restore   F7-Search F8-Options ↑F8-Save

Using Lists of Fields To Enter Field Names

You also can enter the names of merge fields in the merged document by
entering a list of fields. Although this method may take a little longer, it is
more accurate than relying on your memory to recall the exact field names.
Because accuracy of field names is vital for the merge to work, this method
can save trouble in the long run.

To enter a field name using a list, follow these steps:

1. Within the merge document, place the cursor where you want the
   field name inserted.

2. Press Alt-F7.

12

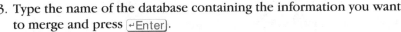

```
    Data file name: D:\QA\FILE\

    Dear *First Name*,

        We've moved!  The Generic Computer Store has moved to
    110 North Market Street.  To celebrate our move, we're
    having a housewarming party featuring 20% off all games
    and small business software.  Stop by and join the party!

└┴┴┴┴┴┴┴┴┴Ts┴┴T┴┴┴T┴┴┴T┴┴┴┴T┴┴┴T┴┴┴T┴┴┴T┴┴┴T┴T17┴┴┴┴┴┴
NEWADDR.DOC                 Num         0 % 57  Line 10 of Page 1 of 1

Esc-Exit                                        ← Continue
```

You are prompted for the database name you want to use.

3. Type the name of the database containing the information you want to merge and press ⏎Enter.

```
    ┌───────────────────┐
    │    FIELD NAMES    │
    ├───────────────────┤
    │ Address           │
    │ City              │
    *First Name* *Last Name*   First Name
    *Address*             Last Name
    *City*, *State* *Zip*   State
                          Zip
    Dear *First Name*,

        We've moved!  The Generic Computer Stor
    110 North Market Street.  To celebrate our
    having a housewarming party featuring 20% o
    and small business software.  Stop by and j
    └───────────────────┘

└┴┴┴┴┴┴┴┴┴Ts┴┴T┴┴┴T┴┴┴T┴┴┴┴T┴┴┴T┴┴T┴┴┴T┴┴┴T┴T
NEWADDR.DOC                 Num         0 % 57  Line 10 of Page 1 of 1

Esc-Exit        A-Z  ↑  ↓  PgUp  PgDn  Home  End        ← Continue
```

A list of fields in the selected database is displayed.

4. Press the cursor-movement keys to highlight the field name you want to insert.

   To scroll the list of field names, press ⬇ or PgDn.

5. Press ↵Enter.

   The selected field name enclosed in asterisks is inserted in the document.

Completing the Retrieve Spec and Printing Your Document

After you furnish the appropriate field names and select the database from which to retrieve the information, you can begin the printing process. Printing a mail merge is a two-step process. First you must specify how the document is to be printed using the Print Options screen. Then you must select the records you want merged into the document using the Retrieve Spec screen.

To begin the mail merge printing process, follow these steps:

1. Open the completed merge document.

2. Press F2 to go to the Print Options screen.

   Make sure that all settings on this screen are correct for your computer. If you used the list method of filling in the field names, notice that the Name of Merge File field contains a file name. Q&A automatically filled this field when you entered the name of the database in the dialog box. If you did not use the list of field names method to enter merge fields, you must type the name of the database.

You can press F8 to access a Sort Spec screen. Use this screen to sort your documents alphabetically or numerically.

```
First Name:
Last Name:
Address:
City:
State:
Zip:




ADDRESS.DTF                    Sort Spec              Page 1 of 1
Esc-Exit  F1-Help  F6-Expand  Alt+F8-List  ↑F8-Save  F9-Retrieve  F10-Continue
```

12

4. After all the Retrieve Spec screen values are correct, press F10.

```
NEWADDR.DOC  will be merged with
4     record(s) from ADDRESS

Make sure the printer has paper, and
is properly aligned before continuing.

Press ↵ to continue, or Esc to cancel.
```

Esc-Exit   F10-Continue

A message box is displayed and tells you how many forms were selected for printing.

5. Make sure that the printer is turned on and ready to print.

6. Press ↵Enter to indicate you want to begin the merge.

The forms selected for printing appear on-screen briefly before they are printed. After all selected forms are printed, you return to the merge document, which you can edit if you want.

Printing Mailing Labels

The same principles that you used in mail merge also apply to mailing labels. Mailing labels use field names enclosed in asterisks, and addresses are retrieved from a database in the File module and combined with the format and design of the label. To create mailing labels, you use a label document accessed from the Mailing Labels option on the Write menu.

To learn how to use mailing labels, you must have labels in your printer. Keep the box of labels handy because you need the dimension information contained on the box to select the correct label.

For this example, use the EMPLOYEE.DTF database that comes with the Q&A software. To begin this process, follow these steps:

1. From the Write menu, select Mailing Labels and press ⏎Enter.

12

A list of mailing labels that is already designed appears on-screen.

```
                        LIST OF MAILING LABELS

 Avery 5260 2 5/8" x 1" HP          Pin fed 4" x 1 15/16" - 1 up
 Avery 5260 2 5/8" x 1" HP II       Pin fed 4" x 1 7/16" - 1 up
 Avery 5261 4" x 1" HP              Pin fed 4" x 1 7/16" - 2 up
 Avery 5261 4" x 1" HP II           Pin fed 4" x 15/16" - 1 up
 Avery 5262 4" x 1 1/2" HP          Pin fed 4" x 2 15/16" - 1 up
 Avery 5262 4" x 1 1/2" HP II       Pin fed 5" x 15/16" - 1 up
 Avery 5351 1 X 2-3/4 2 Up          Q&A User Group Newsletter Label
 Pin fed 2 1/2" x 15/16" - 3 up     Shipping Label - DOW 4X2.5 2 Up
 Pin fed 3 1/2" x 1 7/16" - 1 up
 Pin fed 3 1/2" x 15/16" - 1 up
 Pin fed 3" x 15/16" - 4 up
 Pin fed 3.3" x 15/16" - 4 up
 Pin fed 4 1/2" x 3" - 1 up
 Pin fed 4" x  15/16" - 2 up


            Enter name: Avery 5260 2 5/8" x 1" HP
 _____

 Esc-Cancel  F1-Info  F3-Delete  F5-Copy  F7-Search  F8-Rename  F10-Continue
```

If you are using Avery labels, you can read the number on the box and match it with the list of label documents. For labels other than Avery that are sheet fed, use the dimensions that appear to the right of the Avery label number.

Pin fed (tractor fed) labels are the next group shown on this listing. These labels attach to pins in your printer for feeding. Use the dimensions shown to determine which label document you will use.

2. Select the correct label document for your labels, based on the size and type of your label.

3. Press F10 to continue.

```
 ▐
 ▌
 *First name* *Last name*
 *Address*
 *City*, *State* *Zip*




 ╚s⊥⊥⊺⊥⊥⊥⊥₁⊥⊥⊥⊺⊥⊥⊥₂⊥⊥⊥⊺⊥⊥⊥3⊥⊥⊥⊺₁⊥┘
 Avery 5161 1              Num          0 %  1   Line 2 of Page 1 of 1

 Esc-Exit   F2-Print   Ctrl+F6-Def label   Alt+F7-List fields    F10-Save & Print
```

12

The label document appears.

```
 *First name* *Last name*
 *Address*
 *City*, *State* *Zip*




 ⊥⊥[⊥⊺⊥₁⊥⊥⊥⊥⊺⊥₂⊥⊥⊥⊥⊺⊥3⊥⊥⊥⊥ ⊥⊥
 Pin fed 3 1/                  0 %   Line 4 of Page 1 of 1

 Esc-Exit   F2-Print   Ctrl F6-Def label   Alt F7-List fields   F10-Save & Print
```

The label document resembles the size of your label, but it is distorted slightly. The document already contains field names.

Using Define Label To Determine Label Size

When the field names match your database and the size of the label is correct, you are ready to start printing. At certain times, however, the file names may not match or the label size may be incorrect. Custom printed label sizes vary and may require special dimensions.

To make changes to the mailing labels, follow these steps:

1. Press Ctrl-F6 to access the Define Label screen.

Actual dimensions of the label are shown in a graphic representation.

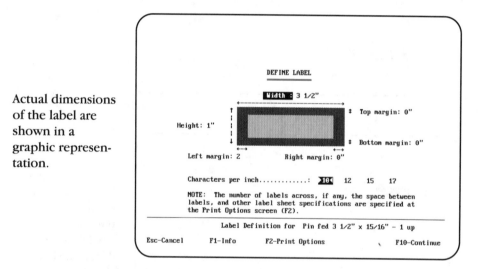

Press Tab to move through the fields on this screen. All settings on the Define Label screen are expressed in inches, except for the left margin; the left margin is expressed in characters. You can change characters per inch by using the last setting at the bottom of the screen. You can print labels with 10, 12, 15, or 17 characters per inch. For labels containing much information such as long names, you may want to use either the 15- or 17-character-per-inch setting.

2. Change any of these settings you feel necessary.

3. Press F2 to activate the Print Options screen.

Mailing Label Print Options

The Mailing Label Print Options screen sends critical information to your computer and printer regarding the location of the printer, specifications of the paper and size of the labels.

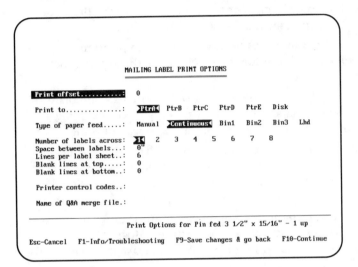

```
                  MAILING LABEL PRINT OPTIONS

 Print offset..........:   0

 Print to..............:   PtrA  PtrB  PtrC  PtrD  PtrE  Disk

 Type of paper feed.....:  Manual  Continuous  Bin1  Bin2  Bin3  Lhd

 Number of labels across:  1   2   3   4   5   6   7   8
 Space between labels...:  0"
 Lines per label sheet..:  6
 Blank lines at top.....:  0
 Blank lines at bottom..:  0

 Printer control codes..:

 Name of Q&A merge file.:

 ─────────────────────────────────────────────────────────────
               Print Options for Pin fed 3 1/2" x 15/16" - 1 up

 Esc-Cancel   F1-Info/Troubleshooting   F9-Save changes & go back   F10-Continue
```

The screen also contains space for printer control codes and the name of the merge file.

Most of these settings will be correct, based on the type and dimensions of the label that you selected from the list of labels. If you use a customized label, however, you need to change some of these settings.

Press F2 to access the Mailing Label Print Options screen. You can modify the following settings on this screen:

- **Print Offset** moves the entire body of the labels to the right based on the number of characters that you enter in this field.

- **Print To** indicates the location of your printer. Most printers are PtrA (Printer A).

- **Type of Paper Feed** indicates the type of paper that you use for your labels. Manual stops after each sheet printed; Continuous prints sheets consecutively; Bin1-3 indicates special bin feeders; and Lhd pulls a sheet from Bin1 and the remainder from Bin2.

- **Number of Labels Across** indicates the number of rows of labels contained on your sheet of labels. Most labels are one across, but some may be two, four, or more.

- **Space Between Labels** adjusts the spacing of labels. Most labels on sheets are flush with one another and contain no blank space between labels. Set this field to 0 if you want labels flush with each other. For some pin fed labels, you may need to adjust this setting.

- **Lines Per Label Sheet** indicates how many lines can print on the label. Up to six lines can print for each inch of length, so a one-inch label can contain up to six lines of type.

- **Blank Lines at Top** indicates the number of lines that are left blank at the top of your sheet of labels. Change this setting if you are using a sheet fed type of label where the top 1/4" or 1/2" does not print.

- **Blank Lines at Bottom** indicates the number of lines that are left blank at the bottom of your sheet of labels. Change this setting if there is blank space at the bottom of the sheet of labels that will not contain printing.

- **Printer Control Codes** indicates any special control codes that must be sent to your printer to activate special features. Most of these codes are already included in your print driver. You can leave this field blank if you do not need it.

- **Name of Q&A Merge File** indicates which database is to be used for the address information.

Change any of the settings necessary to reflect your label (if you are using a commercial, standard label, these settings should be correct as shown). Press F10 to continue.

For this example, move the cursor to the Name of Q&A Merge File field and type C:\QA\EMPLOYEE, which is the database that will provide the address information. Press F10 to continue.

Completing the Retrieve Spec

After all settings are correct, then the labels are ready to print. The last step is to indicate which forms are to be used to generate the label. Do you want all forms? Do you want a specific form? You specify these essential settings on the Retrieve Spec.

To access the Retrieve Spec screen, press F2 once the label is correct. Change any options you want on the Print Options screen and press F10. The Retrieve Spec screen is displayed.

288

To print a mailing label, follow these steps:

1. Complete the Retrieve Spec screen so that only the desired forms will be merged. If you want all forms merged, leave the screen blank.

2. Press `F10`.

   A message box is displayed, which tells you how many forms will be merged.

From the Retrieve Spec screen, press `F1` to view the help screen and see basic retrieval information.

```
Pin fed 3 1/ will be merged with
1     form(s) from EMPLOYEE

Make sure the printer has paper, and
is properly aligned before continuing.

Press ←┘ to continue, or Esc to cancel.
```

The program reminds you to check your printer for paper and asks whether you want to continue the process.

3. Press `←Enter` to continue.

   Q&A finds the form, which flashes quickly on your screen, and combines the information in the form with your label document. Next, the label is printed.

   After the printing is complete, you are returned to the label document.

4. Press `⇧Shift`-`F8` to save your label document.

   You can print one label or multiple labels. You can use this feature to generate mailing labels for advertising or bulk mail processing.

5. Press `Esc` until you return to the Q&A Main menu.

Using the Q&A Intelligent Assistant

Q&A Write, File, and Report are powerful, easy-to-use tools. If you use these three modules alone, you will not be taking advantage of two features that make Q&A far more powerful and easier to use than other programs with integrated word processors and database managers.

The Intelligent Assistant (also called the IA) uses sophisticated artificial-intelligence technology to allow you to communicate with the program with plain-English commands rather than menus. You can use English phrases and sentences to query a database, produce columnar or cross tab reports, edit records, and add new records. You can even use plain-English sentences to perform mathematical calculations and ask for the date and time.

The Query Guide helps you build query statements for the Intelligent Assistant, by prompting you to choose menu items and fill in data entry prompts. The Query Guide is simpler to use than the Intelligent Assistant, because you do not have to teach it terms you use when performing data retrievals, as you do with the IA. The Query Guide is limited to Q&A's built-in retrieval vocabulary. But even so, it can help you manage your data in extremely sophisticated ways.

13

Using the Query Guide is an excellent way to become familiar with the Intelligent Assistant, because it teaches you to fill in correctly formatted and worded IA queries.

Key Terms Used in This Chapter	
Query Guide	A system of menus that assist you at filling out a request for the Intelligent Assistant.
Alternate field names	Alternate words and phrases you use to refer to specific fields.
Vocabulary	Contains verbs you use to specify operations for displaying, sorting, and searching.

Defining the Intelligent Assistant

The Intelligent Assistant is a language processor or interpreter that has a built-in vocabulary of about 600 words. You can teach the IA new words, and the IA can prompt you to teach it new words it finds in your database. Using the Intelligent Assistant is similar to asking a human assistant to locate, organize, change, analyze, or report information. If, for example, you had a file of employees and wanted to list the employees who live in Boston, you might ask the IA to **Display the Boston forms**.

To answer your requests, the IA depends on built-in knowledge and on information it learns from your databases. Before you teach the IA about a database, it already knows the following items:

- The time of day
- The current date
- How to conduct mathematical calculations
- A vocabulary of about 600 words

After you teach the IA about your database, it also knows the following items:

- Database field names
- Field contents and data types
- Field descriptions (which fields contain locations, for example)
- Relationships between fields (that the first-name and last-name fields combine to form a complete name, for example)

- Synonyms for field names and contents
- Additional vocabulary words that you teach it

Defining the Query Guide

The Query Guide is a system of menus that assists you at every step of filling out a request on the IA's query entry screen. (You can think of the Query Guide as training wheels for the IA.)

In the beginning, you may find it quicker to use the Query Guide, because you won't have to teach it about search terms or phrases. After you have used both modules, you may find yourself using the Intelligent Assistant to perform report and retrieval functions with which you are familiar. When you are not quite sure of the phrasing of a request, the Query Guide provides help by listing your options at each step.

Guidelines for Using the Intelligent Assistant

Whether you are just beginning to experiment with the IA or use it regularly for your applications, the following guidelines will help you avoid problems:

- Keep a current backup copy of your database file (DTF). If your computer is turned off or accidentally loses power while you are using the IA, you may not be able to access your database file.
- Pay close attention to the Intelligent Assistant's prompts. After you enter a request, if the prompts indicate that the IA is unable to complete the task, do not proceed with the operation.
- Leave the Intelligent Assistant by pressing Esc from the IA menu to return to the Q&A Main menu.

Teaching the Query Guide

Setting up the Query Guide is easier than setting up the Intelligent Assistant. The first time you use the QG, Q&A automatically learns about the field names in your file. You need to tell the QG only which text and key fields, if any, you will be using to search for data.

To teach the Query Guide about the database you want to search, follow these steps:

   1. At the Q&A Main Menu, choose Assistant.

13

The Assistant
menu is
displayed.

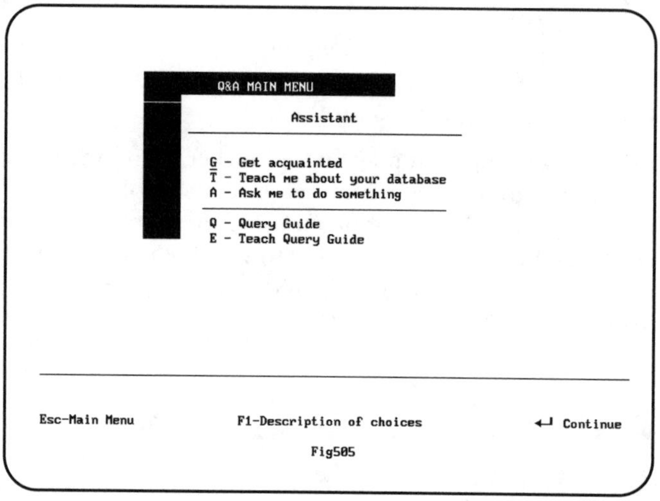

```
                    ┌─────────────────────┐
                    │    Q&A MAIN MENU     │
                    └─────────────────────┘
                          Assistant
                    ─────────────────────────────

                    G - Get acquainted
                    T - Teach me about your database
                    A - Ask me to do something
                    ─────────────────────────────
                    Q - Query Guide
                    E - Teach Query Guide
```

   Esc-Main Menu   F1-Description of choices   ↵ Continue

                              Fig505

   2. Choose Teach Query Guide.

      Q&A asks for the name of a database. Type a name or press ⏎Enter to select from a list.

      If you have never used the Query Guide with your database, and you choose Query Guide, Q&A asks whether you want to teach the Query Guide to recognize field names and values from your database. Press Y to start the learning process, or N to proceed and use the Query Guide without teaching it about field names and values.

   3. Q&A displays a copy of your database form in the Query Guide Teach screen and enters the letter Q in each text or keyword field.

```
┌─────────────────────────────────────────────────────────┐
│ Last name: Q              First name:                     │
│ Address:                                                  │
│ City: Q                   State: Q      Zip: Q            │
│                                                           │
│ Sex: Q    Alma Mater: Q                                   │
│ Hobbies: Q                                                │
│                                                           │
│                                                           │
│ Hired date:           Department: Q     Position: Q       │
│ Classification:       Manager: Q                          │
│                                                           │
│ R  Type "Q" in each text or keyword field that you wish to index │
│ R  for use by the Query Guide.  For example, if you wish to have │
│    access to a scrollable list of cities in your database while in │
│    the Query Guide, type a "Q" in the "City" field.       │
│                                                           │
│ E  SUGGESTION: Start by pressing F5 to mark all fields indexable by the │
│ S  query guide with "Q"s.  Then, remove the "Q"s from those fields that │
│ N  you do not wish to index.  To unteach the database, remove all Q's. │
│ P                                                         │
│   ────────────────────────────────────────────────────   │
│ EMPLOYEE.DTF           Query Guide Teach        Page 1 of 1 │
│                                                           │
│ Esc-Exit       F3-Clear spec      F5-Select all    F10-Continue │
│                      FIG11-2                              │
└─────────────────────────────────────────────────────────┘
```

The Query Guide
Teach screen is
displayed

13

Remember, you cannot teach the QG about numerical or date fields.
This is a prudent feature of Q&A's design, because there may be
many different dates and numbers in such fields, and it makes little
sense to specify data by searching through hundreds of numbers or
dates with the cursor.

4. Move the cursor to each text or keyword field that you will use with
   the QG, and type a Q. To clear all fields, press F3.

   If you are not sure which fields you will use, press F5 to enter a Q
   into every text and keyword field. You can later redisplay this screen
   and remove unneeded items.

5. Press F10 to exit the Query Guide Teach screen. Q&A displays the
   first Query Guide menu.

You can now use the Query Guide to fill out an Intelligent Assistant task
statement. While you work with the Query Guide, you can back up to a
previous screen at any point by pressing Esc. Q&A erases the most recently
added phrase from the statement in the task box. Press Esc again and Q&A
backs up another screen and erases the next element from the task statement.
Later in this chapter, you learn how to enter a complete QG query.

Querying a Database

Suppose that you want to find out how many employees live in the city of
Boston. You can use the Intelligent Assistant to complete the search. Begin by
selecting the IA from the Q&A Main menu. When the Assistant menu is displayed, choose the Ask me to do something option. When Q&A asks you to
indicate the file containing the data you want to search, type the file name.
The request window appears, and you can type a simple sentence, such as
Display the Boston forms.

The IA screen
with a query
entered.

```
Display the Boston forms_




        Type your request in English in the box above, then press ←.

        Examples:

        "List the average salary and average bonus from the records
         on which the sex is male and the department is sales."

        "Get the records of the Administration employees, sorted by city."


                    Press F1 for more information.


EMPLOYEE.DTF

Esc-Exit      F1-Help      F6-See words      F8-Teach word      ← Continue
                              FIG11-4
```

When you press ←Enter, the Intelligent Assistant analyzes your sentence. A
simple sentence such as "Display the Boston forms" is easy for the Intelligent
Assistant to understand because the sentence contains words that come from
the IA's built-in vocabulary or are defined in your database. In addition, the IA
can process the request because the IA understands the plural of *form* and
makes assumptions about your request—assumptions that are based on
knowledge of your database and databases in general. After successfully
analyzing the sentence, the Intelligent Assistant displays a request to confirm a
query prompt before proceeding.

13

```
┌──────────────────────────────────────────────────────┐
│  ┌──────────────────────────────────────────────┐     │
│  │DISPLAY THE BOSTON FORMS                        │     │
│  │                                                │     │
│  └──────────────────────────────────────────────┘     │
│  ┌──────────────────────────────────────────────┐     │
│  │         Shall I do the following?             │     │
│  │                                                │     │
│  │      Select and show the records on which      │     │
│  │         the City is BOSTON.                    │     │
│  │                                                │     │
│  │     _Yes - Continue     No - Cancel request    │     │
│  └──────────────────────────────────────────────┘     │
│                                                        │
│                                                        │
│  ─────────────────────────────────────────────        │
│  EMPLOYEE.DTF                                          │
│                                                        │
│  Esc-Cancel                          ↵ Continue        │
│                    FIG11-05                            │
└──────────────────────────────────────────────────────┘
```

IA requests you to confirm a query.

13

Notice that the prompt tells you that the Intelligent Assistant has analyzed your sentence and gives you an opportunity to cancel the request if you find the analysis wrong. In the example, however, the Intelligent Assistant has analyzed the sentence correctly; you want the IA to select and view the forms on which the city field entry is Boston. By pressing ↵Enter, you direct the Intelligent Assistant to display employees who live in Boston. Because Boston is a value in only one field, the IA assumes that you want the search to be conducted on that field. The IA displays the same initial form that is displayed when you manually request the Boston employees by using the Search function in the File module. After the Intelligent Assistant displays the first record that meets the Boston Employee criterion, you can press F10 (Continue) to display other records for Boston employees.

When you have reviewed all records that meet the criterion, you can display the records again or press Esc to return to the IA. When the Intelligent Assistant screen is displayed, you can enter other questions for sorting or searching your database. One of the Intelligent Assistant's most sophisticated features is the capacity to modify the database. You can, for example, ask the IA to change the telephone number on one of your forms, as follows:

Change Blackson's telephone number to "363-886-3980"

After you press ⏎Enter, the Intelligent Assistant analyzes your request, asks you to confirm its interpretation, and searches the forms in the database for the specified record. When the IA displays the forms you want to change, you press ⇧Shift-F10 to change the data and save the modifications.

13 | Using the Query Guide

Using the Query Guide is very similar to using the Intelligent Assistant, except that the Query Guide builds a correctly formatted request statement for you. At the Main menu, select Assistant, and press Q at the Assistant menu to run the Query Guide. The last option on the screen—Teach Query guide—sets up the Query Guide so that it can display lists of text or keyword data from your database as suggested selections for completing your query guide statements. This option is discussed later in this chapter.

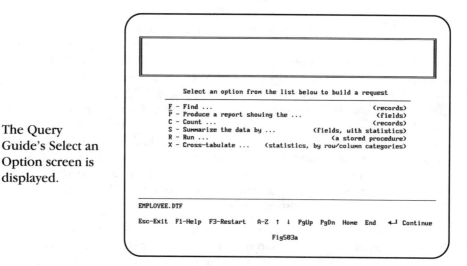

The Query Guide's Select an Option screen is displayed.

```
                 Select an option from the list below to build a request

          F - Find ...                                           (records)
          P - Produce a report showing the ...                    (fields)
          C - Count ...                                          (records)
          S - Summarize the data by ...            (fields, with statistics)
          R - Run ...                                (a stored procedure)
          X - Cross-tabulate ...    (statistics, by row/column categories)




        EMPLOYEE.DTF

        Esc-Exit  F1-Help  F3-Restart   A-Z ↑ ↓  PgUp  PgDn  Home  End   ↵ Continue

                                    Fig503a
```

Move the cursor to the first prompt F-Find...(records). Press ⏎Enter.

```
┌─────────────────────────────────────────────────────────────┐
│  ┌──────────────────────────────────────────────────────┐   │
│  │Find                                                  │   │
│  │                                                      │   │
│  │                                                      │   │
│  └──────────────────────────────────────────────────────┘   │
│                                                             │
│        Select an option from the list below to build a request │
│       ─────────────────────────────────────────────────     │
│        R - the records where ...                            │
│        A - ALL the records ...                              │
│        C - the current record.          (last record entered) │
│                                                             │
│                                                             │
│                                                             │
│       ─────────────────────────────────────────────         │
│   EMPLOYEE.DTF                                              │
│                                                             │
│   Esc-Backup  F1-Help  F3-Restart  A-Z ↑ ↓ PgUp PgDn Home End ← Continue │
│                         FIG11-07                            │
└─────────────────────────────────────────────────────────────┘
```

The Find...(records) screen is displayed.

Move the cursor to the prompt R–the records where.... Notice that as you proceed from one screen to the next, Q&A adds your latest query restriction to the Intelligent Assistant query box displayed in the upper part of the screen. In effect, you are using the Query Guide to operate the Intelligent Assistant, by entering pre-edited statements in the IA query screen.

Press ↵Enter. Q&A displays the Select a Field screen. In the list of field names, move the cursor to Zip by pressing Z. Press ↵Enter to display the Select a Constraint screen.

```
┌─────────────────────────────────────────────────────────────┐
│  ┌──────────────────────────────────────────────────────┐   │
│  │Find the records where                                │   │
│  │                                                      │   │
│  │                                                      │   │
│  └──────────────────────────────────────────────────────┘   │
│                                                             │
│                        Select a field                       │
│       ─────────────────────────────────────────────         │
│            Accrued Vacation                                 │
│            Address                                          │
│            Alma Mater                                       │
│            Bonus                                            │
│            Bonus factor                                     │
│            City                                             │
│            Classification                                   │
│            Department                                       │
│            Eligible                                         │
│            Evaluation                                       │
│            First name                              ↓        │
│       ─────────────────────────────────────────────         │
│   EMPLOYEE.DTF  24 FIELDS                                   │
│                                                             │
│   Esc-Backup  F1-Help  F3-Restart  A-Z ↑ ↓ PgUp PgDn Home End ← Continue │
│                         FIG11-08                            │
└─────────────────────────────────────────────────────────────┘
```

The Select a Field screen is displayed.

299

13

The Select a
Constraint screen
is displayed.

```
┌─────────────────────────────────────────────────────────────────┐
│ ╭───────────────────────────────────────────────────────────╮   │
│ │Find the records where Zip                                  │   │
│ │                                                            │   │
│ ╰───────────────────────────────────────────────────────────╯   │
│                                                                  │
│              Select a constraint on the text or keyword field    │
│         ─────────────────────────────────────────────────────    │
│         = - equals ...                      (a value in the database) │
│         B - begins with ...                 (a character sequence) │
│         E - ends with ...                   (a character sequence) │
│         C - contains ...                    (a character sequence) │
│         M - matches ...                     (a character sequence) │
│         S - matches the SOUNDEX pattern ...    (a letter sequence) │
│         A - appears alphabetically ...     (before/after/first/last) │
│         N - does not ...                       (one of the above) │
│         I - is ...                       (blank or correctly formatted) │
│                                                                  │
│         ─────────────────────────────────────────────────────    │
│   EMPLOYEE.DTF                                                    │
│                                                                  │
│   Esc-Backup  F1-Help  F3-Restart  A-Z  ↑  ↓  PgUp  PgDn  Home  End  ↵ Continue │
│                            FIG11-09                              │
└─────────────────────────────────────────────────────────────────┘
```

The Intelligent Assistant query box at the top of the display should now read
Find and show the records where Zip. Subsequent screens display the
following questions, which you can answer by pointing to one of the listed
field names, or by typing your responses in a blank screen:

Query Guide Screen Item	User Response
R—the records where...	Zip
A—appears alphabetically...	
A—after...	89999
A—and the...	Zip
A—appears alphabetically...	
B—before...	93001

At this point, the statement in the IA query box reads:

> Show me the records where Zip appears alphabetically
> after "89999" and Zip appears alphabetically before "93001"

Choose the following menu item to execute the query statement:

.—. [execute the command]

Q&A displays the first record in your database that meets the query constraints. At any time while building a Query Guide statement, you can go back one screen at a time by pressing [Esc], or erase the query and start over by pressing [F3] (Restart). As you back up through your query, Q&A erases the parts of the query statement that were entered at each screen.

The Query Guide is nearly as complex as Q&A itself, with thousands of pathways through the prompts and menus. Describing all the possible QG requests requires reviewing most of Q&A's features. Therefore, this book shows you just how to build a complex retrieval statement. Using the Employee database, you will construct and execute the following statement:

13

> Cross-tabulate the total and the count of values for Bonus by Position and Department from ALL the records.

1. At the Query Guide Select an Option screen, press [X] to choose Cross-tabulate... (statistics, by row/column categories).

```
┌────────────────────────────────────────────────────────────┐
│                                                             │
│  Cross-tabulate                                            │
│  ┌───────────────────────────────────────────────────────┐ │
│  │                                                       │ │
│  └───────────────────────────────────────────────────────┘ │
│                                                             │
│          Select statistic(s) for the field to be analyzed   │
│      ──────────────────────────────────────────────────     │
│      S - all statistics for ...              (field)       │
│      A - the average ...                                    │
│      T - the total ...                                      │
│      G - the maximum ...                                    │
│      L - the minimum ...                                    │
│      V - the variance ...                                   │
│      D - the standard deviation ...                         │
│      C - the count of values ...                            │
│                                                             │
│                                                             │
│   ─────────────────────────────────────────────────────     │
│  EMPLOYEE.DTF                                               │
│                                                             │
│  Esc-Backup  F1-Help  F3-Restart  A-Z ↑ ↓  PgUp  PgDn  Home  End  ↵ Continue │
│                        FIG11-011                            │
│                                                             │
└────────────────────────────────────────────────────────────┘
```

The Select Statistics screen is displayed.

Notice that Q&A has entered the first element of the search in the dialog box at the top of the screen: Cross-tabulate.

2. Press [T] to choose the total.... Q&A displays the Total screen.

13

```
┌─────────────────────────────────────────────────────────────┐
│ ┌───────────────────────────────────────────────────────┐   │
│ │Cross-tabulate the total                               │   │
│ │                                                       │   │
│ │                                                       │   │
│ └───────────────────────────────────────────────────────┘   │
│                                                             │
│            Select an option from the list below to build a request │
│          ──────────────────────────────────────────────── │
│          A - and the average ...                           │
│          G - and the maximum ...                           │
│          L - and the minimum ...                           │
│          V - and the variance ...                          │
│          D - and the standard deviation ...                │
│          C - and the count of values ...                   │
│          F - for ...                              (field)  │
│                                                             │
│                                                             │
│          ──────────────────────────────────────────────── │
│   EMPLOYEE.DTF                                             │
│                                                             │
│   Esc-Backup  F1-Help  F3-Restart  A-Z ↑ ↓  PgUp  PgDn  Home  End  ←┘ Continue │
│                       FIG11-012                           │
└─────────────────────────────────────────────────────────────┘
```

The Total screen
is displayed.

3. Choose C—and the count of values.... Q&A adds this element to the
   statement in the dialog box and displays the Count of Values screen.

```
┌─────────────────────────────────────────────────────────────┐
│ ┌───────────────────────────────────────────────────────┐   │
│ │Cross-tabulate the total and the count of values       │   │
│ │                                                       │   │
│ │                                                       │   │
│ └───────────────────────────────────────────────────────┘   │
│                                                             │
│            Select an option from the list below to build a request │
│          ──────────────────────────────────────────────── │
│          A - and the average ...                           │
│          G - and the maximum ...                           │
│          L - and the minimum ...                           │
│          V - and the variance ...                          │
│          D - and the standard deviation ...                │
│          F - for ...                              (field)  │
│                                                             │
│                                                             │
│                                                             │
│          ──────────────────────────────────────────────── │
│   EMPLOYEE.DTF                                             │
│                                                             │
│   Esc-Backup  F1-Help  F3-Restart  A-Z ↑ ↓  PgUp  PgDn  Home  End  ←┘ Continue │
│                       FIG11-013                           │
└─────────────────────────────────────────────────────────────┘
```

The Count of
Values screen is
displayed.

Because Q&A knows about the field names in your database, it
displays a list of the field names.

```
┌─────────────────────────────────────────────────────────┐
│                                                         │
│  ┌──────────────────────────────────────────────────┐  │
│  │Cross-tabulate the total and the count of values for│  │
│  │                                                    │  │
│  │                                                    │  │
│  └──────────────────────────────────────────────────┘  │
│                                                         │
│  ────────────── Select the field to be analyzed ─────── │
│                                                         │
│         Accrued Vacation                                │
│         Bonus                                           │
│         Bonus factor                                    │
│         Classification                                  │
│         Evaluation                                      │
│         Salary                                          │
│                                                         │
│                                                         │
│  ─────────────────────────────────────────────────────  │
│  EMPLOYEE.DTF  6 FIELDS                                  │
│                                                         │
│  Esc-Backup F1-Help F3-Restart A-Z ↑ ↓ PgUp PgDn Home End ↵ Continue │
│                      FIG11-014                          │
└─────────────────────────────────────────────────────────┘
```

The List of Field
Names screen is
displayed.

4. Press ⍈B⍈ to move the cursor to the Bonus field name in the list, and
   press ⍈↵Enter⍈ to add the field name to the request statement in the
   dialog box. Q&A now displays the Select Sort Direction screen.

```
┌─────────────────────────────────────────────────────────┐
│                                                         │
│  ┌──────────────────────────────────────────────────┐  │
│  │Cross-tabulate the total and the count of values for Bonus│  │
│  │                                                    │  │
│  │                                                    │  │
│  └──────────────────────────────────────────────────┘  │
│                                                         │
│        Select a sort direction for (top-to-bottom) row headings │
│      B - by ...                  (increasing values from the field) │
│      D - by decreasing ...          (values from the field) │
│                                                         │
│                                                         │
│                                                         │
│                                                         │
│  ─────────────────────────────────────────────────────  │
│  EMPLOYEE.DTF                                            │
│  Esc-Backup F1-Help F3-Restart A-Z ↑ ↓ PgUp PgDn Home End ↵ Continue │
│                      FIG11-015                          │
└─────────────────────────────────────────────────────────┘
```

The Select Sort
Direction screen
is displayed.

5. Choose B—by... (increasing values from the field) to sort row heading in ascending order. Q&A displays the Select a Row Title screen.

The Select a Row Title screen is displayed.

```
┌─────────────────────────────────────────────────────────────────┐
│ ┌─────────────────────────────────────────────────────────────┐ │
│ │Cross-tabulate the total and the count of values for Bonus by│ │
│ │                                                             │ │
│ │                                                             │ │
│ └─────────────────────────────────────────────────────────────┘ │
│                                                                   │
│                      Select a row title (field)                   │
│               ────────────────────────────────────────────────   │
│               Accrued Vacation                                    │
│               Address                                             │
│               Alma Mater                                          │
│               Bonus                                               │
│               Bonus factor                                        │
│               City                                                │
│               Classification                                      │
│               Department                                          │
│               Eligible                                            │
│               Evaluation                                          │
│               First name                                       ↓  │
│                                                                   │
│               ─────────────────────────────────────────────────  │
│  EMPLOYEE.DTF  24 FIELDS                                           │
│                                                                   │
│  Esc-Backup  F1-Help  F3-Restart  A-Z ↑ ↓  PgUp  PgDn  Home  End  ↵ Continue │
│                            FIG11-016                              │
└─────────────────────────────────────────────────────────────────┘
```

6. Press ⃞P to move the cursor to Position and press ⃞↵Enter to put Position in the request. Q&A displays another Select Sort Direction screen, for left-to-right column headings. Press ⃞& to select And... (increasing values from the field). Q&A displays the Select a Column Title screen.

The Select a Column Title screen is displayed.

```
┌─────────────────────────────────────────────────────────────────┐
│ ┌─────────────────────────────────────────────────────────────┐ │
│ │Cross-tabulate the total and the count of values for Bonus by Position│ │
│ │                                                             │ │
│ │                                                             │ │
│ └─────────────────────────────────────────────────────────────┘ │
│                                                                   │
│            Select a sort (left to right) direction for column headings │
│            ───────────────────────────────────────────────────── │
│            & - and by ...              (increasing values from the field) │
│            D - and decreasing ...               (values from the field)   │
│                                                                   │
│                                                                   │
│                                                                   │
│                                                                   │
│            ─────────────────────────────────────────────────────  │
│  EMPLOYEE.DTF                                                      │
│                                                                   │
│  Esc-Backup  F1-Help  F3-Restart  A-Z ↑ ↓  PgUp  PgDn  Home  End  ↵ Continue │
│                            FIG11-017                              │
└─────────────────────────────────────────────────────────────────┘
```

7. Press D to choose Department and press ⏎Enter. Q&A displays the Option screen.

```
┌──────────────────────────────────────────────────────────────────────┐
│ ┌──────────────────────────────────────────────────────────────────┐ │
│ │Cross-tabulate the total and the count of values for Bonus by Position and│ │
│ │by                                                                  │ │
│ └──────────────────────────────────────────────────────────────────┘ │
│                                                                        │
│                      Select a column title field                       │
│              ─────────────────────────────────────────                 │
│              Accrued Vacation                                          │
│              Address                                                   │
│              Alma Mater                                                │
│              Bonus                                                     │
│              Bonus factor                                              │
│              City                                                      │
│              Classification                                           │
│              Department                                                │
│              Eligible                                                  │
│              Evaluation                                               │
│              First name                                      ↓          │
│              ─────────────────────────────────────────                 │
│  EMPLOYEE.DTF  24 FIELDS                                                │
│                                                                        │
│  Esc-Backup  F1-Help  F3-Restart  A-Z ↑ ↓  PgUp  PgDn  Home  End  ↵ Continue│
│                              FIG11-018                                  │
└──────────────────────────────────────────────────────────────────────┘
```

The Option screen.

8. Press **A** to select ALL records from the database.

Q&A now displays the completed statement and immediately executes the request. The cross tab report is displayed on the screen.

```
┌──────────────────────────────────────────────────────────────────────┐
│ ┌──────────────────────────────────────────────────────────────────┐ │
│ │Cross-tabulate the total and the count of values for Bonus by Position and│ │
│ │by Department from ALL the records.                                 │ │
│ └──────────────────────────────────────────────────────────────────┘ │
│                                                                        │
│                                                    Department          │
│                      ─────────────────────────────────────────────    │
│  Position             ACCNT    ADMIN     EXEC      LEGAL      OPS       │
│  ──────────────  ───  ─────    ─────     ────      ─────      ───       │
│  Assistant       Tot  $0.00  $1,080.00   $0.00     $0.00     $0.0       │
│                  Cnt      0         1        0         0        0       │
│                                                                        │
│  Attorney        Tot  $0.00     $0.00     $0.00  $6,750.00   $0.0       │
│                  Cnt      0         0        0         1        0       │
│                                                                        │
│  Chief Counsel   Tot  $0.00     $0.00     $0.00  $8,000.00   $0.0       │
│                  Cnt      0         0        0         1        0       │
│                                                                        │
│  Clerk           Tot  $0.00  $1,680.00   $0.00     $0.00     $0.0       │
│                  Cnt      0         1        0         0        0       │
│  ──────────────────────────────────────────────────────────────────   │
│  EMPLOYEE.DTF                                                           │
│                                                                        │
│  Esc-Exit      F2-Reprint      ⟨ → ← ↓ ↑ PgUp PgDn ⟩-Scroll    F10-Continue│
│                              FIG11-019                                  │
└──────────────────────────────────────────────────────────────────────┘
```

The completed report is displayed.

To view other sections of the report, you can scroll the screen vertically and horizontally using the PgUp, PgDn, and arrow keys.

Teaching the Intelligent Assistant about Your Database

13

You can use the Intelligent Assistant without expanding its built-in vocabulary or teaching it specific information about your database. As long as your questions contain words from the Intelligent Assistant's built-in vocabulary and the field names and values in your database, you can enter a wide range of requests. But if a request contains a word the Intelligent Assistant doesn't recognize, the IA stops processing the request and prompts you to supply information about the unknown word. Depending on the word's context, the Intelligent Assistant may not be able to process the request.

The best way to make sure that the Intelligent Assistant can process most of your data management and reporting requests is to use the Teach option. Even though you can forgo that step and still use the IA to answer simple requests and produce reports, for more complicated tasks you will need to teach the IA to recognize words that are unique to your database. When you use the Teach option to expand the Intelligent Assistant's information bank, you gain three important benefits:

- You can substitute alternative field names so that you can enter the same request many different ways. You can, for example, teach the IA to recognize three other names for the Alma Mater field in the Employee database: college, university, and school.

- Teaching the IA a set of alternate search words enables other users to search the database without having to use the same terms.

- The more the Intelligent Assistant knows about your database, the faster the IA can process your requests. When the Intelligent Assistant encounters an ambiguous word or a word not included in the IA's vocabulary, processing stops. This delay can waste valuable time.

Methods for Teaching the IA about Your Database

If you like to plan an activity thoroughly before you begin, you can take the time to teach the Intelligent Assistant about your database before you begin using it to make requests. If you do not want to plan your requests in advance, though, you can teach the IA interactively. You can bypass the Teach option and go directly to entering requests that contain vocabulary the IA does not understand. When the Intelligent Assistant comes to something it cannot process, it stops and asks for help, giving you a chance to expand the IA's vocabulary. After you add the new term to the IA's vocabulary, the IA continues to process your request and stores the new word or phrase for future requests. As you continue to enter questions, you gradually enlarge the Intelligent Assistant's vocabulary.

A third method for teaching the IA combines the first two. Begin by teaching the Intelligent Assistant as much as you can about your database, then begin entering requests and add to the information in the IA's vocabulary by responding as it requests help with words that it does not understand.

When you select Teach me about your database from the Assistant menu, the IA responds with a Basic Lessons menu that includes five choices:

- What this database is about
- Which fields identify a form
- Which fields contain locations
- Alternate field names
- Advanced lessons

Selecting Advanced Lessons displays another menu with five selections:

- What fields contain people's names
- Units of measure
- Advanced vocabulary: adjectives
- Advanced vocabulary: verbs
- Exit lessons

You may not need to use all these options, but you should select those that best prepare the Intelligent Assistant for your particular kinds of requests. The time you spend working through the Teach lessons greatly increases the IA's efficiency.

Although the Intelligent Assistant's flexibility allows for various types of questions, you can save time and avoid problems by putting requests in the simplest form possible. You may want to keep a printed set of your often-used requests for querying, sorting, and changing the form and data in the database. When you design these requests, keep in mind the following guidelines:

13

- Use the shortest form possible.
- Use direct requests rather than complex questions.
- Use math symbols to simplify requests.

You can replace a question such as

> Which sales leads are not current customers?

with

> List current customers = N.

Notice that the latter request uses a command rather than a question and math symbols rather than full English syntax. Check for any ambiguities and revise to ensure the correct interpretation.

Preparing the IA for Your Requests

As mentioned previously, the IA Teach option includes two sets of lessons: basic and advanced. The lessons fit into the following categories:

- Providing synonyms for your database and its fields (basic lessons 1 and 4)
- Teaching the IA concepts related to fields (basic lessons 2 and 3; advanced lessons 1 and 2)
- Relating verbs and adjectives to the fields in your database (advanced lessons 3 and 4)
- Telling the IA what to include when you make requests for specific information rather than complete forms (basic lesson 2)

To select an option from the Basic Lessons menu or the Advanced Lessons menu, type the number or move the cursor to the selection and press `Enter`. Many options display help screens that explain how you can use that particular option. For many selections, the Intelligent Assistant prompts you to enter numbers, words, phrases, and abbreviations that expand the IA's vocabulary and indicate relationships between information and fields in your database.

Preparing the IA for Your Vocabulary

Lessons 1 and 4 on the Basic Lessons menu prepare the Intelligent Assistant for the range of requests you will enter about your database. Lesson 1, What this database is about, helps the IA process requests that refer to the subject of your database. Lesson 4, Alternate field names, prepares the IA for the alternate words and phrases you will use to refer to specific fields. The following sections explain these lessons as they relate to the sample Employee database.

When you select the second option on the Basic Lessons menu, What this database is about, the Intelligent Assistant prompts you to list all words, phrases, abbreviations, and acronyms that you might use to refer to the subject of the database. When you display this screen for the Employee database, you see that 11 terms have already been listed.

```
┌─────────────────────────────────────────────────────────────────┐
│ ┌───┐ ┌─────────────────────────────────────────────────────┐     │
│ │La │ │ "Each record contains information about a particular _____." │
│ │Ad │ │                                                       │     │
│ │Ci │ │ Are there any words or phrases that could be used to complete │
│ │   │ │ the above sentence?  If YES, type them in the blanks below. │
│ │Se │ │ If NO, press F10 to continue.  If you're NOT SURE, press F1 │
│ │Ho │ │ for more explanation.                                 │     │
│ └───┘ └─────────────────────────────────────────────────────┘     │
│                    <Employee        >                             │
│ ┌───┐              <worker          >                             │
│ │Hi │              <person          >                             │
│ │Ci │              <people          >                             │
│ └───┘              <staff member    >                             │
│ ┌───┐              <staffer         >                             │
│ │Re │              <individual      >                             │
│ │Re │              <body            >                             │
│ └───┘              <human being     >                             │
│                    <human           >                             │
│ ┌───┐              <soul            >                             │
│ │Ev │                                                             │
│ │Sa │                                                             │
│ │No │                                                             │
│ │Phone:│                                                          │
│ └───┘──────────────────────────────────────────────────────────  │
│ EMPLOYEE.DTF                                                       │
│                                                                    │
│ Esc-Exit          F1-Examples and explanation        F10-Continue  │
│                         FIG11-020                                  │
└─────────────────────────────────────────────────────────────────┘
```

The first Teach screen is displayed.

After you have listed all possible words and word combinations, press F10 to save the words. With many synonyms listed in the What this database is about screen, the Intelligent Assistant can process your requests with fewer interruptions.

Entering Alternate Field Names

When you select the Alternate field names lesson from the Basic Lessons menu, the IA displays a screen where you can enter up to nine alternative field names.

13

The Alternate Field Names screen is displayed.

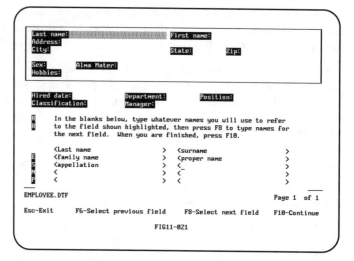

```
 ┌─────────────────────────────────────────────────────────────┐
 │ Last name:▓▓▓▓▓▓▓▓▓▓▓▓▓▓▓▓▓▓  First name:░░░░░           │
 │ Address:                                                     │
 │ City:                          State:       Zip:            │
 │                                                             │
 │ Sex:      Alma Mater:                                       │
 │ Hobbies:                                                    │
 │                                                             │
 │                                                             │
 │ Hired date:          Department:       Position:           │
 │ Classification:      Manager:                              │
 │                                                             │
 │ R   In the blanks below, type whatever names you will use to refer │
 │ R   to the field shown highlighted, then press F8 to type names for │
 │     the next field.  When you are finished, press F10.     │
 │                                                             │
 │     <Last name          >  <surname             >         │
 │ E   <family name        >  <proper name         >         │
 │ S   <appellation        >  <                     >         │
 │ N   <                    >  <                     >         │
 │ P   <                    >  <                     >         │
 │                                                             │
 │ EMPLOYEE.DTF                                 Page 1  of 1   │
 │                                                             │
 │ Esc-Exit    F6-Select previous field   F8-Select next field   F10-Continue │
 │                          FIG11-021                          │
 └─────────────────────────────────────────────────────────────┘
```

The alternative names can be words, phrases, or abbreviations. The original field name is shown as the first entry in the prompt box.

When displaying a columnar report in response to your requests, the IA uses the original field names unless you change the entry by using the Alternate field names screen. If, for example, you want the Department field name to be displayed in capital letters, select Alternate Field names from the Basic Lessons menu, press [F8] 10 times to move the highlight to the Department field, move the cursor to the first entry in the Alternate Field names screen, and change the entry in the prompt box to all capital letters.

You can provide synonyms for any field in the form. To move the cursor to succeeding fields, press [F8]; for previous fields, press [F6]. Keep in mind, however, that Q&A does not accept the same alternative field name in different fields. You cannot, for example, use *Company Rating* to refer to two fields named *Insurance Rating* and *Product Rating*. When you teach the Intelligent Assistant alternative field names, keep in mind the following suggestions:

- Consider abbreviations and long forms of existing field names.
- Include special symbols or acronyms if someone else will use these in requests.
- When you have finished entering synonyms, press [F10] to return to the Basic Lessons menu.

Teaching the IA To Relate Fields

The Intelligent Assistant needs your help to make connections between basic vocabulary items and the information in your database. Several lessons help you teach the IA about people's names (advanced lesson 1), locations (basic lesson 3), and units of measure (advanced lesson 2).

Identifying Name Fields

If your database includes fields that store the names of individuals—prospective customers, current customers, clients, employees, consultants—you will probably want to make requests for these names. The Employee database, for example, has three fields that contain either full names or parts of names: Last name, First name, and Manager. Before the IA can respond to a request like

> Who is the manager in Dubuque?

you must teach it to recognize which fields contain people's names. To do so, choose option 1, What fields contain people's names?, from the Advanced Lessons menu. When you select this option, the IA displays a prompt asking you to press F1 if any fields contain a person's name. When you press F1, the Intelligent Assistant directs you to number each field that contains a name.

```
┌─────────────────────────────────────────────────────────┐
│ Last name: _              First name:                    │
│ Address:                                                 │
│ City:                     State:        Zip:             │
│                                                          │
│ Sex:        Alma Mater:                                  │
│ Hobbies:                                                 │
│                                                          │
│ Hired date:          Department:        Position:        │
│ Classification:      Manager:                            │
│                                                          │
│    Are there any fields that contain a person's name?    │
│                                                          │
│    If YES, then press F1 so that I can tell you what I need to know. │
│                                                          │
│    If NO, then just press F10 to continue to the next lesson. │
│                                                          │
│ Phone:                                                   │
│ ──────────────────────────────────────────────────────  │
│ EMPLOYEE.DTF                          Page 1  of 1       │
│                                                          │
│ Esc-Exit          F1-Examples and explanation   F10-Continue │
│                        FIG11-023                         │
└─────────────────────────────────────────────────────────┘
```

The People's Names screen is displayed.

To tell the Intelligent Assistant which fields are parts of a single name and should be combined into one composite name, enter the same number in each field, followed by a single-letter code to indicate whether the field contains the last name (L), first name (F), middle name (M), or title (T). If a field contains the whole name, use W. Notice in the previous figure that 1L and 1F are the codes to identify each part of the employee's name. 2W identifies the whole name for the manager. You can program the IA to recognize up to nine separate names in each record.

Specifying Location Fields

If your database contains fields that store address, city, or state information, you need to teach the Intelligent Assistant that these fields refer to locations. To help the IA process a question such as **Who is the manager in Nashville?**, for example, use the third option from the Basic Lessons menu (Which fields contain locations) to identify the Address, City, State, and ZIP fields as location fields. When you select the third option on the Basic Lessons menu, the Intelligent Assistant prompts you to number each field that refers to a location. In Employee database, for example, you can identify four fields that refer to locations: Address, City, State, and Zip.

To identify fields that refer to locations, choose number 3 from the Basic Lessons menu. The Intelligent Assistant then asks you to number each field in the order you want the items to appear in the IA's response.

The Location screen with fields numbered.

```
Last name: _                        First name:
Address: 1
City: 2                   State: 3         Zip: 4

Sex:           Alma Mater:
Hobbies:

Hired date:        Department: 5     Position:
Classification:    Manager:

Revi     Are there any fields on your form that contain locations,
Revi     such as addresses, cities, or states?

         If YES, then number them in the order in which you would
         like them to appear in reports.  If NO, press F10 to
Eval     continue.
Sala
Note     If you're NOT SURE, press F1 for explanation and examples.
Phon

EMPLOYEE.DTF                                          Page 1  of 1

Esc-Exit              F1-Examples and explanation       F10-Continue
                            FIG11-024
```

As you can see, the location fields have been numbered so that they will appear as displayed on the original sales lead form.

Identifying Units of Measure Fields

13

You also can help the Intelligent Assistant answer questions that relate to units of measure. Before you can ask the IA questions containing the word *months*, for example, you must teach the IA about this concept. From the Advanced Lessons menu, choose lesson 2, Units of measure, to identify the units of measure for all numeric fields.

Because the Employee database does not contain a field that uses units of measure, you will use the Property database (PROPERTY.DTF), supplied with Q&A, for this example. When you select Units of measure from the Advanced Lessons menu, the Intelligent Assistant asks you to indicate the particular unit for the highlighted field and displays a screen that explains how to specify the units of measure for the field. In the Property database, for example, you can enter acres as the unit of measure for the Lot Size field. To move the cursor between fields, press F8 and F6. After you have identified the measurement types for the fields, press F10 to save the information.

```
                      SHATTUCK REAL ESTATE SERVICE

    Address:                               Price:

                             DESCRIPTION

    Style                 Rooms      ############ Lot Size   ####### acres
    Floors   ############ Bedrooms   ############ Sq Ft      ##############
    Age      ##### years  Baths      ############ Loan Balance
    Condition             Basement                Payment
    Heat                  Garage                  Yearly Taxes


         Is the field shown highlighted measured in some kind of unit?
         If YES, type the unit in the blank below.  If NO, press F8 to
         select any other number fields that have units, or F10 to
         continue to the next lesson.  If you're NOT SURE, press F1 for
         examples and explanation.

         Unit of measure: Room          >

         Example units: mpg, inches, yards, tons, cups.

    PROPERTY.DTF                                   Page 1  of 1

    Esc-Exit     F6-Select previous field    F8-Select next field   F10-Continue

                             FIG11-025
```

The Units of measure screen is displayed.

13

Teaching the IA Adjectives and Verbs

Initially, the Intelligent Assistant's vocabulary is smaller than a young child's. The more sophisticated the sentence structure you attempt to use in your queries, the more difficulty the IA has in processing your requests. When you use adjectives and verbs that are new to the IA, it asks for your help in relating the words to the information in your database. Advanced lessons 3 and 4 help you teach the IA to connect the special adjectives and verbs in your requests with the information in your database.

Table 13.1.
Adjectives in the Built-In Vocabulary

above	below	under
big	bigger	biggest
early	earlier	earliest
few	fewer	fewest
great	greater	greatest
high	higher	highest
large	larger	largest
late	later	latest
little	littler	littlest
long	longer	longest
low	lower	lowest
many	more	most
maximum		minimum
much	less	least
small	smaller	smallest
top		bottom

To teach the IA the special adjectives you plan to use in your requests, select lesson 3, Advanced vocabulary: adjectives, from the Advanced Lessons menu. Highlight the field to which the adjectives will relate by pressing F6 to move

the cursor into the preceding field or F8 for the next field. When you select
this lesson, the Intelligent Assistant displays a screen that explains the purpose
and method for using the lesson. Below the explanation are blanks on which
you enter pairs of adjectives or single adjectives to convey high or low values.
For the Employee database, in the Salary field, for example, you can enter the
following adjectives:

rich	poor
successful	unsuccessful
prosperous	struggling
hot	
overpaid	underpaid

```
    ┌
    │    Will you use adjectives in your questions about the highlighted
    │    field? If YES, type them in the blanks below.  If NO press F8 to
    │    select other fields that have adjectives, or F10 to continue.  If
    │    you're NOT SURE, press F1 for examples and explanation.
    │
    │    High value: <good         >  Low value: <bad          >
    │                 <excellent    >             <poor         >
    └                 <_            >             <             >
                      <             >             <             >

    Review date:
    Review comments

    Evaluation:############# Bonus factor:############## Eligible:
    Salary:################# Bonus:##################### Accrued Vacation:########
    Note:
    Phone:
    ─────────────────────────────────────────────────────────────────
    EMPLOYEE.DTF                                        Page 1  of 1

    Esc-Exit      F6-Select previous field    F8-Select next field   F10-Continue

                          FIG11-026
```

The Adjectives
screen.

You can enter adjectives in one or both columns; you do not need to provide
pairs of adjectives in every case. You can, for example, enter the adjective *hot*
so that you can use the query **"Which employee is the hottest?"** but you do
not have to supply an opposite. You do not need to enter the *-est* form of the
adjective when you enter the word in the prompt box; Q&A understands
automatically. If you want to use the same adjective to refer to more than one
field, you must enter the adjective for each field. When you use the same
adjective to refer to more than one field, you must specify the field in your
requests. If you do not make the field reference clear, the IA assumes that you
mean the first field that contains the adjective.

13

The Intelligent Assistant can respond easily to a request for the highest or lowest value in a field. If you ask the Intelligent Assistant to determine whether a range of values is high or low, however, the IA can interpret high or low values only as they relate to an average value. If, for example, you ask **"Which employees are prosperous?"**, the Intelligent Assistant interprets your request as *"Which employees have above the average salary?"*.

Entering Special Verbs

The Intelligent Assistant's built-in vocabulary contains verbs that you can use to specify operations for displaying, sorting, searching, calculating, or changing data (see table 13-2). In addition, the IA includes a number of other verbs that are used often in requests. When you enter a verb that the Intelligent Assistant does not recognize, however, the IA needs you to define the word and its relationship to the field it references.

Table 13.2.
Verbs in the IA's Built-in Vocabulary

add	define	find	print
set	blank	delete	get
remove	show	change	display
increase	replace	sum	count
divide	list	report	total
create	enter	make	run
decrease	erase	multiply	search

When you select the Verbs lesson from the Advanced Lessons menu, the IA asks you to enter the verbs you will use to refer to the fields in your database.

```
┌─────────────────────────────────────────────────────────────┐
│                                                             │
│  Last name:                    First name:                  │
│  Address:                                                   │
│  City:                         State:▒▒▒▒▒   Zip:           │
│                                                             │
│  Sex:          Alma Mater:                                  │
│  Hobbies:                                                   │
│                                                             │
│  ─────────────────────────────────────────────────────     │
│  Hired date:          Department:        Position:          │
│  Classification:      Manager:                              │
│  R   If you need help, press F1.  If not, type verbs you wish to use │
│  R   with the field shown highlighted, then press F8 to teach me verbs │
│      for the next field, if desired.  Press F10 when done.  │
│                                                             │
│      <is from            >  <lives            >             │
│  E   <lives in           >  <_                >             │
│  S   <                   >  <_                >             │
│  N   <                   >  <                 >             │
│  P   <                   >  <                 >             │
│                                                             │
│  EMPLOYEE.DTF                              Page 1  of 1     │
│                                                             │
│  Esc-Exit     F6-Select previous field    F8-Select next field    F10-Continue │
│                       FIG11-027                             │
└─────────────────────────────────────────────────────────────┘
```

The Verbs screen.

13

Although you can enter verbs for any field in your database, you cannot enter the same verb in more than one field. Move to the field you want by pressing F8 for the next field and pressing F6 for the preceding field.

When you have finished entering verbs for the fields, press F10 to save the entries. If you plan to use any irregular verbs (verbs that do not have regular endings, such as *-s*, *-es*, *-en*, *-ed*, or *-ing*), you must enter all forms of the verb. The verb *pay* plus its irregular past tense form *paid* must be entered in reference to the Salary field. This entry enables you to ask the IA a question such as "**Who gets paid most in Chicago?**".

Controlling the Display of Columnar Reports

The Intelligent Assistant responds to your requests by displaying complete forms or by listing the results in columnar format. When you ask the IA to "**Display all forms for employees in San Francisco**", however, the IA displays each form. On the other hand, if you ask the IA to answer "**Which employees are in PA?**", the IA produces a single-column list of those employees. No other information is displayed unless you specify that the IA should include certain fields each time it displays a columnar report.

317

Using the request **"Display all forms for employees in San Francisco"**.

```
Last name: Billingsgate              First name: Rudy
Address: 767 Turk St.
City: San Francisco                  State: CA     Zip: 93247

Sex: MALE    Alma Mater: UC Berkeley
Hobbies: reading; theology

Hired date: Apr 9, 1983   Department: ADMIN   Position: Manager
Classification: 6         Manager: John Smith

Review date: Oct 10, 1985
Review comments  Good management skills.


Evaluation: 6            Bonus factor: 10         Eligible: Y
Salary: $29,000.00       Bonus: $2,900.00         Accrued Vacation: 45.7
Note:
Phone: (419) 555 - 0612
_____
EMPLOYEE.DTF   Retrieved form 1     of --     Total Forms: 32    Page 1  of 1

Esc-Exit   F1-Help      Alt+F6-Table     F7-Search     F8-Calc    F10-Continue
                              FIG11-028
```

Using the request **"Which employees are in PA?"**.

```
Which employees are in PA?



   Full name              Department
_____        _____
Darwin Charles            R&D
Foobah Dorian             PROMO
Eisenstein Joseph         LEGAL
Brothers John             EXEC
Johnson Nick              SALES
Jones Jane                SALES
Smith John                EXEC




_____
EMPLOYEE.DTF
xxxxxxxxxxxxxxxxxxxxxxxxxxxxxxx   END OF REPORT  xxxxxxxxxxxxxxxxxxxxxxxxxxxxxxxxxx
Esc-Exit       F2-Reprint      ( → ← ↓ ↑ PgUp PgDn )-Scroll       F10-Continue
                              FIG11-029
```

To specify which fields you want the IA to display in columnar reports, select the second option (Which fields identify a form) from the Basic Lessons menu. On the screen that appears, you can specify the order of the fields in the columnar report. Suppose, for example, that you want the Intelligent Assistant to display the name and title of the employee, the department name, and the phone number each time a columnar report is produced. To indicate that you want those fields included, number the fields in the order you want them to appear.

```
┌─────────────────────────────────────────────────────────────┐
│ Last name: 1              First name: 2                       │
│ Address:                                                      │
│ City:                     State:        Zip:                  │
│                                                               │
│ Sex:        Alma Mater:                                       │
│ Hobbies:                                                      │
│                                                               │
│ Hired date: 3      Department: 4_   Position:                 │
│ Classification:    Manager:                                   │
│                                                               │
│    If you ask me to make a report, are there columns I should │
│    ALWAYS include to help you identify which forms the        │
│    information comes from?                                    │
│                                                               │
│    If YES, type "1" in the field which would be the first     │
│    column of identifying information, "2" in the second, "3"  │
│    in the third, etc.                                         │
│                                                               │
│    If NO, just press F10.  If you're NOT SURE, press F1 for   │
│    more info.                                                 │
│                                                               │
│ EMPLOYEE.DTF                              Page 1  of 1        │
│                                                               │
│ Esc-Exit          F1-Examples and explanation    F10-Continue │
│                         FIG11-030                             │
└─────────────────────────────────────────────────────────────┘
```

The Field Identifier screen.

For reports generated from the Employee database, the Last name field has been numbered as 1, First name as 2, Telephone as 3, and Department as 4. To save your settings, press F10. Now each time you produce a columnar report, the IA includes those fields.

Displaying Additional Columns

You can add columns to summary reports—without changing the information—using basic lesson 2. Suppose, for example, that you decide to display the Alma Mater in addition to the name, department, and telephone number. You can enter the request **List all employees and display Alma Mater**. The Intelligent Assistant understands from this request that you want an additional column displayed in the report.

Restricting Columns

The Intelligent Assistant can "hide" columns of information that you do not want to appear in a summary report. To suppress the column display, you simply add one of three acronyms at the end of your request.

319

13

The acronyms used to hide columns are as follows:

Acronym	Meaning	Purpose
WNIC	With No Identification Columns	Suppress columns listed in basic lesson
2WNRC	With No Restriction Columns	Suppress restriction columns
WNEC	With No Extra Columns	Suppress extra columns

You can suppress the display of the columns you specified in basic lesson 2 (Which fields identify a form) so that only the columns affected by your request are displayed. If, for example, you want the Intelligent Assistant to display only Department and Salary columns when you request a report of all employees with salaries between $50,000 and $200,000, you can enter the request **List employes with salaries between 50000 and 200000. WNIC.**

The IA asks for confirmation that you want only `employees and revenues` displayed.

Using the acronym *WNEC* (with no extra columns), you can tell the Intelligent Assistant to display only the columns you specify in your request. You can, for example, have the IA display only the employees that have a salary between $50,000 and $200,000 by entering **List employees with salaries between 50000 and 200000.WNEC.**

Using the Ask Option To Enter Requests

When you want to ask the Intelligent Assistant to process a request, select the Ask me to do something option from the Assistant menu. Before your first request can be analyzed, the IA must analyze your database. That process may take a few minutes, depending on the size of your database and the hardware you use.

After the IA has analyzed your database, you can enter requests in the box at the top of the screen. The center of the screen is reserved for messages and prompts that help you use the Intelligent Assistant. The bottom of the screen shows the file name of your database and lists explanations of the special keys. The IA has context-sensitive help screens that you can display access from any program screen by pressing F1.

Tips for Entering Requests

You can use the Intelligent Assistant to search, sort, change, add, and calculate data. The IA also can create new forms, produce reports, and delete existing forms. The IA can even respond to requests regarding the date and time and can operate as a calculator for simple equations. This section lists tips for using the Intelligent Assistant to your best advantage.

When you ask the IA to change information in a text field, enclose the new entry in double quotation marks. Suppose that you want to change the value in the Manager field for all Atlanta employees. You enter the request **Change Manager to "Jim Stevens" in all forms where City = Atlanta**.

Only text fields require that the new information be enclosed in double quotation marks; you can specify number, date, and time fields in the usual way. In the request **Change the Bonus factor to 2 for the San Francisco employees**, for example, the numeric value needs no quotation marks.

Save time and keystrokes by using follow-up questions. Instead of typing a new request every time you query the Intelligent Assistant, you can use phrases that refer to a previous request. If you last requested the IA to list all employees with a bonus factor greater than 5, your next request can be **Change these to 12 bonus factor**.

Use math symbols to simplify your requests. Although you probably will want to use English phrases in most of your requests, you can use math symbols to reduce your typing time and help the IA process faster. Compare the different versions of these two requests:

> Display annual revenues that are greater than $3,000,000.
>
> Annual revenue >$3,000,000.
>
> Display sales leads entered between 4/15/88 and 7/1/88.
>
> Display leads for date entered >4/15/88 and <7/1/88.

The shorter versions not only include math symbols but also have been written with as few words as possible. The shorter your request, the quicker the IA can respond.

Use the word "define" in the request box to teach the IA new synonyms. In addition to teaching the IA new words by using the Teach option, you can enter synonyms with requests such as **Define address as address, city, state, and zip**. After you enter this request, the Intelligent Assistant displays the Address, City, State, and ZIP fields whenever you ask for address.

321

To have the IA display a yes/no field in a columnar report, include the word *field* in your request as follows:

> **Show employees from the Philadelphia area and the Bonus factor field.**

Updating the IA's Knowledge of Your Database

As you enter requests to the IA, you will probably need to add to the information you originally specified with the Teach option. Instead of returning to the Teach option, however, you can add to the IA's vocabulary and help the IA process requests while you are working by using the Ask option on the request screen. By pressing F1, you can display a help screen that lists the function keys available for reviewing and adding vocabulary. The Intelligent Assistant provides two options for updating information. First, you can use the F6 and F8 function keys when entering a request. Second, you can update the IA when it is unable to process a request because of an unknown or ambiguous term.

Getting Started in the Utilities Module

This chapter teaches you how to use the features in the Utilities module to install printers, set default directories, issue DOS commands from within Q&A, and run other programs from the Q&A Main menu.

Although you may view some of the operations discussed in this chapter as advanced topics, you eventually will need to understand these concepts so that you can use Q&A to the fullest extent. A basic understanding of the File module is helpful in completing some of the exercises in this chapter. You should be somewhat familiar with DOS, the disk operating system, to complete the exercises on DOS file facilities. Specifically, you should be familiar with the DELETE, COPY, and RENAME commands.

Installing printers

Setting global defaults

Making default directories

Issuing DOS commands in Q&A

Key Terms Used in This Chapter

Parallel port	An external connection that contains the cable from the computer to your printer.
DOS	The Disk Operating System that controls your computer's performance.
Drive path	A "road map" that tells DOS where to find files on your computer. This road map is comprised of directories and subdirectories.
Defaults	Settings that are used for all new files, documents, reports, or other items that you generate within Q&A. Defaults apply to many Q&A operations you perform, but you can adjust the settings to match your own preferences.
Toggle	An option that turns a software function on and off.
Printer drivers	Special modules that tell Q&A how to use various models of printers.

Understanding the Utilities Menu

The Utilities menu is the fifth selection on the Q&A Main menu. With this module, you can perform special functions such as maintaining files within Q&A, installing printers, and setting global defaults. Although these functions are important, you do not use them frequently. Understanding Utilities, however, enables you to use Q&A to its fullest potential.

To enter the Utilities module, follow these steps:

1. From the Q&A Main menu, select Utilities.

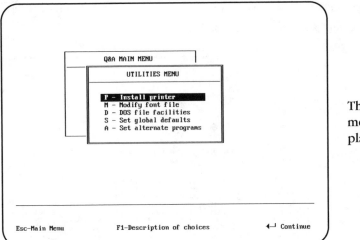

The Utilities menu is displayed.

14

The Utilities menu contains the following options:

- Select Install printer to set up printers to use with your software. You must install a printer prior to printing.

- Select Modify font file to set up files for those fonts you want to make available to Q&A. Not all fonts have font files developed for them within Q&A. For those that need font files to print correctly, use this option to develop them.

- Select DOS file facilities to execute DOS commands from within Q&A. Files can be copied, renamed, and deleted using this selection.

- Select Set global defaults to indicate storage areas for your databases and word processing documents.

- Select Set Alternate programs to request that programs appear on the Q&A Main menu.

Installing Printers in Q&A

Before you can print any information on paper, you must install your printer. The installation process tells the software which printer you are using. All relevant data about your printer and how it reads special commands is contained in a file called a *printer driver*. Without this file, your printer would be confused when it received special commands and would not be able to execute those commands. Each printer has its own unique printer driver that enables it to give you the highest quality printed document.

325

To install a printer, follow these steps:

1. From the Utilities menu, select Install Printer.

The Printer
Selection screen
is displayed.

```
                              PRINTER SELECTION
                              _____

       A "Q&A PRINTER" is a combination of a PORT and a specific PRINTER MODEL
       and MODE (e.g. draft or letter).  Press F1 if you want more explanation.

       Highlight the Q&A PRINTER you want to install by pressing ↑ or ↓, then
       press ◄┘.

       ┌──────────────────┬────────┬────────────────────────────────────────┐
       │ Q&A PRINTER      │ PORT   │ PRINTER MODEL AND MODE                  │
       ├──────────────────┼────────┼────────────────────────────────────────┤
       │ Printer A (PtrA) │ LPT1   │ Basic (Vanilla) Non-Laser Printer       │
       │ Printer B (PtrB) │ LPT1   │ Basic (Vanilla) Non-Laser Printer       │
       │ Printer C (PtrC) │ LPT1   │ Basic (Vanilla) Non-Laser Printer       │
       │ Printer D (PtrD) │ COM1   │ Basic (Vanilla) Non-Laser Printer       │
       │ Printer E (PtrE) │ COM2   │ Basic (Vanilla) Non-Laser Printer       │
       └──────────────────┴────────┴────────────────────────────────────────┘


    _____

    Esc-Exit                        F1-Help               ◄┘ Continue
```

The Printer Selection screen lists all the printers that are installed for your
software. This screen contains three columns of information regarding printers. The first column lists the printers you can install. Q&A can support up to
five printers. The next column of information tells the software which port
(output device) you are using to send the commands to the printer. Most
ports are parallel ports (LPT1). Serial printers, however, use the COM setting.
Serial printers use a different cable type and a different data transfer method
to communicate with the computer. The last column of information shows the
model of your printer and the mode of printing. Modes include draft or
standard, letter or legal, and portrait or landscape.

Note that completing the printer installation process is not essential due to
Q&A's "plain vanilla" printer driver, which works with just about anything that
connects to a computer and puts inks on paper. If you have not installed any
printers, the Printer Selection screen indicates that all printers (Printer A
through E) are Basic (Vanilla) Printers. This setting sends the characters and
some enhancements to your printer, but usually does not contain specific
enough information for the printer to execute special enhancements.

2. Press ⏎Enter to confirm the installation of the first printer, Printer A
   (PtrA).

   After you confirm that you want to install PtrA, press ⏎Enter and the
   cursor moves to the center section of the screen under the Port
   column.

326

```
                        PORT SELECTION

   Highlight the PORT you wish to assign to the Q&A PRINTER by pressing
   ↑ and ↓.  Press ←┘ to select the highlighted PORT.


  ┌────────────────────┬──────────┬───────────────────────────────────┐
  │ Q&A PRINTER        │  PORT    │  PRINTER MODEL AND MODE           │
  ├────────────────────┼──────────┼───────────────────────────────────┤
  │ Printer A (PtrA)   │  LPT1    │  Basic (Vanilla) Non-Laser Printer│
  │                    │  LPT2    │                                   │
  │                    │  LPT3    │                                   │
  │                    │  COM1    │                                   │
  │                    │  COM2    │                                   │
  │                    │  FILE    │                                   │
  │                    │          │                                   │
  └────────────────────┴──────────┴───────────────────────────────────┘


  Esc-Exit        F1-Help      F8-Special Ports      F9-Go back   ←┘ Continue
```

The Port Selection screen is displayed.

14

Only the printer you just selected appears on the Port Selection screen. The cursor is located in the Port column. A *port* is the output device (an electrical socket) on the back of your computer. This socket holds the cord to your printer. The back of the computer contains two types of output devices. One is a parallel port and one is a serial port. Generally, the parallel port is the larger of the two ports and is used for most printers. Check your printer manual to determine which of these two ports you should use.

You can select special ports by pressing F8, as shown on the key assignment line. You use this option with special items such as a fax machines. Q&A can send a fax when it is used with a fax board or card. The board or card must be installed in your computer.

3. Select the appropriate port and press ←Enter.

    The cursor is highlighting the LPT1 port. LPT1 is the "address" of a parallel port. If your printer manual instructs you to use a parallel port, select LPT1. If your manual instructs you to use a serial port, select COM1 from the list. LPT ports are parallel, COM ports are serial, and FILE ports print documents to a disk instead of paper.

```
              LIST OF PRINTER MANUFACTURERS

   Basic (Vanilla)        Cordata              IBM
   Adler                  CPT                  IDS
   Alps                   DaisyWriter          Juki
   AMT                    Dataproducts         Kyocera
   Amadex                 Datasouth            Mannesmann Tally
   Apple                  Diablo               NEC
   AST                    Diconix              Okidata
   AT&T                   Digital              Olivetti
   Brother                DTC                  Olympia
   BusinessLand           Epson                Output Technology
   C. Itoh                Fortis               Panasonic
   Canon                  Fujitsu              PaperJet
   Citizen                Gemini               PMC
   Comrex                 Hewlett Packard      Primage

   ┌──┐      Press ↑ ↓ ← → or the space bar to select your   ┌────┐
   │  │           printer's manufacturer, then press ◄┘       │PgDn│
   └──┘                                                       └────┘

   Esc-Exit       F1-Help          F9-Go back         ◄┘ Continue
```

A list of printer manufacturers appears.

14

Your software contains printer drivers for most models of printers. The list of printers that appears on-screen is two pages long. Press PgDn to see the second page of the list. Select your printer manufacturer from the list.

4. Select your printer manufacturer and press ◄Enter.

```
              LIST OF HEWLETT PACKARD PRINTERS

   2603A (IBM Printwheel)        DeskJet500 (Landscape, Legal)
   2603A (Other Printwheel)      LaserJet (Portrait)
   DeskJet (Portrait, Letter)    LaserJet (Portrait, Legal Size)
   DeskJet (Landscape, Letter)   LaserJet (Landscape)
   DeskJet (Legal)               LaserJet (Landscape, Legal)
   DeskJet (Envelope)            LaserJet (Envelope)
   DeskJet + (Portrait, Letter)  LaserJet IID (Portrait,Duplex)
   DeskJet + (Portrait, Legal)   LaserJet IID (Port,Leg,Duplex)
   DeskJet + (Landscape, Letter) LaserJet IID (Landscape,Duplex)
   DeskJet + (Landscape, Legal)  LaserJet IID (Land,Leg,Duplex)
   DeskJet + (Envelope)          LaserJet II/D/P/III (Port)
   DeskJet500 (Portrait, Letter) LaserJet II/D/P/III (Port, Leg)
   DeskJet500 (Portrait, Legal)  LaserJet II/D/P/III (Land)
   DeskJet500 (Landscape, Letter)LaserJet II/D/P/III (Land, Leg)

   ┌──┐      Press ↑ ↓ ← → or the space bar to select a     ┌────┐
   │  │              printer, then press ◄┘                  │PgDn│
   └──┘                                                      └────┘

   Esc-Exit       F1-Help       F9-Reselect Manufacturer    ◄┘ Continue
```

A list of printers from the manu-facturer you chose appears. In this example, you see the list of available Hewlett-Packard printers.

Most printer drivers display the mode of printing to the right of the printer model. You can select from portrait, landscape, envelope, legal, and letter. Some printers even enable you to select specific character styles. The available options depend on the type of printer you are using.

This page is taller than it is wide. The orientation is Portrait.

Portrait mode is used for correspondence, reports, and memos.

14

This page is wider than it is tall. The orientation is landscape.

Landscape mode is used for graphs, charts, and tables.

5. Select your printer model and mode of printing.

   If your printer is not on the list, press `PgDn` to view the entire list of printers. If you cannot find your printer after reviewing the list, call or write Symantec Corporation for further instructions. They may be able to send you the printer driver or suggest a printer driver on the list that will translate the print commands correctly.

6. Press `↵Enter` to confirm your selection.

   A brief synopsis of your printer appears. The synopsis includes any special information you may need to know regarding the printer.

In this example, the HP LaserJet is selected, and Q&A provides specific information about cartridges for that printer.

```
                    LIST OF HEWLETT PACKARD PRINTERS
    2603A (IBM Printwheel)              DeskJet500 (Landscape, Legal)
    2603A (Other Printwheel)           LaserJet (Portrait)
    DeskJet (Portrait, Letter)         LaserJet (Portrait, Legal Size)
    DeskJet (Landscape, Letter)        LaserJet (Landscape)
    DeskJet (Legal)                    LaserJet (Landscape, Legal)
    D
    D            Hewlett Packard LaserJet (Portrait, Legal Size)
    D
    D   * For portrait orientation printing on legal size paper    *
    D   * NOTE: A font cartridge is needed except for non-bold, non- *
    D   * italic pica. Suggested cartridges: Pica pitch 92286A,C,L,  *
    D   * Q. Elite: 92286D,E,J,M, or N. Compressed: 92286C,J, or L.  *
    D
    D    ↵ to confirm      F8 for Special Options      Esc to cancel

  ┌─┐              Press ↑ ↓ ← → or the space bar to select a    ┌────┐
  └─┘                      printer, then press ↵                 │PgDn│
                                                                 └────┘

  Esc-Main Menu              F1-Description of choices           ↵ Continue
```

7. Press ↵Enter to confirm the selection.

Q&A asks whether you want to install another printer. Make your choice and press ↵Enter.

```
        Your printer has been installed.

        Do you want to install another?

           Y - Yes      N - No
```

```
  Esc-Cancel                                        ↵ Continue
```

Using Special Printer Options

Before you confirm your printer choice, you also can select special printer options. These options enable you to change several technical settings for your printer. If your printer was on the list of printers, the special printer option settings are correct and you do not need to change them. If your printer is not a standard printer, however, you may need to modify some of the settings. Because these settings are rather technical, you may need to consult your printer documentation or call the printer manufacturer for specific instructions.

Press F8 to select the Special Printer Options screen.

```
                    SPECIAL PRINTER OPTIONS
                    ──────────────────────

        Use this screen if you have problems with your printer or want to
        change your default font file.

        Check for printer timeout?......:   Yes  ▶No◀

        Length of timeout (in seconds)..:   0

        Check for printer ready signal?.:   Yes  ▶No◀

        Check for paper out?............:   Yes  ▶No◀

        Formfeed at end of document?....:   Yes   No

        Font file name..................:   HPLASERJ.FNT



        Esc-Exit              F9-Reselect printer          F10-Continue
```

The Special Printer Options screen is displayed.

The Special Printer Options screen contains the following fields:

- When set to Yes, the Check for printer timeout option tells you whether the printer is responding to the commands you send.

- The Length of timeout (in seconds) option changes the frequency with which the software checks printer response. A 15-second setting, for example, means that the software checks every 15 seconds to see that the printer is reading commands correctly.

- The Check for printer ready signal option sends a message to the software telling it when it is ready to receive print commands. If your printer does not send this message, you should change this setting to No.

- The Check for paper out option informs the software that it cannot respond to print commands because it is out of paper. If you receive a message that your printer is out of paper, but it has paper in the tray, this setting may need to be changed.

- The Formfeed at end of document option ejects the last page of a document when it is finished printing. Some printers do not eject the last page automatically.

14

- The Font file name displays the appropriate font file name, if one exists for your printer. Font files contain font descriptions about the size and style of fonts used when printing. If you are using a customized or special font file, you should enter the name of that file. Most printer drivers set these selections to the appropriate setting, and modifications may not be necessary.

To reselect your printer, press F9. To exit this process, press Esc. You also can continue setting special printer options by pressing F10.

Using a Cut-Sheet Feeder and Setup Strings

A cut-sheet feeder is a paper tray that holds single sheets of paper like a copy machine. You must specify this set up to your printer. After you select your printer and press F10, you see the More Special Printer Options screen.

The series of codes you see on this screen are called escape codes.

```
                    MORE SPECIAL PRINTER OPTIONS

         Use this screen if you want to use a cut sheet feeder or printer
         setup strings.

         Bin 1 setup code.:  27, 38, 108, 49, 72

         Bin 2 setup code.:  27, 38, 108, 52, 72

         Bin 3 setup code.:  27, 38, 108, 54, 72

         Eject page code..:  27, 38, 108, 48, 72

         Start of document code.:

         End of document code...:

         Envelope height........:  24


   Esc-Exit                F9-Reselect printer              F10-Continue
```

Escape codes send many commands to your printer, such as telling it to print portrait or landscape or to eject a page after printing is finished. The commands are issued using a numeric representation. If you select your printer from the manufacturer list, these settings should be correct. If you experience problems printing your documents, however, you may need to modify these settings. Review the instruction manual for your printer before you change any of these codes.

Setting Global Options

Global options are automatic settings that apply to all parts of Q&A. These settings enable you to define where Q&A can find default directories, database and word processing files, change command operation from manual to automatic, and determine network identification.

To set up global options, follow these steps:

1. From the Utilities menu, select Set global defaults.

```
                        SET GLOBAL DEFAULTS
                        _____

           Type the Drive and, optionally, the Path where the following
           kinds of files will be stored.  This will save you extra typing
           because Q&A will always know where to look first for these files:

                  Q&A Document files : C:\QA\
                  Q&A Database files : C:\QA\
                  Q&A Temporary files: C:\QA\

           You can make the program execute menu items as soon as you type the
           first letter of the selection.  (If you select this option, you may
           have to re-record macros that expect ENTER after the letter.)

                  Automatic Execution:   Yes   No

           Type your name and phone number for network identification purposes:

                  Network ID........: Network id not set


           Esc-Exit                                          F10-Continue
```

The Set Default Directories screen is displayed.

The screen is divided into three sections. The first section applies to default directories. The second section changes command execution to Automatic. The third section stores identification information for networked copies of Q&A.

Making Default Directories

Default directories are areas of your computer that store word processing documents, database files, or temporary working files. Database files are stored separately from word processing files. You should set up your computer so that each software package has its own directory. Directories can be compared to file drawers. Each file drawer (or directory) can contain different types of information such as correspondence or topic-specific files. Each type of information is a subdirectory, or a further definition of the contents of the file drawer.

Subdirectories can be compared to the individual file folders within a file drawer, where each folder is concentrated on a different topic. Word processing documents or database files are like these folders.

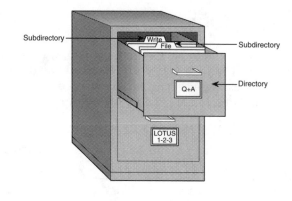

You serve two purposes by using directories and subdirectories. First, because documents and databases are stored in another part of the computer, you do not have to worry about losing this data when you update software. Second, when backing up your system, you only need to back up the subdirectories, not the directory that contains the software. Software files are already backed up on the original disks that you used to load the software. Backing up only subdirectories can save you disks and time. You should store your word processing documents and database files in subdirectories. You may want to name these directories FILE (for databases) and WRITE (for word processing documents). Therefore, the names of the subdirectories match the names of the modules in Q&A to which they apply.

If you have not made directories, you must exit Q&A and return to DOS to create the directories. Refer to your DOS manual for instructions on creating directories. You will need two subdirectories (FILE and WRITE) under the directory holding the Q&A software (QA). The structure of these directories should resemble the following:

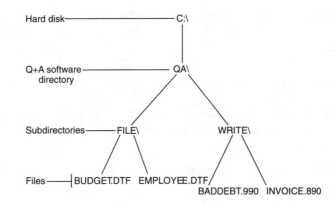

The "road map" that your computer uses to locate files is called a drive path and consists of the directory and subdirectory information.

If you already have subdirectories developed to hold documents and databases, substitute the names of your directories in the following steps. If you are using Q&A on a network, check with your system administrator before using this option.

After you create directories and subdirectories with DOS, you need to tell Q&A the name of the drive path for the directories.

```
                        SET GLOBAL DEFAULTS

     Type the Drive and, optionally, the Path where the following
     kinds of files will be stored.  This will save you extra typing
     because Q&A will always know where to look first for these files:

            Q&A Document files : C:\QA\
            Q&A Database files : C:\QA\
            Q&A Temporary files: C:\QA\

     You can make the program execute menu items as soon as you type the
     first letter of the selection.  (If you select this option, you may
     have to re-record macros that expect ENTER after the letter.)

            Automatic Execution:   Yes  No

     Type your name and phone number for network identification purposes:

            Network ID........: Network id not set


     Esc-Exit                                          F10-Continue
```

The cursor appears in the first section of the screen on the Q&A Document files option.

The following exercise assumes that the software is in a directory named QA and word processing and database files are in subdirectories named WRITE and FILE.

Q&A Document Files

With the first field of information, you tell the software where you want to store all word processing documents. The information that you enter here is called the *drive path*.

Change the prompt so that it reads

     C:\QA\WRITE\

When your computer looks for or stores documents created in WRITE, it will go to this location automatically, unless you instruct it differently. When you back up your word processing documents, you only need to copy the contents of the WRITE subdirectory.

Q&A Database Files

The second selection tells the software where you want to store all database files. This information also is called the drive path.

Change the prompt so that it reads

     C:\QA\FILE\

When your computer looks for or stores database information created in FILE, it will go to this location automatically, unless you instruct it differently. When you back up your database information, you only need to copy the contents of the FILE subdirectory.

Q&A Temporary Files

The last screen selection tells the software where you want to store all temporary files that Q&A creates as it performs functions such as sorts. These files are erased when the process is complete. Generally, these files are stored in the same directory as your software; therefore, you do not need to change this prompt.

If the prompt is not set for the QA directory currently, change it so that it reads C:\QA\.

Keep in mind that setting these defaults does not mean that you cannot access data that is stored in other subdirectories. To access other data files or software packages, just change the drive path when you are prompted to type a file name. The directories that you selected here are merely suggestions; you can change them at any time.

Specifying Automatic Execution

The second section of this screen changes execution from manual to automatic. Manual execution requires you to press ⏎Enter to confirm each selection; automatic execution executes selections when you press the first letter of a menu item name. Automatic execution makes menu navigation quick and easy.

Remember that when you change to automatic execution, existing macros may execute differently. An extra, unnecessary Enter keystroke may execute in the macros.

To change execution from manual to automatic, highlight Yes in the Automatic Execution field. You can change execution from automatic to manual by highlighting No in the field.

Specifying Network Identification

You use the last section of this screen to specify that you use Q&A in a networked environment. Networks are groups of computers that are linked together electronically. Each computer can access information on the network and can share information with other network users. If you are using a stand-alone computer that is not networked, you can skip this step. If you are using a network version, consult your system coordinator for further details on this setting.

This screen shows that this computer is not part of a network.

```
                        SET GLOBAL DEFAULTS
                        _____

        Type the Drive and, optionally, the Path where the following
        kinds of files will be stored.  This will save you extra typing
        because Q&A will always know where to look first for these files:

                Q&A Document files : C:\QA\WRITE
                Q&A Database files : C:\QA\FILE
                Q&A Temporary files: C:\QA\
        _____
        You can make the program execute menu items as soon as you type the
        first letter of the selection.  (If you select this option, you may
        have to re-record macros that expect ENTER after the letter.)

                Automatic Execution:  Yes  No

        Type your name and phone number for network identification purposes:

                        Network ID........: Network id not set
        _____

    Esc-Exit                                            F10-Continue
```

Press F10 to save your changes and return to the Utilities menu.

Installing Alternate Programs

Because most people with computers use more than one kind of software, Q&A gives you the option of adding software options to the Q&A Main menu. The Main menu splits into two sections, with one side offering the standard Q&A modules and the other side offering other software packages that are resident on your computer.

This screen shows an example of a menu with macros and alternate programs available.

```
                        Q&A MAIN MENU
        _____
        |  F - File          |  Q - QUICKEN            |
        |  R - Report        |  L - LOTUS 123          |
        |  W - Write         |  S - SALES-MONTHLY      |
        |  A - Assistant     |                         |
        |  U - Utilities     |                         |
        |  X - Exit Q&A      |                         |
        _____


    Q&A Version 4.0  112N   Copyright (C) 1985-1990, Symantec   All rights reserved.

    X-Exit to DOS            F1-Description of choices          ↵ Continue
```

This feature has the advantage of permitting you to run other programs without exiting Q&A, returning to DOS, running the program, and reloading Q&A. When exiting other programs, you are returned to Q&A automatically.

The following steps are based on two alternate programs and one macro. This example uses samples that may not exist on your computer. You can use them, however, to see how alternate program selection works. Assume that you have both Lotus 1-2-3 and Quicken on your computer. You want to access both these programs directly from Q&A without having to exit to a DOS prompt.

To install alternate programs, follow these steps:

1. From the Utilities menu, select Set Alternate Programs.

14

```
                        ALTERNATE PROGRAMS
                        ──────────────────

        You can install up to six alternate programs for the Main Menu.
        You can then execute those programs by selecting them at that menu.
        When you exit from these programs, you will return automatically
        to the Main Menu.

                    Alternate program 1:
                    Menu selection.....:
                    Alternate program 2:
                    Menu selection.....:
                    Alternate program 3:
                    Menu selection.....:
                    Alternate program 4:
                    Menu selection.....:
                    Alternate program 5:
                    Menu selection.....:
                    Alternate program 6:
                    Menu selection.....:



    Esc-Exit                                    F10-Continue
```

The Alternate Programs screen is displayed. You can install up to six other programs or macros.

2. Select the Alternate Program 1 field. Type the drive path for the alternate program you want to add. Don't forget to add any toggle that is needed to activate the program. The drive path should always start at your hard disk drive. For most users, the hard drive is drive C.

   Supposing that you want to add Lotus 1-2-3, type C:\123\123. This drive path assumes that the Lotus 1-2-3 software is on drive C and in a directory named *123*. The second *123* is the toggle that activates the program.

3. Select the Menu selection field for Alternate Program 1. Type the description that will appear on the Q&A Main menu. Try to choose a name, therefore, that starts with a letter other than the standard Q&A menu selections.

In this example, type **LOTUS 123**. Remember that you can navigate the menus by typing letters to activate your selection.

4. Select Alternate program 2.

For this example, type **C:\QUICKEN2\Q**.

This drive path assumes that Quicken software is on drive C and in a directory named *Quicken2*. The *Q* is the toggle that activates the program.

5. Select the Menu selection field for Alternate Program 2.

Type **QUICKEN** as the description for Quicken. This description will appear as a selection on the Q&A Main menu.

This screen shows the drive paths and startup names you entered.

```
                      ALTERNATE PROGRAMS
                      ══════════════════

        You can install up to six alternate programs for the Main Menu.
        You can then execute those programs by selecting them at that menu.
        When you exit from these programs, you will return automatically
        to the Main Menu.

             Alternate program 1: C:\123\123
             Menu selection.....: LOTUS 123
             Alternate program 2: C:\QUICKEN2\Q
             Menu selection.....: QUICKEN
             Alternate program 3:
             Menu selection.....:
             Alternate program 4:
             Menu selection.....:
             Alternate program 5:
             Menu selection.....:
             Alternate program 6:
             Menu selection.....:
        _____


        Esc-Exit                                        F10-Continue
```

6. Press F10 to save the defaults.

You are returned to the Utilities menu.

7. Press Esc once to return to the Q&A Main menu.

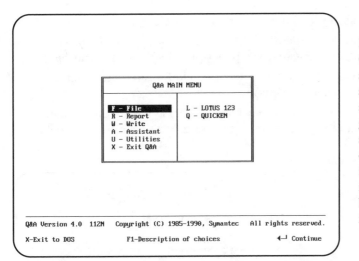

LOTUS 123 and QUICKEN appear as Main menu selections. If the alternate programs are installed in the directories you indicated, you can run the software by selecting it from this menu.

Installing a Macro as an Alternate Program

In addition to software, you also can activate macros from the Q&A Main menu. If you are not familiar with macros, refer to Chapter 13 for an explanation of how to write macros and what they can do. You should have a basic understanding of macros before you continue in this section.

To install macros on the Q&A Main menu, follow these steps:

1. From the Q&A Main menu, select Utilities.

2. Select Set alternate programs.

   Assume that you have a macro that runs a weekly report showing all sales for the current quarter. The report must be run weekly, and the steps are always the same. A macro has been written that runs this report automatically, and it is activated by pressing Alt-S (for *Sales*). This macro will be the third alternate program on the Main menu.

3. Move the cursor to the Alternate Program 3 field.

   This field usually contains the drive path and toggle needed to activate another software program. When you install macros, however, you enter the macro identifier. The macro identifier is the key combination that starts the macro; in this case, it is the Alt-S key combination.

4. With the cursor in the Alternate Program 3 field, type **ALTS**.

   You must enter both identifier keys on this line to start the macro. Do not add characters such as a plus (+) or hyphen (-) in this field.

5. Move the cursor to the Menu selection field for Alternate Program 3 and type the macro description.

   The description of the macro, which appears as a Main menu selection, can be up to thirteen characters long. For this example, type **SALES REPORT**.

The Alternate Programs screen now shows the macro assignment.

```
                          ALTERNATE PROGRAMS

          You can install up to six alternate programs for the Main Menu.
          You can then execute those programs by selecting them at that menu.
          When you exit from these programs, you will return automatically
          to the Main Menu.

                 Alternate program 1: C:\123\123
                 Menu selection.....: LOTUS 123
                 Alternate program 2: C:\QUICKEN2\Q
                 Menu selection.....: QUICKEN
                 Alternate program 3: ALTS
                 Menu selection.....: SALES REPORT
                 Alternate program 4:
                 Menu selection.....:
                 Alternate program 5:
                 Menu selection.....:
                 Alternate program 6:
                 Menu selection.....:


    Esc-Exit                                              F10-Continue
```

6. Press F10 to save the new menu assignments.

   You are returned to the Utilities menu.

7. Press Esc once to return to the Q&A Main menu.

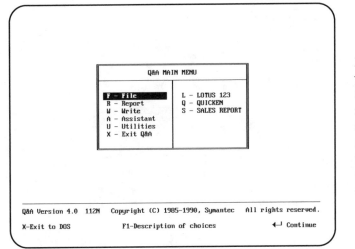

In this example, you see that the Sales Report macro has been added to the Main menu, along with the Lotus 1-2-3 and Quicken options.

14

You now can run the macro that generates the Sales Report by selecting it from the Q&A Main menu.

Issuing DOS Commands in Q&A

One of the selections from the Utilities menu offers DOS file facility commands. Generally, you issue these commands from DOS (when you are at the C: prompt), and they require that you type the command and press Enter to initiate the request. DOS commands help you maintain and archive files. You can use DOS commands to delete, copy, rename, and move text. You can accomplish some of these housekeeping chores without leaving Q&A.

To issue DOS commands from within Q&A, follow these steps:

1. From the Utilities menu, select DOS file facilities.

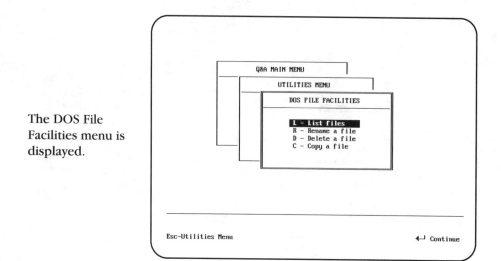

The DOS File
Facilities menu is
displayed.

14

This menu offers the following DOS functions:

- List files lists all files stored in the directory specified.
- Rename a file renames or changes the name of existing files.
- Delete a file removes files from storage that you no longer need.
- Copy a file copies a file from one location to another.

2. Select List files on the DOS File Facilities menu.

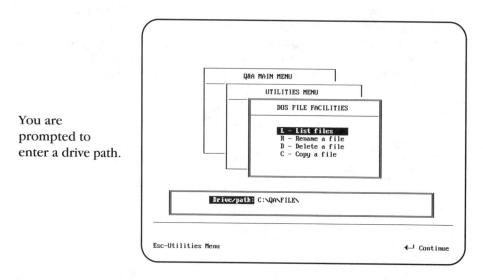

You are
prompted to
enter a drive path.

3. Press ⏎Enter to view the files that are contained in the displayed drive path.

```
┌─────────────────────────────────────────────────────────────┐
│                                                               │
│  ┌─────────────────────────────────────────────────────────┐ │
│  │           LIST OF FILES IN C:\QA\FILE\*.*                │ │
│  │  ▓▓▓▓▓▓▓▓▓                                               │ │
│  │  \..                                                     │ │
│  │  BUDGET.DTF                                              │ │
│  │  BUDGET.IDX                                              │ │
│  │  DOW.DTF                                                 │ │
│  │  DOW.IDX                                                 │ │
│  │                                                          │ │
│  │                                                          │ │
│  │  ┌───┐  ┌──────────────────────────────────┐   ┌───┐    │ │
│  │  │   │  │ File name: C:\QA\FILE\            │   │   │    │ │
│  │  └───┘  └──────────────────────────────────┘   └───┘    │ │
│  └─────────────────────────────────────────────────────────┘ │
│                                                               │
│  Esc-Exit   F1-Help   F3-Delete   F5-Copy   F7-Search        │
│             F8-Rename   F10-Continue                          │
└─────────────────────────────────────────────────────────────┘
```

A list of files is displayed. Notice that the key assignment line shows the available DOS functions.

4. Press F1 to view the help screen for this menu.

```
┌─────────────────────────────────────────────────────────────┐
│  ═══════════════ USING A LIST ═══════════ Appendix B ═══════  │
│  Type or select the name of the file, document, print spec,  │
│  or report that you want to use and press ◄┘. To select a    │
│  name, type ↓ ↑ → ← or the SPACE BAR.                         │
│  At a list of DOS files, you can subset the list. NOTE:      │
│  Specs (Print, Report, Retrieve, Etc.) are not DOS files;    │
│  they cannot be subsetted.                                    │
│  ┌─────────────────────────────────────────────────────────┐ │
│  │         HOW TO SUBSET A LIST OF DOS FILES               │ │
│  │  Type * or ? in various combinations followed by ◄┘ to  │ │
│  │  show a subset of the files in a directory, just as you │ │
│  │  can with DOS. For example:                             │ │
│  │  *.doc  to show all the files in the directory with a   │ │
│  │         "doc" extension.                                │ │
│  │  p??.*  to show all files that have a 3-character name  │ │
│  │         and begin with "p".                             │ │
│  ├──────────────────────────┬──────────────────────────────┤ │
│  │  HOW TO RENAME/DELETE/COPY│   HOW TO SEARCH FOR A NAME   │ │
│  │  Type or select a name,   │ Type the first few unique    │ │
│  │  then press:              │ letters of a name followed   │ │
│  │                           │ by two periods, then press   │ │
│  │  F3 - to delete it        │ F7 (SEARCH). For example,    │ │
│  │  F5 - to make a copy of it│ type "m.." then F7 to find   │ │
│  │  F8 - to rename it        │ the first name in the list   │ │
│  │                           │ that begins with "m".        │ │
│  └──────────────────────────┴──────────────────────────────┘ │
│  Esc-Exit                                                     │
└─────────────────────────────────────────────────────────────┘
```

The Help screen is displayed.

5. Press Esc to clear the Help screen.

6. Select the file you want to modify. If you prefer, you can type the name in response to the File name prompt.

You also can use the following function key assignments:

Key	Function
F1	Displays a Help screen for DOS commands.
F3	Deletes a file from the list of files.
F5	Copies a file on the list.
F7	Segments the list to specific files.
F8	Renames a file on the list.
F10	Continues the process requested and returns you to the Utilities menu.

Copying a File

Copying a file is an easy process. You can use this procedure to back up files on floppy disks. Assume that you want to copy the first file on your list and rename the copy. For this example, use your first name to rename the new file.

To copy a file, follow these steps:

1. From the Q&A Main menu, select Utilities.
2. Select DOS File Facilities.
3. Select Copy a file.
4. At the Copy from prompt, type a file name or press ↵Enter to see a list of files.
5. Highlight the file you want to copy.

```
                  LIST OF FILES IN C:\QA\FILE\*.*

    \..
    BUDGET.DTF
    BUDGET.IDX
    DOW.DTF
    DOW.IDX




    ┌─┐   ┌────────────────────────────────────────┐   ┌─┐
    │ │   │ File name: C:\QA\FILE\BUDGET.DTF        │   │ │
    └─┘   └────────────────────────────────────────┘   └─┘

    BUDGET.DTF     Size: 25,600     Date edited: 11/07/90    Time edited: 16:46
    No description available.  Press F6 to add one.
    Esc-Exit   F1-Help   F3-Delete   F5-Copy   F7-Search   F8-Rename   F10-Continue
```

The status line tells you the file name, size, date, and time edited.

14

6. Press F5 to initiate the copy process.

```
                  LIST OF FILES IN C:\QA\FILE\*.*

    \..
    BUDGET.DTF
    BUDGET.IDX
    DOW.DTF
    DOW.IDX




    ┌─┐   ┌────────────────────────────────────────┐   ┌─┐
    │ │   │ File name: C:\QA\FILE\BUDGET.DTF        │   │ │
    │ │   │ Copy to: C:\QA\FILE\                    │   │ │
    └─┘   └────────────────────────────────────────┘   └─┘

    BUDGET.DTF     Size: 25,600     Date edited: 11/07/90    Time edited: 16:46

    Esc-Exit   F1-Help   F3-Delete   F5-Copy   F7-Search   F8-Rename   F10-Continue
```

The prompt box requests that you enter a name for the copied file.

The new file requires a new name. The name can be up to eight
characters long and must not be the same as the source file. For this
example, use your first name as the new file name. If your name is
longer than eight characters, use only the first eight characters. If
your name is shorter than eight characters, you do not have to use all
eight spaces.

7. Press F10 to continue the copy process.

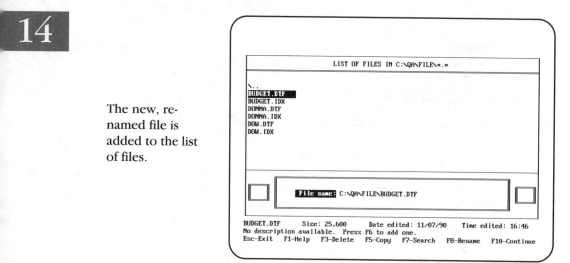

The new, re-
named file is
added to the list
of files.

Note: When you are copying a database file, both the IDX and DTF files are
included in the copy process.

Renaming a File

Use the Rename feature to change a file name. Remember that every file name
must be unique. If you select an existing file name, Q&A writes the renamed
file over the existing file. Use caution when you rename files.

To rename a copied file, follow these steps:

1. From the Q&A Main menu, select Utilities.

2. Select DOS File Facilities.

3. Select Rename.

4. Type a file name or press ⏎Enter to see a list of files.

5. Press ⏎Enter or F8 to rename the file.

```
          LIST OF FILES IN C:\QA\FILE\*.*

  \..
  BUDGET.DTF
  BUDGET.IDX
  DONNA.DTF
  DONNA.IDX
  DOW.DTF
  DOW.IDX




  ┌─┐   ┌──────────────────────────────────────┐  ┌─┐
  │ │   │   File name: C:\QA\FILE\DONNA.DTF     │  │ │
  └─┘   │  Rename to: C:\QA\FILE\               │  └─┘
        └──────────────────────────────────────┘

  DONNA.DTF      Size: 25,600    Date edited: 11/17/90   Time edited: 14:28

  Esc-Exit   F1-Help   F3-Delete   F5-Copy   F7-Search   F8-Rename   F10-Continue
```

A prompt appears at the bottom of the screen and asks for the new name for this file.

14

6. Enter the new name for this field.

7. Press `F10` to continue.

```
          LIST OF FILES IN C:\QA\FILE\*.*

  \..
  BUDGET.DTF
  BUDGET.IDX
  DOW.DTF
  DOW.IDX
  DOWDLE.DTF
  DOWDLE.IDX




  ┌─┐   ┌──────────────────────────────────────┐  ┌─┐
  │ │   │  File name: C:\QA\FILE\DOWDLE.DTF     │  │ │
  └─┘   │                                      │  └─┘
        └──────────────────────────────────────┘

  DOWDLE.DTF     Size: 25,600    Date edited: 11/17/90   Time edited: 14:28
  No description available.  Press F6 to add one.
  Esc-Exit   F1-Help   F3-Delete   F5-Copy   F7-Search   F8-Rename   F10-Continue
```

The file is re-named and added to the list in alphabetical order.

Deleting Files from the File List

You can use the F3 function key to remove files from the List of Files screen from within File, Write, Report, or the Intelligent Assistant. If you delete a file, it is gone and you cannot retrieve it without using a special utility program. Do not use the delete feature carelessly. When you delete database files, both the IDX and DTF files are deleted.

To delete a file, follow these steps:

1. From the DOS File Facilities menu, select Delete a File.

2. At the file name prompt, press ⏎Enter to accept the displayed name or erase the name and type a name. You also can press ⏎Enter to see a list of files.

A warning box appears and asks you to confirm the deletion.

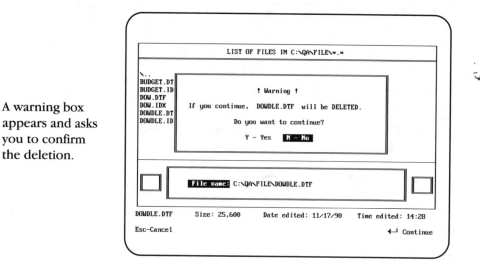

```
                    LIST OF FILES IN C:\QA\FILE\*.*

  \..
  BUDGET.DT
  BUDGET.ID              ! Warning !
  DOW.DTF
  DOW.IDX       If you continue,  DOWDLE.DTF  will be DELETED.
  DOWDLE.DT
  DOWDLE.ID              Do you want to continue?

                        Y - Yes   N - No


      File name: C:\QA\FILE\DOWDLE.DTF


  DOWDLE.DTF    Size: 25,600    Date edited: 11/17/90    Time edited: 14:28
  Esc-Cancel                                             ⏎ Continue
```

3. Select Yes to delete the file or No to return to the file name prompt.

    The file is deleted from the List of Files.

4. Press Esc until you return to the Utilities menu.

5. Press Esc to return to the Q&A Main menu.

    The file is renamed and added to the list in alphabetical order.

Creating Macros and Menus

This chapter introduces you to Q&A macros and custom menus. Using macros can decrease the time you spend entering repetitive keystrokes. Macros can save you a great deal of work.

A macro is a function that stores a series of commands or text and then "plays them back" when you press a single keystroke. You can use macros in Q&A File, Write, Report, or the Intelligent Assistant to automate command sequences and data-entry.

You can create macros to save a text file, enter special print settings, and print a report. Macros also are ideal for inserting frequently used paragraphs, sentences, or phrases into your documents. You can use macros to reassign the keys on your keyboard so that Q&A works like other programs with which you are familiar.

You can name your macros and list them in a menu with descriptions that tell what each macro does. You then can run your macros by choosing them from the menu, so you don't have to remember their invocation keys.

You also can create menus that extend or replace Q&A's own menus. This feature enables you to customize Q&A so that other users can choose a menu item to perform complex tasks such as printing monthly reports or mailing labels.

Key Terms Used in This Chapter

Macro	Enables you to store repetitive keystrokes and to play them back.
Nested macro	The process of placing one macro command within another macro.

Creating Macros—The Basics

15

You can create Q&A macros in two ways:

- You can have Q&A record a series of keystrokes as you type them. To use the recording method, you simply tell Q&A when to begin recording keystrokes, when to stop, and specify a name for the recorded keystrokes.

- You can type each command separately. To use this interactive method, you must open a text file and type special commands that represent each keystroke and indicate where the macro begins and ends. You can use the interactive method to edit macros created with the recording method.

Defining Macros in Record Mode

In most cases, creating macros by recording keystrokes is quicker, easier, and more accurate than creating macros by typing commands. When you record a macro, you don't have to leave the current document, and all of Q&A's normal keystrokes are available for defining the macro. After you complete the keystroke sequence, you simply turn off the recording feature. With the recording method, no programming is involved.

Recording Macros

Q&A makes recording macros easy:

1. Press ⌖Shift⌫-F2 to display the Macro menu.

2. Select Define Macro from the menu.

   Q&A prompts you for a macro name. You can name a macro three ways:

352

- With an invocation key such as Alt-A
- With a name such as Print Reports
- With both a name and an invocation key

If you choose a single-key identifier, such as Alt-A, you can run the macro by pressing the identifier key without selecting the macro from a menu. You also can run the Alt-A macro from a menu of macros.

If you choose a name for your macro, you can run the macro only from Q&A's Macro names list.

In either case, you can enter a description for the macro on the Macro Names list.

15

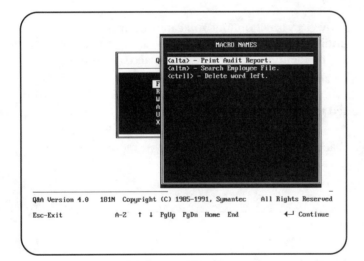

The Macro names list.

3. If you want to use a macro identifier key, press that key (for example, Alt-A).

By combining Ctrl or Alt with a letter, you can choose from more than 80 possible macro identifier keys. Table 15.1 lists the keys and combinations already used by Q&A for Write, File, Report, and Intelligent Assistant operations. When you define macros, use identifier keys other than those listed in the table unless you want to override a key's Q&A assignment. (If, for example, you named a macro Ctrl-F for use within the Write module, you would disable Write's regular use of Ctrl-F for moving the cursor from one word to the next.)

If you type the key of an existing macro, Q&A asks whether you want to overwrite it or choose a different identifier key. Select **Yes** to redefine that key combination.

If you want to give the macro a name so that you can run it by selecting its name from a list of macros, press ⤶Enter without typing an identifier key. When you finish recording, you can name the macro and give it a description, both of which appear on the list of macros whenever you play back the macro.

4. Type the keystrokes that you want to record.

You can enter Q&A commands or type text. Q&A displays a flashing square at the bottom of the screen to remind you that macro recording is turned on.

You can record any Q&A function, but you cannot start recording a second macro until you finish the first one. You can, however, "nest" macros by typing the identifier keys of existing macros as you record.

If you want the macro to pause for input during playback (for example, while you type a response at a Q&A prompt), press Alt-F2. Type the required text at the prompt and press Alt-F2 to end the pause.

When you play back the macro, Q&A pauses for you to type the input and press ⤶Enter to end the pause.

5. Press ⤒Shift-F2 to turn off macro recording.

Q&A displays the Macro Options box.

```
                     ┌──────────────────────────────────┐
                     │          Q&A MAIN MENU           │
                     │      ┌───────────────────┐       │
                     │      │   MACRO OPTIONS   │       │
                     │      └───────────────────┘       │
                     │                                  │
                     │ Macro name.........: <alta> - Print Audit Report. │
                     │                                  │
                     │ Show screen........:   Yes  ▶No◀ │
                     │ End with menu......: Main Menu    │
                     │                                  │
                     │                                  │
                     └──────────────────────────────────┘

   Q&A Version 4.0    181N  Copyright (C) 1985-1991, Symantec    All Rights Reserved

   Esc-Exit                  Alt+F7-List of menus               F10-Continue
```

6. At the `Macro Description` prompt, Q&A displays a code for the macro identifier key, if you entered one. At this point you have two options:

   You can move the cursor to the right of the identifier code, enter a space, and type a description for the macro. The macro's identifier and description can contain up to 31 characters.

   You can move the cursor to the left end of the line and type over the code at the name prompt. The new identifier key goes into effect.

7. At the `Show Screen` prompt, tell Q&A whether you want screens to be displayed while the macro runs. If you choose No, the macro plays back faster.

8. At the `End with Menu` prompt, type the name of a Q&A or custom menu that you want to display when the macro finishes running. (For more details, see "Naming Menus" later in this chapter.)

   Or, press [Alt]-[F7] to display a list of existing Q&A program menus and custom menus that you designed for the current macro file, highlight the name of the menu in the list, and press [↵Enter].

   If you enter a name at the End with Menu prompt, Q&A displays the menu you name after the macro runs. (For example, you can have a macro that runs a spell check, then displays the Write Print Options menu.).

9. Press [F10] to end the macro recording process.

   Q&A displays the name of the currently loaded macro file; the default macro file name is QAMACRO.ASC.

   Press [↵Enter] to accept the default, or type a new macro file name and press [↵Enter].

   At the macro file name prompt you can press [Esc] to avoid saving the macro, but when you turn off your computer or Get another macro file, any macros in memory are lost.

   You can save any macros in memory at any point by pressing [⇧Shift]-[F2] to display the Macro Menu and choosing Save Macros. (For more information, see "Saving Recorded Macros" later in this chapter.)

15

Table 15.1
Macro Key Combinations Used by Q&A

Ctrl-A	Ctrl-Bksp	F1	Shift-F1	Del
Ctrl-C	Ctrl-PrtSc	F2	Shift-F2	End
Ctrl-D	Ctrl-F2	F3	Shift-F3	Home
Ctrl-E	Ctrl-F5	F4	Shift-F4	Ins
Ctrl-F	Ctrl-F6	F5	Shift-F5	PgDn
Ctrl-G	Ctrl-F7	F6	Shift-F6	PgUp
Ctrl-H	Ctrl-F8	F7	Shift-F7	Ctrl-I
Ctrl-[	F8	Shift-F8	Ctrl-M	Ctrl-Home
F9	Shift-F9	Ctrl-R	Ctrl-PgDn	F10
Shift-F10	Ctrl-S	Ctrl-PgUp	Shift-Bksp	Bksp
Ctrl-T	Alt-F2	Shift-Esc	Esc	Ctrl-V
Alt-F5	Shift-Enter	Enter	Ctrl-W	Ctrl-Z
Alt-F8	Shift-Tab	Tab	Ctrl-Y	Alt-F9

Playing Back and Changing Recorded Macros

To play back the macro you just created, you can use one of three methods:

- Press its invocation key from anywhere in Q&A.
- Press (Alt)-(F2) to display the macro list. Move the cursor to the macro's name and press (↵Enter).
- Press (⇧Shift)-(F2) to display the Macro menu and choose Run Macro.

If the macro doesn't work properly, press (Esc) to stop execution.

To redefine the macro, press (⇧Shift)-(F2) to display the Macro menu. Select Define Macro and press the macro's identifier key. Q&A warns you that the key has already been defined. You can choose to redefine the key by ignoring the warning and typing new macro keystrokes for the identifier. After you record the new keystrokes, press (⇧Shift)-(F2) to end macro recording.

You also can change a macro by editing its file in the Write module. The procedure for importing a macro file to Write is described later in this chapter, in "Creating and Editing Macros Interactively."

Saving Recorded Macros

When you create a recorded macro, you can use the macro for the current work session only or save the macro for future use. If you use a macro to perform a calculation on a field for a one-time application, you don't need to save it. If you create a macro to perform a recurring function, such as inserting a heading on personal letters, you need to save the macro to disk. Macros created with the recording method are stored in RAM.

If you haven't saved your macro during the recording sequence, press `Shift`-`F2` and select Save Macros from the Macro menu. Enter a macro file name at the prompt. You can use any name that follows DOS conventions: up to eight characters with an optional three-character extension.

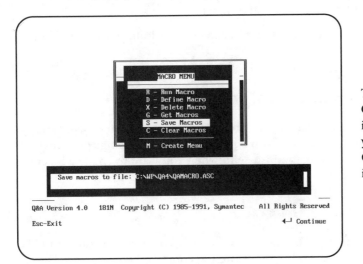

The default name, QAMACRO.ASC, is used only if you load QAMACRO.ASC into RAM first.

Don't save a new macro to a macro file until you load that macro file into RAM with the Get macros command on the Macro menu. If the macro file isn't loaded in RAM and you save a new macro using a file name assigned to previously stored macros, Q&A replaces the existing file with a new file containing only your new macro. To save your macros without losing any valuable information, follow these rules:

- Load the macro file into memory before you record any macros.

- Resave the file after you add new macros.

- Make backups of macro files (Q&A does not make automatic back-ups).

- Save macro files with names that are easy to identify. (Give them an .ASC or .MAC extension, for example.)

Clearing Recorded Macros from Memory

After you save a set of macros to disk, you can choose Clear from the Macro menu to remove the macros from RAM. This command does not delete macros that you have saved to disk.

The Clear command returns all your macro keys and key combinations to their original values. Clearing macros from RAM enables you to work on another set of macros or return the keyboard to its default state. This command is useful when you have defined macros for a specific database and want to use or define another set of macros for another database.

You can create and save any number of macro sets, as long as you use different file names.

Defining Macros in Q&A Write (Interactive Mode)

In addition to recording macros, you can define macros by using Q&A Write to create a file of macro commands. You type the commands using codes that can be read by Q&A. This method is useful when you want to create a macro that is too long or complex to edit by retyping all of the keystrokes.

Writing Interactive Macros

When you create a macro in Define macro mode, Q&A creates a command file for you. In the interactive mode, you create the command file yourself. The following example shows a simple macro file that takes the user from Q&A's Main menu into File, then displays the Retrieve Spec for the file named EMPLOYEE. The commands are displayed in unbroken lines on the Write edit screen, but here they are split apart so they are easier to read.

```
<begdef>
<altm>
<name>"<caps,>altm<caps.><sp>-
<sp>Search<sp>Employee<sp>file.<sp>"
```

<vidoff>

fsemployee<enter>

<enddef>

Each macro begins with the code *<begdef>*, which stands for "begin definition."

The identifier key is entered next, followed by the keystrokes. Each keystroke is enclosed within angle brackets (<>) and typed in lowercase letters. Text that is to appear literally is not enclosed.

In the sample macro, the identifier key is Alt-**M**. The *<name>* command introduces the macro's name as it is displayed in the macro list. Everything between quotation marks is part of the macro's listed key assignment and description.

The *<vidoff>* command tells Q&A that you have selected **N**o for the Show Screen option on the Macro Options menu (at the end of the macro recording process). Choosing <vidoff> suppresses screen displays while the macro runs.

fsemployee selects **F**ile from the Q&A Main menu and **S**earch from the File menu, and then chooses Employee as the database to be searched. *<enter>* presses the Enter key after the file name (employee) is typed at the prompt.

The code *<enddef>* tells Q&A to "end definition."

You also can create or edit macros in the Write edit screen. To edit an existing macro, choose Get from the Write menu, type the name of the macro file, and press Enter. Q&A 4 converts files stored in standard Q&A Write document format to ASCII format when you use the Macro menu to Run or Get a macro file.

When you write macros interactively, follow these rules:

- An asterisk (*) must separate each macro from the preceding macro in the macro file. The first macro in the file is not preceded by an asterisk.

- Angle brackets are used to enclose each element of the macro. Do not insert spaces between elements.

- Let Q&A word-wrap the macro codes. Here, the commands are separated with carriage returns to make them easier to read; when editing macros, do not press Enter at the end of a line.

15

The following table describes the elements of a Q&A macro:

Table 15.2
Q&A Macro Elements

Code	Purpose
<begdef>	Indicates the start of a macro.
<Keystroke ID> | <nokey>	If you do not assign a macro invocation key, <nokey> appears here; otherwise, enter the invocation key (<alta>, for example).
<name>	The macro's name. The name is enclosed in quotation marks (not angle brackets). This name appears in Q&A's list of macros when you choose Run a Macro from the Macro menu. If you do not assign a macro name, do not enter anything.
<vidon> | <vidoff>	Tells Q&A whether to display screens while a macro runs. If you don't enter a code, Q&A assumes <showscreen>, described below.
recorded keystrokes...	The keystrokes that the macro plays back.
<call>	Followed by a menu name, it tells Q&A to display the named menu after the macro runs.
"Menu Name"	The name of the menu invoked with <call>. The menu name is enclosed in quotation marks.
<wait>	An optional code that tells Q&A to pause while the user types text. Macro playback resumes when the user presses ⏎Enter or <keyname>, as described below.
<keyname>	An optional code used with <wait> to tell Q&A to end a pause when the user presses the key named in <keyname>.
<enddef>	Ends the macro.

When you write and edit interactive macros, the following special keys and key combinations must be entered in a specific format:

Key/Combination	Written as
Alt -A	\<alta>
Alt -5	\<alt5>
Alt - F2	\<altf2>
◆Backspace	\<bks>
Ctrl - Home	\<ctrlhom>
Ctrl - PgUp	\<ctrlpgu>
Ctrl - ↵Enter	\<ctrlent>
↓	\<dn>
↑	\<up>
Esc	\<esc>
Ins	\<ins>
←	\<lft>
→	\<rgt>
↵Enter	\<enter>
⇧Shift - F1	\<capsf1>
⇧Shift - Tab⇄	\<capstab>
Tab⇄	\<tab>

Not all of the keys used to edit macros are shown in the table, but they are entered in similar formats. For example, all function keys (normal, shifted, or with the Alt key) can be entered by following the F1 and F2 examples in the table. For example, F10 is entered as \<f10> and Alt - F10 is \<Altf10>. If in doubt about how to enter command keystrokes, try what seems logical; Q&A tells you if the combination doesn't work.

If you cannot figure out how to construct a key sequence, save the macro and display the Macro menu with ⇧Shift - F2. Choose Define Macro and enter the keystrokes you want to add to your interactive macro. Save the macro to a tempo-

15

361

rary file. Now you can load this file into Write and see how Q&A constructed the sequence. Then you can insert the file into the interactive macro or type the sequence.

Saving Interactive Macros

Saving macro files you've created in Write is simple. Just save the macro as a Q&A Write document.

When you want to use a set of macros, press ⌖Shift - F2 and choose Get Macros from the Macro menu. Enter the macro file name at the prompt (be sure to include the path), and Q&A loads the set of macros.

Using Write To Solve Macro Problems

If your recorded macro doesn't work, you can use Write to fix the problem. Suppose that the final command in a macro tells Q&A to exit to DOS. You cannot save that macro, because the final command returns you to DOS before you can choose Save a Macro.

Solve the problem by ending the recorded definition before the last command and selecting the Save a Macro option. Then enter the macro file through Q&A Write, find the macro, and add X<enter> before the end of the definition (<enddef>). Save the file. Now the macro exits Q&A from the Main menu as the final step.

The interactive method is also helpful when you need to create a series of macros that perform very similar functions. To avoid repeating the same keystrokes, you can use Write's block-copying capabilities to copy the repeated keystrokes to each macro.

Reloading Macro Files

You can create as many macro files as you have room for on your disk. To retrieve the file you want to use, press ⌖Shift - F2 for the Macro menu and select Get Macros. Enter the macro file name at the prompt; the macro file is then loaded into RAM and ready to use.

Protecting Macro Files and Applications

You can protect your macros and custom applications (described in "Creating Custom Menus and Applications" later in this chapter) so that other users

362

cannot tamper with them. When Q&A protects a macro file or application, the user can run the macros, but cannot edit them in Write or overwrite them by recording a new macro with the same name or invocation key. Protected macro files cannot be edited, nor can a user get, create, delete, save, or clear macros while the protected file is loaded.

To protect a macro file or an application, follow these steps:

1. From the Q&A Main menu, choose File, and at the File menu, choose Design File.

   Q&A displays the Design menu.

2. Select Customize Application.

   Q&A displays the Customize Application menu.

3. Select Protect Macro File.

   Q&A displays the Protect Macro box.

4. Enter the name of the macro file you want to protect.

5. Type a new name for the protected macro file.

   Be careful. If you type the name of the old macro file, that file is overwritten by the new, protected version, and you cannot edit it again.

6. To load the protected file, press ⇧Shift-F2 to display the Macro menu, and choose Get Macros.

Using Autostart Macros

Q&A loads the macro file called QAMACRO.ASC at startup. If you want a different macro file to load when you start Q&A, name that file QAMACRO.ASC. When the program is booted, Q&A searches for that macro file. Only one macro file can be in memory at a time.

If you want to use a macro file with a name other than QAMACRO.ASC, choose the Get command from the Macro menu to load the file after the system has been booted and the autoloading macros have executed.

To have Q&A load a different macro file at startup, type the following line at the DOS prompt to load Q& A:

    QA -AL<macro filename>

To make a file other than QAMACRO.ASC the permanent default startup macro file, type

> QA -AD<macro filename>

at the DOS prompt. Be sure to type a space between QA and the code -AL or -AD.

Creating Custom Menus and Applications

You can run a macro in the following ways:

- Press its invocation key (for example, ⌨Alt⌨-**A** or ⌨Alt⌨-**Q**).
- Choose **R**un Macro from the Macro Menu (press ⌨⇧Shift⌨-⌨F2⌨ , **R**), and select the macro from the list that Q&A displays.

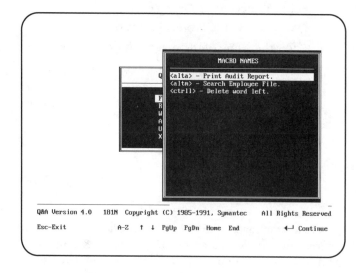

Running a macro from the macro list.

- Press ⌨Alt⌨-⌨F2⌨ from any Q&A screen to display the list of macros, then choose the macro from the list and press ⌨↵Enter⌨.
- Run the macro from a custom menu of your own design.

Creating Custom Menus

To create a custom menu, follow these steps:

1. From any Q&A screen, press ⌨⇧Shift⌨-⌨F2⌨ to display the Macro menu.
2. Select Create **M**enu.

   Q&A displays a list of existing custom menus.

```
                    MACRO MENU OPTIONS

                                    ┌─────────────────────────────────────────┐
        Menu name..........:        │           Q&A MENU NAMES             ↑   │
        Display.............:       │                                          │
        Status..............:       │ Assistant Menu                           │
        Menu returns........:       │ Basic Lessons Menu                       │
        On Escape, show menu.:      │ Center button                            │
                                    │ Columnar Global Options Menu             │
        ┌───────────────────────────┤ Copy Menu                                │
        │          Menu Title...:   │ Cross tab Global Options Menu            │
        │                           │ Customize Application Menu               │
        │ Item 1: Salaries by Department │ Customize Menu                       │
        │ Item 2: Monthly Billings  │ Design Menu                              │
        │ Item 3:                   │ Dos File Facilities Menu                 │
        │ Item 4:                   │ Export Menu                              │
        │ Item 5:                   │ File Menu                                │
        │ Item 6:                   │ File Rename Delete Copy Menu             │
        │ Item 7:                   │ Global Options Menu                      │
        │ Item 8:                   │ Import Menu                          ↓   │
        │ Item 9:                   └─────────────────────────────────────────┘

    Esc-Exit           A-Z  ↑ ↓  PgUp PgDn  Home  End        ↵ Continue
```

The Q&A Menu
Names list.

3. To create a new menu, choose New Menu. To edit an existing menu, choose its name from the list.

   Q&A displays the Macro Menu Options screen.

```
                    MACRO MENU OPTIONS

        Menu name..........: Reports
        Display.............: ▶Full screen◀   Overlay
        Status..............: ▶Active◀        Inactive
        Menu returns........:    Yes     ▶No◀
        On Escape, show menu.: Main Menu

        ┌──────────────────────────────────────────────────────────┐
        │          Menu Title...: Custom Reports                    │
        │                                                           │
        │ Item 1: Annual Audit        Macro Name: <alta>            │
        │ Item 2: Draft Statements    Macro Name: <altb>            │
        │ Item 3: Monthly Billings    Macro Name: <altc>            │
        │ Item 4:                     Macro Name:                   │
        │ Item 5:                     Macro Name:                   │
        │ Item 6:                     Macro Name:                   │
        │ Item 7:                     Macro Name:                   │
        │ Item 8:                     Macro Name:                   │
        │ Item 9:                     Macro Name:                   │
        └──────────────────────────────────────────────────────────┘

    Esc-Exit         F1-Help         Alt+F7-List of...      F10-Continue
```

The Macro Menu
Options screen.

Answer the following prompts:

Prompt	Response
Menu Name	Type the name you want to use to calling the menu from macros and from other menus.
Display	Choose Full Screen to display the menu in a blank screen. Choose Overlay to display the menu in a box over the current Q&A screen.
Status	Choose Active to display the menu. If you choose Inactive, the menu can be called from a macro, but is not displayed.
Menu Returns	Choose Yes to display the menu after a menu item runs.
On Escape, Show Menu	Type the name of the menu you want to display when the user presses Esc at this menu.
Menu Title	Type the title to display at the top of the menu. This title need not be the same as the menu name you gave at the top of the screen.
Item1..9	Type the text to appear next to the menu item.
1..9.Macro Name	Type the name or key identifier of the macro to be run by the menu item. To choose a macro from the current macro, press Alt-F7, highlight the macro, and press ↵Enter. When you finish with the Macro Menu Options screen, press F10. Q&A saves the menu.

Naming Menus

Be careful naming macros and menus. If you name a custom menu "File Menu," Q&A replaces its own File menu with your custom menu. Then, whenever you choose File from the Main menu, Q&A runs your custom menu. Some Q&A menus have duplicate names—for example, the Global Options menus have identical names in Write, Report, and File Print. If you need to call one of these Q&A menus with a macro or custom menu, use the following names:

Menu	Name to Use in Macro or Custom Menu
Rename/Delete/Copy (File)	File, Print, Rename/Delete/Copy
Rename/Delete/Copy (Report)	Report, Rename/Delete/Copy
Print Global Options	File, Print, Global Options
Report Global Options	Report, Global Options
Columnar Global Options	Report, Global Options, Columnar Global Options
Crosstab Global Options	Report, Global Options, Crosstab Global Options
Write Global Options	Write, Utilities, Global Options
Assistant Menu	Assistant Menu (use this name, not a customized name you've assigned to the Intelligent Assistant)

Creating and Editing Menus Interactively

Just as you can create and edit macros interactively (described in this chapter's "Defining Macros in Q&A Write" section), you can create and edit menus by editing a macro file in Q&A Write's editing screen. Custom menus that you create are stored in the Q&A macro file that is loaded when you save them.

A menu has the following macro structure:

```
<begdef>
<nokey>
<name>"Menu Name"
<vidon>
<menu>
"Menu Title: Item1/Item1macro,Item2/Item2macro...Itemn/Itemnmacro/"
<enddef>
```

The following table explains the codes:

Code	Purpose
<begdef>	Begins the menu.
<nokey>	Every menu must have a <nokey> code in this position.
<name>	Menu name follows. Every menu must have a name.
"Menu Name"	The menu name of up to 31 characters, enclosed in quotation marks. (You cannot use quotation marks within the name itself.) Q&A uses this name to call the menu from a macro, etc. The name cannot be the same as "Menu Title," which is described below.
<menu>	Indicates that the menu structure follows.
"Menu Title"	The list of choices that appear in the menu, with the macros that each choice invokes.
	The menu structure is enclosed in quotes, but cannot contain quotes. You can specify up to nine menu choices with 255 characters total, but cannot use spaces or carriage returns within the menu structure codes. A colon separates the menu title from the choices and their associated macros. Separate each choice from its macro with a slash. Use commas to separate menu choices.

Building Custom Applications

Building a customized Q&A application is a simple process, involving two steps:

- Write macros for the functions that you want to assign to menus.
- Using Q&A's automated menu creation process, assign your macros to menus that supplement or replace Q&A's menus.

Suppose that you want to replace the Report menu with a customized menu from which the user can print several reports by selecting their names from a menu. First, write a macro that prints each report. You can use macro pauses (described earlier in this chapter) to enable the user to make retrieval specifications, adjust the Print Spec, and make other entries while the macro runs.

After you write and test the macro, you can assign it to a custom menu. You also can tell Q&A that when it finishes printing a report it should redisplay the custom menu, display one of Q&A's own menus, or run a macro that exits Q&A. These procedures were described earlier in this chapter, in "Creating Custom Menus."

The macros you create can be used in every module of Q&A. You will discover many time-saving applications for macros, whether you define them by recording keystrokes or by editing them in Q&A Write. This section explains a few of the advanced techniques that add to Q&A's macro capability.

15

Macros within Macros

Suppose that you create a macro that types the name of your regional manager, Jonathan T. McGillicuddy, and you assign the macro to Alt-**N**. Then you want to create another macro that types his name and address. This macro is assigned to Alt-**A**.

When you record the new macro, rather than typing your manager's name again, type Alt-**N** to enter the old macro as part of the new macro's definition. Then you can add address information to finish the macro. In Q&A Write, these macros appear as follows:

<begdef>
<altn>
<name>
<vidoff>
Jonathan T. McGillicuddy
<enter>
<enddef>*
<beg def>
<alta>
<altn>
, Regional Manager
<enter>
Titan Technologies

<enter>

1234 Main Street

<enter>

Lumberyard, P A 12534

<enter>

<enddef>*

Q&A accepts up to five levels of "nested" macros. This example has only one level.

Using Other Word Processors To Create Q&A Macros

You can create Q&A macro files in any word processing program whose files you can convert for use by Q&A .

You could write Q&A macros with WordPerfect 5.1, for example, then use Q&A Write's Import feature to import the macro files.

Sample Macro Applications

Q&A macros can make your work in any of the program's modules easier. This section offers a few ideas for macro applications and may inspire you to create additional macros. All of the macros in this section have been designed to start from the Q&A Main menu, but you can write macros that begin at any point within Q&A. If you record a macro from within a Q&A module, however, remember in which module it originates; if you run the macro from some other point in Q&A, the macro keystrokes may perform undesirable actions.

If you start each macro with <ShiftF10><Esc><Esc><Esc>, you return to the Q&A Main menu from virtually anywhere in Q&A.

Querying the Intelligent Assistant

The following macro accesses the Intelligent Assistant, enters the name of the Employee database (EMPLOYEE .DTF), activates the file, and asks the Intelligent Assistant for a current list of employees in the database.

```
<begdef>
<alts>
<name>
"RUNIA"
<vidoff>
a
<enter>
a employee.dtf
<enter>
Show me the employees in the database.
<enter>
y
<enter>
<enddef> *
```

The <begdef> code tells Q&A that you are starting a new macro. [Alt]-S is the identifier key (the one you use to start the macro). The <name> code followed by "RUNIA" tells Q&A what name to display for this macro. (Every macro must have a name.) The <vidoff> code tells Q&A to suppress screen display during playback. The first letter a and [↵Enter] keystrokes select the Intelligent Assistant from the Main menu. The second letter a selects the Ask option from the Intelligent Assistant menu. EMPLOYEE.DTF tells Q&A the name of the database. The query "Show me the employees in the database" tells Q&A to display a report of the specified data. The remaining entries in the macro are responses to prompts about the query.

If you plan to use a macro repeatedly, type the file name rather than using the arrow keys. The arrow keys work when you define the macro, but if you add a database file, the arrow keystrokes may move the cursor to the wrong point in the list and access the wrong file.

The same macro can be used to ask the Intelligent Assistant questions. Rather than including the name of the database file and query in the macro, you can insert a <wait> code so that the program waits for input. The macro then appears as follows:

<begdef>
<alts>
<name>
"RUNIA"
<vidoff>
a
<enter>
<wait>
<enter>
Show me the employees in the database.
<enter>
y
<enter>
<enddef> *

Printing Reports

Macros, such as the following example, can enable you to print a report by pressing only one key.

<begdef>
<altr>
<name>
"Report Printout"
<vidoff>
r
<enter>
p
employee.dtf
<enter>
employee directory
<enter>
<enter>
<enddef> *

After the <begdef> code, Alt-**R** is specified as the identifier key and "Report Printout" as the name; <vidoff> tells Q&A to suppress menu display during playback; **r** tells Q&A to select **R**eport from the Main menu, and **p** tells Q&A to **P**rint a file; employee.dtf is the name of the database. Employee directory is the name of the report, and the remaining ↵Enter keystrokes complete the process.

The following macro uses the Intelligent Assistant to create a report from the Employee database. The macro tells Q&A to select employees from Boston and to print a report of the findings.

<begdef>

<altf8>

<name>

"IA IN Employee Report"

<vidoff>

a

<enter>

a<enter>

employee.dtf

<enter>

Who are the Boston employees

<enter><enter>

<f2>

<home>

<f8>

<tab><tab><tab><tab><tab><tab><tab>

Employees in Boston

<F10>

<esc><esc>

<enddef> *

This macro is more complicated than previous examples. The letter **a** selects the Intelligent Assistant; the database file EMPLOYEE.DTF is specified. The macro then asks the Intelligent Assistant "Who are the Boston employees" and answers the prompts with ⏎Enter keystrokes. The report is then displayed, and the F2 keystroke in the macro sends results to the printer. The Print Options screen appears before the report is printed, and the destination is changed from SCREEN to LPT1. The macro moves the cursor to a place where a title or header can be entered. In this example "Employees in Boston" is the title. The F10 in the macro prints the report. The concluding Esc keystrokes return the user to the Main menu.

15

Getting Started on a Network

This chapter helps you set up Q&A on a network system. A network is a group of computers that are linked together with cable. The linked computers can exchange information, and every person using a computer on the network can use the same databases and documents with Q&A.

Working on a network enables you to assign passwords to databases, just as you can password-protect your databases in a stand-alone system. This chapter includes a brief description of networks and instructions for setting password protection. You also learn to control read/write access to data and maintain password lists.

The chapter does not include detailed instructions for installing and setting up a network. For more information on installing Q&A on a network, see the "Q&A Network Administrators Guide," which is supplied with the network version of Q&A.

To understand this chapter completely, you must have a good working knowledge of Q&A's File and Write modules. Understanding basic DOS terminology is useful also. Unless you are the person who manages the network, you may not have access to all the screens and functions described.

16

Key Terms Used in This Chapter

Database Administrator	The person responsible for Q&A databases stored on the network. This person assigns passwords and configures Q&A for the network.
Network	A group of computers linked together with cable. Linked computers can access the same Q&A databases.
Network Administrator	The person responsible for administering a network, particularly for handling hardware and software setup and maintenance.
Network ID	A 20-character code that identifies each user to the network, regardless of which software package is being used.
Password	A 10-character secret code that grants the user access to password-protected Q&A databases.
User ID	A 20-character code that identifies a user to Q&A and grants the user access to networked Q&A databases.

Introduction to Network Facilities

You can use Q&A on a stand-alone computer or on a local area network (LAN). Networked computers can share Q&A databases and other types of information. Most offices benefit from a network structure because this setup enables several people to use the same software and access the same databases simultaneously. The advantage is that all users have access to up-to-date information from the database. Data can be maintained in one location. Instead of trading disks to update a database, you can access quickly the same database as other users and view the most current information.

Because they require additional funding and maintenance, however, network environments are not for everybody. Your work conditions may not warrant additional expenditures. For multiple-user environments in which networks are not practical or necessary, sneaker-nets are quite effective. A sneaker-net refers to the process of copying a database on a disk and walking it to another user, who in turn, uses the information contained on the disk.

You can establish a network by linking computers together in a ring or assigning one central computer to hold files that can be accessed from any networked computer.

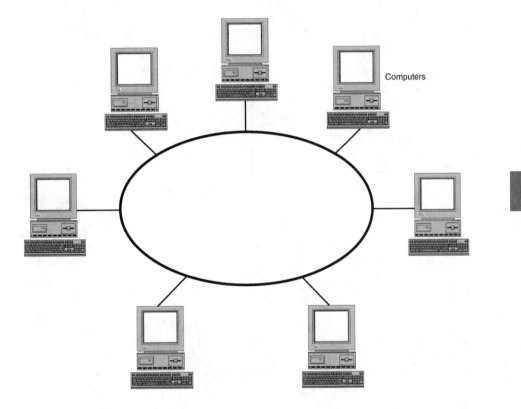

Computers

16

A ring or "distributed" network contains no central computer to hold files accessible to all the network users; instead, files are stored on the individual computers that belong to the network.

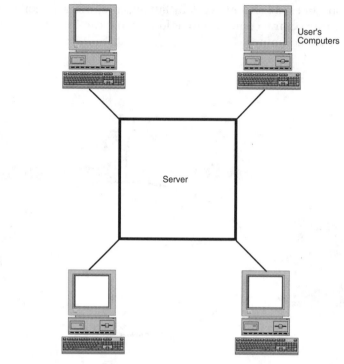

16

The file server uses special software, such as the network version of Q&A, to control access to those central files.

If you are not using a network environment, you still can use some of the features detailed in this chapter. You do not need a physical network to assign password protection to a database or to restrict access rights. These features also work for stand-alone computers.

Understanding Record Locking

In a networked environment, many users can access the same database simultaneously. At any given moment, more than one person can be looking at different forms in the database. What happens when one form is requested by more than one person? If two people try to update the same form at the same time, the network software prevents the second person from doing so by locking the record that is currently in use. The second user can view the form as it's being changed, but may not make changes. Record locking permits only one user at a time to update a form. When a user exits the form, Q&A unlocks the form and access is permitted to another user.

Access to database records can be controlled on a network in other ways as well. With Q&A's password option, you control database access. Passwords may permit the user to view but not change forms, to view only certain fields on a form, or to view and change forms at will. This chapter describes the process of selectively setting up passwords to control access to database files.

Ensuring Data Integrity

When many people are using and updating the same database, or have access to your database, data integrity becomes an important issue. Data integrity ensures that entries or changes going into a database are correct and that frequent backups are handled properly. You can imagine the problems that arise when no procedure is established for backing up data and the system experiences a mechanical failure!

Which users can access databases that contain important or confidential information also is critical, especially on a network. You may not want to grant all users access to your database. Passwords can permit view-only access, update ability, or no access at all. Which activities the password permits are determined at the time that the password is added to Q&A.

16

Using Q&A on a Network

If each user on a network has an individual copy of Q&A, database files can be stored on a central network server and shared among network users. To enable multiple users to share the Q&A program files, one individual copy of Q&A and one or more networked versions (Q&A Network Packs) must be installed on the central network server. Each Network Pack allows three users to access Q&A in addition to the first user.

No fundamental differences exist between the single-user version of Q&A and the networked version. The single-user software supports shared data access and even record locking to ensure that two or more users don't try to modify the same record at the same time. The multiuser version asks you to provide your Network ID (usually your name) and a password for some operations. Q&A displays messages to tell you when you try to perform an operation that another user is doing.

After you install either version of Q&A on the network and create data files, few apparent differences exist for the user between single-user access and multiuser access. Several aspects of Q&A, such as printing and file access, however, operate somewhat differently on a network. The following sections describe some differences that you should be aware of when you use Q&A under multiuser access.

Data Access

With most LANs, the network server is accessed as one or more additional disk drives from the users' PCs. DOS sets aside drives A through E as local drives, so the first network drive is drive F. To access Q&A files or programs from the network, set the appropriate drive default (probably F or above) and run Q&A as if it were on your local drive. Q&A and file access should function virtually the same in the network environment as they do on a single-user PC.

Although most Q&A networked operations are open to all users sharing a database at any time, some networked operations can be performed by only one user at a time. Table 16.1 shows operations that are limited to a single user on a shared file. Although multiple users can access the shared file, only one user at a time can perform each operation listed.

Table 16.1
Single-User Functions on a Shared File

Module	Function
File	Design a Print Spec
	Assign passwords
	Assign user rights
	Use named specs
Report	Design a report
Intelligent Assistant	Teach

Other operations are critical to database integrity and directly affect the view other users have of the database. These functions are considered single-user functions on a locked file and completely lock the file against access by any other user. The operations that lock the file are listed in table 16.2.

380

Table 16.2
Single-User Functions on a Locked File

Module	Function
File	Redesign a file
	Customize a file
	Copy/design forms
	Mass file update
	Posting
	Remove file forms
	Delete duplicate records
Intelligent Assistant	Teach
	Mass file update
Utilities	Database recovery
	DOS commands

How Q&A Functions in a Multiuser Environment

A shared printer can serve only one user (one print job) at a time. Your network software handles competing requests for the printer by queuing print jobs in a RAM cache or on disk. When you send a job to a networked printer, you should see no difference between printing on a LAN and printing in a single-user environment. In addition, during report preparation Q&A makes a copy ("snapshot") of the database at the time you request a report. In this way you can access data for a printout without interfering with other users who may be modifying the data. Of course, your report will not reflect any changes made to the database after the report is started.

Q&A Write in a Multiuser Environment

If you installed a Network Pack, you can share the Write module in a network. You can view or modify a Write document and then save it to a network server, where another user can access the document. Note that Write documents are essentially single-user files. Two or more users cannot have access to the same Write document simultaneously.

The Intelligent Assistant in a Multiuser Environment

The Intelligent Assistant operates the same in a shared environment as it does in a single-user environment, except for the Teach option. Only one user at a time can access the Teach facilities of the Intelligent Assistant.

Macros in a Multiuser Environment

You can use macros on a network the same as with a single-user environment, with one exception. When the Q&A Main menu is first displayed, press F6 to call up the password box and enter your password. Q&A remembers your password and will not ask for it during other operations. By entering your password first, macros that access password-protected operations do not stop to request your password.

Q&A Network Setups

Q&A works in multiuser environments on most of the popular networks that run under MS-DOS Version 3.1 or later versions, as well as the AppleShare network. Symantec specifically mentions support for the 3Plus network, the IBM PC Network and Token-Ring, and networks that use NetWare software. In fact, any network that adheres to the multiuser procedures of DOS (that is, any network that uses the DOS SHARE program or implements the SHARE protocols) should work with Q&A. Symantec regularly expands the list of supported networks. If you have questions about Q&A support for your specific network, call the network vendor or Symantec.

Without the Network Pack, each Q&A user must have a separate copy of the single-user version of the software. If you want networked users to share Q&A, you must use the Network Pack to enable the multiuser features. Each Network Pack increases the number of users by three. Thus the first Pack permits four users to access the Q&A program simultaneously; a second Pack supports up to seven users. When you use the Network Pack, you install a single-user copy of Q&A on your network server and then install the network portion. This procedure modifies your installed Q&A software so that it runs on a network only. After installing a networked version of the software, you can no longer use the single-user version without violating the terms of your software license. Included with the Network Pack is the Q&A Network Administrator's Guide, which shows you how to configure Q&A programs for shared access and offers some instruction on network management.

Multiuser Databases

Although there are no fundamental differences between the single-user version of Q&A and the networked version of the software, before creating a multiuser networked database you should consider some special factors. For example, you must establish access rights for each database and declare the Sharing mode, as well as assign passwords to each database to restrict user access. Be aware that true multiuser operation in Q&A is restricted to databases and the support programs for them.

A database file can be controlled so that each user can access one record at a time, giving many users simultaneous access to the database file. Networked users also can share word processing files, but only one person can have access to a given file at a time. Controlling how more than one person uses and changes a text-based file is difficult or impossible. Therefore, the multiuser instructions in this chapter apply to database access only.

Network and Database Administrators

The network administrator and the database administrator are responsible for maintaining networks. Depending on your organization, one person may be responsible for both duties. The network administrator is the person responsible for the administration of the network. This person focuses on the hardware and network software demands. The database administrator is responsible for Q&A databases that are stored on the network. This person handles password assignment, updating, and deleting tasks.

Designing Multiuser Databases

The basic concepts of designing a database are essentially the same for single- and multiuser operation. Additional considerations may apply to some database applications, however. In a typical Q&A installation, several data files store different kinds of information. You may have an inventory file, a customer file, one or more sales support files, some accounting or bookkeeping files, and personnel files. After you design these files, you may want to restrict access to some of the information. Not every user should have access to the general payroll files, for example.

16

Assigning IDs

One easy way to control this level of access is to establish user classes or groups. At the simplest level, each member of a group is assigned a group ID and password. This arrangement reduces the number of IDs and passwords that the database administrator must track. Note that this arrangement is less secure than one in which each user is assigned a separate ID and a unique password. Q&A only supports user-based access. Several users can share the same ID and password, but the idea of groups, with each user in the group assigned a unique ID and password, is not supported.

Some networks (such as NetWare), however, do permit simultaneous group and individual ID and password assignments. You can use the security features of your individual network to enhance Q&A's multiuser access control. Refer to your network configuration manual for more information on this technique.

Specifying the Mode

Before multiple users can share a database file, the file must be configured for sharing. Follow these steps to configure the file for sharing:

1. From the Main menu, select File.
2. Select Design file.
3. Select Customize a file.

   You are asked which database you want to customize.

4. Type the name of the database you want to customize and press ⏎Enter.
5. Select Assign Access Rights.

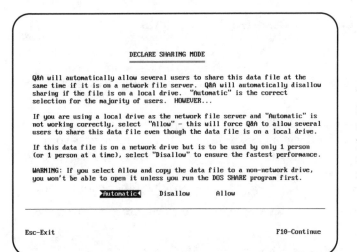

The Security menu is displayed.

6. Select **D**eclare Sharing Mode.

The Declare Sharing Mode screen enables you to set multiuser access for a file.

The screen you see enables you to control concurrent use of Q&A. Concurrent use means two or more users may use the same database at the same time. Selecting Automatic causes the software to check whether you have a network version of Q&A. The Disallow option restricts a database to one user at a time. Other users must wait for access. Allow enables multiple users to access the same database at the same time.

7. Specify Allow to turn on Sharing mode.

Because you were asked to declare which file you wanted to customize before the Customize menu was displayed, the settings on the Access menu apply to one file at a time. Q&A can handle file access automatically by determining whether files are being stored on a server or a local PC. If files are stored on a network server, Q&A assumes that you want to share them. For some applications, forced Sharing or forced Nonsharing mode is desirable. If you want to maintain a private, personal database, for example, you can prevent access to other users by disallowing sharing from the Declare Sharing Mode screen. You may want to force sharing or nonsharing for some applications software.

Specifying Access Rights and Passwords

One method of controlling access to network facilities is to assign each user a unique ID and password. Unless the ID and password are entered correctly, a user is denied access to specific network features, programs, files, and record fields.

Passwords can be chosen by the database administrator or the user. You enter your user ID and password when Q&A requests; then open the password-protected database. Passwords can be up to 10 characters long. Many people select simple passwords, such as a spouse's name, child's name, or pet's name. To ensure security, do not select a password that other people know.

To restrict access to specified files stored on a network server, follow these steps:

1. Follow Steps 1 through 5 for specifying the mode.

2. Select Assign Access Rights.

```
                                   LIST OF USERS/GROUPS
  ████████████████████████████████████████████




















                        Enter name: ACCOUNTING
  _____

  Esc-Exit    F1-Help  F3-Delete  F5-Copy  F7-Search  F8-Rename  F10-Continue
```

Q&A displays the
List of Users/
Groups screen.

3. Type a user ID or group name up to 31 characters long.

   This name is not the user's or group's password, but an unrestricted
   name used for identification in Q&A lists and prompts related to
   network access functions.

4. Press F10 and Q&A displays the Access Control screen.

```
                              ACCESS CONTROL

            Initial Password: AKASHA

  Make the selections below to indicate what rights this person has:

     Can assign password rights?........:    Yes◄  No

     Can change design and program?.....:    Yes◄  No

     Can mass delete?...................:    Yes◄  No

     Can delete individual records?.....:    Yes◄  No

     Can run mass update?...............:    Yes◄  No

     Can Design/Redesign reports?.......:    Yes◄  No

     Can enter/edit data?...............:    Yes◄  No
  _____

  EMPLOYEE.DTF          Access Control Form for ACCOUNTING

  Esc-Exit                      F1-Help                      F10-Continue
```

From this screen,
you assign which
functions a user
can perform.

From this screen, you also assign user passwords. To designate yourself as the data base administrator, for example, you assign yourself the right to assign passwords, change designs and programs, and so on. Other users are assigned fewer rights.

5. Press F10 to exit the Access Control screen.

   Q&A saves your user ID and password and asks whether you want to edit the Access Control screen for another user.

The following table illustrates the function-key assignments for access control.

Table 16.3
Function-Key Assignments for Access Control

Key(s)	Function
F3	Deletes the displayed form and removes it from the database.
Ctrl-F6	Adds the displayed form as a user authorized for the database.
F9	Pages backwards through other Access Control screens.
F10	Pages forwards through other Access Control screens.
Shift-F10	Saves changes or additions to Access Control screens and takes you back to the Access menu.

Field Level Security

Beginning with Q&A version 4.0, you can assign access rights to specific fields of a database form. Assigning access rights to specific fields requires that a person enter a password before being permitted to enter data in a protected field. Other users not assigned to a field security spec can edit any field in the form.

Using the Field Security Spec

To assign access codes to individual fields in a file, follow these steps:

1. From the File menu, select Design file.
2. Select Secure file.

3. At the Security menu, select the file that you want to secure.

4. Select Field level security.

   Q&A displays the List of Field Security Specs.

5. Select a spec from the list or type a name for the security spec.

   Names for security specs can be up to 31 characters long. Choose a descriptive name. An example of a descriptive name is "View without personnel data," which designates a security spec that hides personnel information from certain users. The process of hiding fields is discussed below.

6. Q&A displays the Field Security Spec, which consists of a copy of the database form.

If this is a new Field Security Spec, Q&A enters a W code in each field, indicating that users can presently read and write data in all fields.

7. Q&A overlays the form with a help screen. To remove the help information, press Esc.

8. Type an access code in each field:

Code	Access capability
W	Read & Write. The user can view and change data.
R	Read Only. The user can see but not edit data.
N	No Access. The user cannot see or edit data. The field is hidden during Add and Search operations.

9. Press F10.

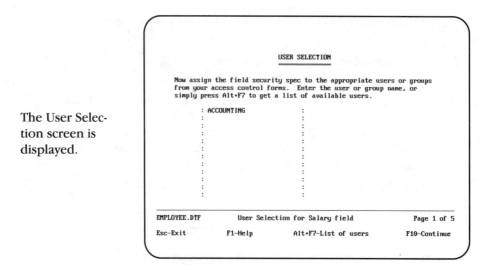

The User Selection screen is displayed.

```
                           USER SELECTION

        Now assign the field security spec to the appropriate users or groups
        from your access control forms.  Enter the user or group name, or
        simply press Alt+F7 to get a list of available users.

                      : ACCOUNTING              :
                      :                         :
                      :                         :
                      :                         :
                      :                         :
                      :                         :
                      :                         :
                      :                         :
                      :                         :
                      :                         :

  EMPLOYEE.DTF          User Selection for Salary field           Page 1 of 5

  Esc-Exit           F1-Help           Alt+F7-List of users        F10-Continue
```

10. Specify the users or user groups to be assigned the field security codes you just specified. In the two columns, type the names of users or groups. You can press Alt-F7 and select existing users or groups from a list by highlighting their names and pressing ↵Enter.

11. Press F10 to leave the User Selection screen and end the field security selection process.

Setting XLOOKUP Passwords

If a user's ID and password are valid for looking up data in one Q&A file but not another, you can allow the user selective password access to the external file for functions that use XLOOKUP to draw data from the external file. The special XLOOKUP password and ID are valid for expressions that use either XLOOKUP or @XLOOKUP. To specify an XLOOKUP password, follow these steps:

1. From the Security menu select Set xlookup password.

```
                    SET XLOOKUP PASSWORD
                    _____


        Enter a User-Id/Password combination that can be used by
        your xlookup statements to access external databases.


                User ID: ACCOUNTING
               Password: AKASHA




        _____


  Esc-Exit              F1-Help                 F10-Continue
```

The Security menu is displayed.

16

2. Type the user ID and password that will allow the user selective access to the external file.

Linking to an SQL Database

Q&A can retrieve data from databases that use SQL (Standard Query Language) protocols compatible with the Oracle Server and Gupta SQLBase mainframe software. Your network workstation must be running the workstation component of the SQL software in order for Q&A to link with the database. SQL databases use a slightly different terminology than Q&A's. In SQL parlance, for example, a field is referred to as a "column" and a record is called a "row."

To import information from an SQL database, follow these steps:

1. From the File Utilities menu, choose Link-to-SQL.

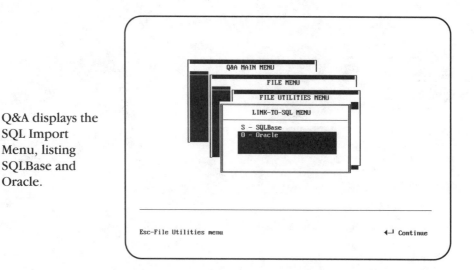

Q&A displays the
SQL Import
Menu, listing
SQLBase and
Oracle.

16

If you choose SQLBase, Q&A asks for a database name, user name,
and password. If you choose Oracle, Q&A prompts you for a user
name, password, server name, and network protocol.

2. Enter the requested information and press F10.

Q&A links to the SQL database and submits your user ID, password,
and so on. If no errors occur, Q&A asks for an SQL table (database)
name and the name of the Q&A database that will receive the transferred records.

3. Type the name of the table and press ↵Enter. You also can press
↵Enter to view a list of tables. Then type the name of the Q&A
database and press ↵Enter or press Enter to select from a list of Q&A
files. If you are importing to an existing database, Q&A displays the
Merge Spec. If you name a new database, Q&A can build the Q&A
database for you and place the fields in the Merge Spec for you. You
can later redesign the form and rearrange the fields.

4. Fill in the Merge and Retrieve Specs. When linking to an SQL database, you may not use the Retrieve Spec functions or MIN and MAX,
but you can press F8 to create a Sort Spec.

5. Press F10 to start the import process. For detailed instructions on
installing Q&A and configuring the package for your computer
environment. For information on purchasing and installing a Q&A
Network Pack for shared program access, call Symantec.

Installing Q&A

The following installation procedures assume that you have made backup copies of the Q&A system disks. If you have not made the recommended copies yet, consult your DOS manual for instructions on how to make duplicates of the disks.

Q&A requires a hard disk for installation. The installation instructions assume that the hard disk is formatted and ready to receive data, the default drive is C, and that the program is copied into a directory named \QA. If the hard disk default is different than drive C, substitute the correct disk drive. To install Q&A, follow these steps:

1. Place a write-protect tab over the notch in the right corner of a 5 1/4-inch disk. If you are using 3 1/2-inch disks, slide the write-protect notch (located on the top right side) so that you can see through the hole in the disk.

2. Turn on the computer. You must be at the C: prompt to begin installation procedures.

3. Type A: and press ⏎Enter.

4. Type Install and press ⏎Enter.

5. Insert Disk #1 in drive A. This disk contains an installation program.

6. The Installation program prompts you for a source drive and a destination drive.

7. You then are prompted for the directory in which you want to install Q&A.

   On-screen prompts indicate when to insert the remaining seven disks.

Creating Data File Subdirectories

After you copy the disks into the QA directory, you should make two more subdirectories to hold the data files and documents you generate using Q&A. Creating separate subdirectories makes backing up easier because only the *data file* subdirectories, not the *software* subdirectories, need to be backed up. When you back up only the data files, you reduce the time and number of disks needed to do a backup of the system. If you are using a network, check with your network administrator before completing the following steps.

To create two separate subdirectories, follow these steps:

1. Start from the QA directory (C:\QA>) and create the FILE subdirectory to hold database files by typing: **MD FILE** and pressing ⏎Enter.

2. Then create the WRITE subdirectory by starting from the QA directory (C:\QA>) and type **MD WRITE** and press ⏎Enter.

Before you begin Chapter 1 exercises, you need to follow the steps in Chapter 6, *Utilities for Setting Global Default,* to indicate that you have created subdirectories to hold the data files.

Configuring the System

Every computer has special instructions that are issued when you first turn on the machine. These configuration instructions tell the system what equipment you are using, such as printer ports, keyboards, monitors, and other general hardware. When you first install Q&A, this configuration file, called CONFIG.SYS, is created for you. In this file, you reserve a certain amount of space on the hard disk to hold files that are created during sorts and calculation processes. This reserved file space is necessary to execute some of the more advanced functions within Q&A.

The CONFIG.SYS file created by Q&A changes the number of files and buffers to the minimum amount required by the software and creates a new file to hold the specialized configuration. If you already have a CONFIG.SYS file, you need to confirm that it has the minimum 20 files and 10 buffers that Q&A requires. If the necessary space does not exist, the system may warn you that not enough room exists to perform sorts or copy files.

Part of the installation procedure asks whether you want to change the CONFIG.SYS file. If you do not want to use DOS, follow the on-screen instructions to have Q&A perform this procedure for you. If a file exists, you are told that the file either meets the minimum standards and does not require modification, or you are advised of the adjustments made to the existing file. (See your DOS manual for instructions on how to alter this file.)

Starting Q&A

To start Q&A , begin in the QA directory. (If you just completed the preceding steps, you should be in the correct location to activate the program.) Next, type QA and then press ⏎Enter. The software is loaded and you are now ready to use Q&A!

Shortcut Keys

Q&A provides special shortcut keys that make using the many functions of the program easier and quicker. The following tables describe the use of function keys within the Q&A menus and how the use of these keys moves you from one menu to another.

File Module

Key(s)	Function
F7	Takes you to the Retrieve Spec option from most screens in the File menu.
Shift-F9	Takes you from the Add or Search/Update option to the Customize Menu option.
Ctrl-F6	Takes you from the Search/Update option to the Add option.
Shift-F9	Takes you from the screen Print option to the Specs option used to complete the printing request.

Write Module

Key(s)	Function
Alt -F8	Takes you to Mailing Labels option.
Ctrl -F8	Exports the document to an ASCII file.

Report Module

Keys	Function
Shift -F9	Takes you from screen Print option to Specs option used to complete printing requests.

Assistant Module

Keys	Function
Shift -F7	Repeats last question asked in question box.

Index

Computer Books From Que Mean PC Performance!

Spreadsheets

1-2-3 Database Techniques	$29.95
1-2-3 Graphics Techniques	$24.95
1-2-3 Macro Library, 3rd Edition	$39.95
1-2-3 Release 2.2 Business Applications	$39.95
1-2-3 Release 2.2 PC Tutor	$39.95
1-2-3 Release 2.2 QueCards	$19.95
1-2-3 Release 2.2 Quick Reference	$ 8.95
1-2-3 Release 2.2 QuickStart, 2nd Edition	$19.95
1-2-3 Release 2.2 Workbook and Disk	$29.95
1-2-3 Release 3 Business Applications	$39.95
1-2-3 Release 3 Workbook and Disk	$29.95
1-2-3 Release 3.1 Quick Reference	$ 8.95
1-2-3 Release 3.1 QuickStart, 2nd Edition	$19.95
1-2-3 Tips, Tricks, and Traps, 3rd Edition	$24.95
Excel Business Applications: IBM Version	$39.95
Excel Quick Reference	$ 8.95
Excel QuickStart	$19.95
Excel Tips, Tricks, and Traps	$22.95
Using 1-2-3/G	$29.95
Using 1-2-3, Special Edition	$27.95
Using 1-2-3 Release 2.2, Special Edition	$27.95
Using 1-2-3 Release 3.1, 2nd Edition	$29.95
Using Excel: IBM Version	$29.95
Using Lotus Spreadsheet for DeskMate	$22.95
Using Quattro Pro	$24.95
Using SuperCalc5, 2nd Edition	$29.95

Databases

dBASE III Plus Handbook, 2nd Edition	$24.95
dBASE III Plus Tips, Tricks, and Traps	$24.95
dBASE III Plus Workbook and Disk	$29.95
dBASE IV Applications Library, 2nd Edition	$39.95
dBASE IV Programming Techniques	$24.95
dBASE IV Quick Reference	$ 8.95
dBASE IV QuickStart	$19.95
dBASE IV Tips, Tricks,and Traps, 2nd Edition	$24.95
dBASE IV Workbook and Disk	$29.95
Using Clipper	$24.95
Using DataEase	$24.95
Using dBASE IV	$27.95
Using Paradox 3	$24.95
Using R:BASE	$29.95
Using Reflex, 2nd Edition	$24.95
Using SQL	$29.95

Business Applications

Allways Quick Reference	$ 8.95
Introduction to Business Software	$14.95
Introduction to Personal Computers	$19.95
Lotus Add-in Toolkit Guide	$29.95
Norton Utilities Quick Reference	$ 8.95
PC Tools Quick Reference, 2nd Edition	$ 8.95
Q&A Quick Reference	$ 8.95
Que's Computer User's Dictionary	$ 9.95
Que's Wizard Book	$ 9.95
Quicken Quick Reference	$ 8.95
SmartWare Tips, Tricks, and Traps 2nd Edition	$24.95
Using Computers in Business	$22.95
Using DacEasy, 2nd Edition	$24.95
Using Enable/OA	$29.95
Using Harvard Project Manager	$24.95
Using Managing Your Money, 2nd Edition	$19.95
Using Microsoft Works: IBM Version	$22.95
Using Norton Utilities	$24.95

Using PC Tools Deluxe	$24.95
Using Peachtree	$27.95
Using PFS: First Choice	$22.95
Using PROCOMM PLUS	$19.95
Using Q&A, 2nd Edition	$23.95
Using Quicken: IBM Version, 2nd Edition	$19.95
Using Smart	$22.95
Using SmartWare II	$29.95
Using Symphony, Special Edition	$29.95
Using Time Line	$24.95
Using TimeSlips	$24.95

CAD

AutoCAD Quick Reference	$ 8.95
AutoCAD Sourcebook 1991	$27.95
Using AutoCAD, 3rd Edition	$29.95
Using Generic CADD	$24.95

Word Processing

Microsoft Word 5 Quick Reference	$ 8.95
Using DisplayWrite 4, 2nd Edition	$24.95
Using LetterPerfect	$22.95
Using Microsoft Word 5.5: IBM Version, 2nd Edition	$24.95
Using MultiMate	$24.95
Using Professional Write	$22.95
Using Word for Windows	$24.95
Using WordPerfect 5	$27.95
Using WordPerfect 5.1, Special Edition	$27.95
Using WordStar, 3rd Edition	$27.95
WordPerfect PC Tutor	$39.95
WordPerfect Power Pack	$39.95
WordPerfect Quick Reference	$ 8.95
WordPerfect QuickStart	$19.95
WordPerfect 5 Workbook and Disk	$29.95
WordPerfect 5.1 Quick Reference	$ 8.95
WordPerfect 5.1 QuickStart	$19.95
WordPerfect 5.1 Tips, Tricks, and Traps	$24.95
WordPerfect 5.1 Workbook and Disk	$29.95

Hardware/Systems

DOS Tips, Tricks, and Traps	$24.95
DOS Workbook and Disk, 2nd Edition	$29.95
Fastback Quick Reference	$ 8.95
Hard Disk Quick Reference	$ 8.95
MS-DOS PC Tutor	$39.95
MS-DOS Power Pack	$39.95
MS-DOS Quick Reference	$ 8.95
MS-DOS QuickStart, 2nd Edition	$19.95
MS-DOS User's Guide, Special Edition	$29.95
Networking Personal Computers, 3rd Edition	$24.95
The Printer Bible	$29.95
Que's PC Buyer's Guide	$12.95
Understanding UNIX: A Conceptual Guide, 2nd Edition	$21.95
Upgrading and Repairing PCs	$29.95
Using DOS	$22.95
Using Microsoft Windows 3, 2nd Edition	$24.95
Using Novell NetWare	$29.95
Using OS/2	$29.95
Using PC DOS, 3rd Edition	$24.95
Using Prodigy	$19.95

Using UNIX	$29.95
Using Your Hard Disk	$29.95
Windows 3 Quick Reference	$ 8.95

Desktop Publishing/Graphics

CorelDRAW Quick Reference	$ 8.95
Harvard Graphics Quick Reference	$ 8.95
Using Animator	$24.95
Using DrawPerfect	$24.95
Using Harvard Graphics, 2nd Edition	$24.95
Using Freelance Plus	$24.95
Using PageMaker: IBM Version, 2nd Edition	$24.95
Using PFS: First Publisher, 2nd Edition	$24.95
Using Ventura Publisher, 2nd Edition	$24.95

Macintosh/Apple II

AppleWorks QuickStart	$19.95
The Big Mac Book, 2nd Edition	$29.95
Excel QuickStart	$19.95
The Little Mac Book	$ 9.95
Que's Macintosh Multimedia Handbook	$24.95
Using AppleWorks, 3rd Edition	$24.95
Using Excel: Macintosh Version	$24.95
Using FileMaker	$24.95
Using MacDraw	$24.95
Using MacroMind Director	$29.95
Using MacWrite	$24.95
Using Microsoft Word 4: Macintosh Version	$24.95
Using Microsoft Works: Macintosh Version, 2nd Edition	$24.95
Using PageMaker: Macinsoth Version, 2nd Edition	$24.95

Programming/Technical

Assembly Language Quick Reference	$ 8.95
C Programmer' sToolkit	$39.95
C Quick Reference	$ 8.95
DOS and BIOS Functions Quick Reference	$ 8.95
DOS Programmer's Reference, 2nd Edition	$29.95
Network Programming in C	$49.95
Oracle Programmer's Guide	$29.95
QuickBASIC Advanced Techniques	$24.95
Quick C Programmer's Guide	$29.95
Turbo Pascal Advanced Techniques	$24.95
Turbo Pascal Quick Reference	$ 8.95
UNIX Programmer's Quick Reference	$ 8.95
UNIX Programmer's Reference	$29.95
UNIX Shell Commands Quick Reference	$ 8.95
Using Assembly Language, 2nd Edition	$29.95
Using BASIC	$24.95
Using Č	$29.95
Using QuickBASIC 4	$24.95
Using Turbo Pascal	$29.95

Teach Yourself
With QuickStarts From Que!

The ideal tutorials for beginners, Que's QuickStart books use graphic illustrations and step-by-step instructions to get you up and running fast. Packed with examples, QuickStarts are the perfect beginner's guides to your favorite software applications.

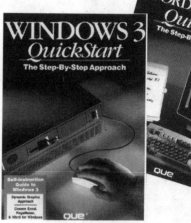

QueCards Put Command Information At Your Fingertips!

WordPerfect 5.1 QueCards

Que Development Group

The convenient flip-card reference for WordPerfect 5.1! Perfect for office or home, *WordPerfect 5.1 QueCards* explains the most frequently used procedures with clear, concise instructions.

Version 5.1

Order #1212   **$19.95 USA**

0-88022-617-X, 60 cards, 6 1/2 X 9

Que's QueCards are the perfect desktop reference for users who want quick and simple command information at a glance. The spiral binding and flip-card format make QueCards easy to use, and each QueCard book comes with a FREE easel.

1-2-3 Release 2.2 QueCards

Que Development Group

Releases 2.01 & 2.2

Order #1211   **$19.95 USA**

0-88022-616-1, 60 cards, 6 1/2 x 9

Q&A QueCards

Que Development Group

Versions 3 & 4

Order #1279   **$19.95 USA**

0-88022-669-2, 60 cards, 6 1/2 x 9

To Order, Call:
(800) 428-5331 OR (317) 573-2510

Find It Fast With Que's Quick References!

Que's Quick References are the compact, easy-to-use guides to essential application information. Written for all users, Quick References include vital command information under easy-to-find alphabetical listings. Quick References are a must for anyone who needs command information fast!

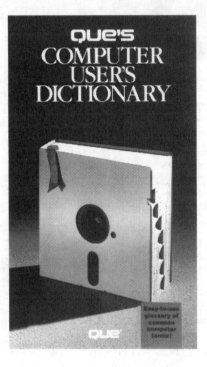

Free Catalog!

Mail us this registration form today,
and we'll send you a free catalog
featuring Que's complete line of
best-selling books.

Name of Book _____

Name _____

Title _____

Phone (___) _____

Company _____

Address _____

City _____

State _____ ZIP _____

Please check the appropriate answers:

1. Where did you buy your Que book?
   - ☐ Bookstore (name: _____)
   - ☐ Computer store (name: _____)
   - ☐ Catalog (name: _____)
   - ☐ Direct from Que
   - ☐ Other: _____

2. How many computer books do you buy a year?
   - ☐ 1 or less
   - ☐ 2-5
   - ☐ 6-10
   - ☐ More than 10

3. How many Que books do you own?
   - ☐ 1
   - ☐ 2-5
   - ☐ 6-10
   - ☐ More than 10

4. How long have you been using this software?
   - ☐ Less than 6 months
   - ☐ 6 months to 1 year
   - ☐ 1-3 years
   - ☐ More than 3 years

5. What influenced your purchase of this Que book?
   - ☐ Personal recommendation
   - ☐ Advertisement
   - ☐ In-store display
   - ☐ Price
   - ☐ Que catalog
   - ☐ Que mailing
   - ☐ Que's reputation
   - ☐ Other: _____

6. How would you rate the overall content of the book?
   - ☐ Very good
   - ☐ Good
   - ☐ Satisfactory
   - ☐ Poor

7. What do you like *best* about this Que book?
   _____
   _____

8. What do you like *least* about this Que book?
   _____
   _____

9. Did you buy this book with your personal funds?
   - ☐ Yes   ☐ No

10. Please feel free to list any other comments you may have about this Que book.
    _____
    _____
    _____

quе

Order Your Que Books Today!

Name _____

Title _____

Company _____

City _____

State _____ ZIP _____

Phone No. (___) _____

Method of Payment:

Check ☐ (Please enclose in envelope.)

Charge My: VISA ☐   MasterCard ☐

American Express ☐

Charge # _____

Expiration Date _____

Order No.	Title	Qty.	Price	Total

You can **FAX** your order to **1-317-573-2583**. Or call **1-800-428-5331, ext. ORDR** to order direct.
Please add $2.50 per title for shipping and handling.

Subtotal _____

Shipping & Handling _____

Total _____

quе

BUSINESS REPLY MAIL
First Class Permit No. 9918   Indianapolis, IN

Postage will be paid by addressee

11711 N. College
Carmel, IN 46032

BUSINESS REPLY MAIL
First Class Permit No. 9918   Indianapolis, IN

Postage will be paid by addressee

11711 N. College
Carmel, IN 46032